A Catholic Spirituality for Business

A Catholic Spirituality for Business

THE LOGIC OF GIFT

Edited by
Martin Schlag & Domènec Melé

Foreword by Cardinal Peter K. A. Turkson

The Catholic University of America Press
Washington, D.C.

The paper used in this publication meets the minimum requirements of
American National Standards for Information Science—
Permanence of Paper for Printed Library Materials,
ANSI Z39.48-1984.
∞

Library of Congress Cataloging-in-Publication Data
Names: Schlag, Martin, 1964– editor. | Melé, Domènec, editor.
Title: A Catholic spirituality for business : the logic of gift / edited by Martin Schlag
and Domènec Melé ; foreword by Cardinal Peter K. A. Turkson.
Description: Washington, D.C. : The Catholic University of America Press, [2019] |
Includes bibliographical references and index.
Identifiers: LCCN 2019010736 | ISBN 9780813231693 (pbk. : alk. paper)
Subjects: LCSH: Business—Religious aspects—Catholic Church. | Spirituality.
Classification: LCC HF5388 .S35 2019 | DDC 261.8/5—dc23
LC record available at https://lccn.loc.gov/2019010736

CONTENTS

PART 2. THE LOGIC OF GIFT IN BUSINESS

FOREWORD

Pope Francis and a New Economic Mindset: The Range and the Extent of the Pope's Message on the Economy

CARDINAL PETER K. A. TURKSON

The Christian faith has a public and social dimension and is thus also relevant for the economic reasoning that pervades most of contemporary public and political discourse. The Christian faith cannot be confined to the individual's private life.[1] Indeed, faith is incomplete without a vision of the world and our place in it. To be a Christian and to have received baptism in the Catholic Church means one partakes in a triple sending or mission: the priestly, pastoral, and prophetic mission.[2] The prophetic mission in particular is a unique phenomenon in the biblical faith: in the name of God, men and women rise to proclaim truth and justice in the face of oppression, injustice, and disinformation, and in so doing they oppose political and economic power.

Pope Francis's pronouncements on the economy are such a prophetic cry. Take, for example, the following frequently quoted passage from his Apostolic Exhortation *Evangelii gaudium*: "Just as the commandment 'Thou shalt not kill' sets a clear limit in order to safeguard the value of human life, today we also have to say 'thou shalt not' to an economy of exclusion and inequality. Such an economy kills. How can

1. Pope John Paul II, speaking about Adolf Kolping at his beatification said, "For him, Christianity was not to be understood simply as a 'prayer room,' but as embedded in everyday life and directed to the formation of the social reality. For him, the places in which human and Christian responsibility must be exercised are: the family, the Church, the workplace, and politics"; *Homily for the Beatification of Father Adolph Kolping*, October 27, 1991; our translation.

2. See Vatican Council II, Dogmatic Constitution *Lumen gentium* (November 21, 1964), nos. 10–12.

it be that it is not a news item when an elderly homeless person dies of exposure, but it is news when the stock market loses two points? This is a case of exclusion. Can we continue to stand by when food is thrown away while people are starving? This is a case of inequality."[3]

Please note that the pope is not against the economy as such but against "such an economy that kills." He is not only fully aware of the fact that the world, and especially the poor of this world, need economy and business; he is moreover also convinced that "the international business community can count on many men and women of great personal honesty and integrity, whose work is inspired and guided by high ideals of fairness, generosity and concern for the authentic development of the human family."[4]

What is the pope's message to businesspeople? It is not an easy task to summarize an ongoing teaching of such an active person as Pope Francis in a few lines. What is clear to identify so far is its consistency in making concerns about the well-being of the human person central to all financial systems, and based on this, I shall try to characterize his thought as best I can, with four general remarks and three specific aims. Of course, the selection of topics is mine, and these remain my thoughts; I do not in any way wish to ascribe to the Holy Father things he has not said.

1. *Business is a noble vocation.* In line with the church's firm conviction that all Christians are called to practice charity in a manner corresponding to their vocation and according to the degree of influence they wield in the *polis*,[5] the former Pontifical Council for Justice and Peace of the Holy See intuited that the church's way of engaging the business community is not to point accusing fingers at it; rather, it adopts the point of view of Pope Francis in recognizing that "the vocation of the business person is a genuine human and Christian

3. Francis, Apostolic Exhortation *Evangelii gaudium* (November 24, 2013), no. 53.

4. Francis, *Message to the Executive Chairman of the World Economic Forum on the Occasion of the Annual Meeting at Davos-Klosters (Switzerland)*, January 14, 2015.

5. Benedict XVI, Encyclical Letter *Caritas in veritate* (June 29, 2009), no. 7.

calling."[6] Indeed, Pope Francis calls business a "noble vocation provided that those engaged in it see themselves challenged by a greater meaning in life; this will enable them to truly to serve the common good by striving to increase the goods of this world and to make them more accessible to all."[7] Accordingly, in his message to the executive chairman of the World Economic Forum in 2014, he wrote, "In fact, 'we must praise the steps being taken to improve people's welfare in areas such as health care, education and communications,' in addition to many other areas of human activity, and we must recognize the fundamental role that modern business activity has had in bringing about these changes, by stimulating and developing the immense resources of human intelligence."[8] He made a similar affirmation of the positive contribution of business before the U.S. Congress in September 2015. There he recognized that the right use of natural resources, the proper application of technology, and the harnessing of the spirit of enterprise are essential elements of an economy that seeks to be modern, inclusive, and sustainable. Subsequently, however, he drew attention to the presence of persistent poverty; development is not always inclusive, and the dignity of people and the common good do not always enjoy a priority of attention. Indeed, "the successes which have been achieved, even if they have reduced poverty for a great number of people, often have led to a widespread social exclusion."[9] According to Pope Francis, this happens because human dignity and the common good, which ought to shape every political and economic decision, at times seem to be little more than an afterthought. Pope Francis's guarded stance is coherent with his program of evangelization.

2. *The pope's remarks form part of his program of evangelization.* It is no coincidence that *Evangelii gaudium*, from where I have taken the

6. Pontifical Council for Justice and Peace, *The Vocation of the Business Leader* (Vatican City: Pontifical Council for Justice and Peace, 2012), no. 6.

7. Francis, *Evangelii gaudium*, no. 203.

8. Francis, *Message to the Executive Chairman of the World Economic Forum*, quoting Francis, *Evangelii gaudium*, no. 52.

9. Ibid.

first quotation, is the post-synodic document on evangelization. Pope Francis does not intend to lecture on economics or give a course on business ethics. He clearly states that neither the church nor the pope possesses a monopoly on the interpretation of social facts. However, the good news of the gospel cannot be spread without a serious reflection on the practical consequences of faith in social and economic life and dealings.[10] Political, social, and economic injustice, wherever it appears, summons Christians to action, and this summoning is part of evangelization. Whoever sincerely endeavors to follow Christ takes to heart Jesus' words: "Then the king will say to those on his right, 'Come, you who are blessed by my Father. Inherit the kingdom prepared for you from the foundation of the world. For I was hungry and you gave me food, I was thirsty and you gave me drink, a stranger and you welcomed me, naked and you clothed me, ill and you cared for me, in prison and you visited me.'"[11]

3. *Service of mammon, idolatry of money, exclude from the Kingdom of God.* "You cannot serve God and mammon" (Mt 6:24). Practical materialism and consumerism are the great and constant threats to Christian life, everywhere in the world and in history, but perhaps especially in the civilized world we inhabit. St. Paul wrote that the "spirit of the world" blocks the gifts of the spirit (1 Cor 2:12–14). Pope Francis echoes him by saying, "The great danger in today's world, pervaded as it is by consumerism, is the desolation and anguish born of a complacent yet covetous heart, the feverish pursuit of frivolous pleasures, and a blunted conscience.... God's voice is no longer heard, the quiet joy of his love is no longer felt, and the desire to do good fades."[12] Pope Francis's ideal of a "poor church for the poor" is not to be understood in a pauperistic way but in the sense that poverty in spirit, which is

10. Recall how the Second Vatican Council urged dialogue of the church with humanity about all its problems; see, for example, Vatican Council II, Pastoral Constitution *Gaudium et spes* (December 7, 1965), no. 3.

11. Mt 25:34–36.

12. Francis, *Evangelii gaudium*, no. 2.

only real if it touches the flesh of Christ in the poor and marginalized, keeps supernatural hope, and thus growth and joy, burning and alive.

4. *Globalization has reduced poverty but increased inequality.* Pope Francis's message to the executive chairman of the World Economic Forum in 2014 is worth reading in this regard. The Holy Father is concerned about growing inequality. The original Spanish word *inequidad* expresses his concern better than the English translation: what he criticizes is unjust inequality, inequality that is the result of hardheartedness or exclusion. We all know that the prospect of reaping the fruits of one's own labor is highly motivating and that different degrees of effort will result in different outcomes and thus just differences. However, whoever rigs the rules or tips the scales to his own advantage, whoever inclines the playing field so that it is no longer level for all, whoever burns the ladders he himself has climbed in order to exclude others, creates unjust inequalities. Unfortunately, our world is full of them. Integral and sustainable development for all is what Pope Francis desires.

This leads me to three specific aims of the economy Pope Francis mentions in his pronouncements.

1. His vision of the economy is one that includes the poor structurally and fights poverty by encouraging the creation of prosperity for all. "The need to resolve the structural causes of poverty cannot be delayed, not only for the pragmatic reason of its urgency for the good order of society, but because society needs to be cured of a sickness which is weakening and frustrating it, and which can only lead to new crises. Welfare projects, which meet certain urgent needs, should be considered merely temporary responses."[13] This ideal is shared by attempts in the business community not only to redistribute wealth after it has been created, but to make capitalism inclusive, to spread the idea of impact in business and investment at the "bottom of the pyramid,"

13. Ibid., no. 202.

and to create shared value in the process of production and the value chain. Also, the notions of corporate social responsibility, corporate citizenship, sustainability, with its triple bottom line, and many other recent models demonstrate that something is changing in the world of business. A paradigm shift seems to be under way toward a new mindset of an economy that includes the poor. It means that businesspeople do very well to care for the needs of their employees and stakeholders but should also be aware of their important contribution to the whole of society. Their work can be sanctified if it is put to the service of the common good and exercised with the wish to honor God.

This recalls his address at the Conferral of the Charlemagne Prize. There he desired a shift to a person-centered economy, a form of *social economy*, saying, "It would involve passing from an economy directed at revenue, profiting from speculation and lending at interest, to a social economy that invests in persons by creating jobs and providing training. We need to move from a liquid economy prepared to use corruption as a means of obtaining profits to a social economy that guarantees access to land and lodging through labor. Labor is in fact the setting in which individuals and communities bring into play 'many aspects of life: creativity, planning for the future, developing talents, living out values, relating to others, giving glory to God.'"[14] He promoted the same person-centered or *social economy* when addressing the popular movements in Santa Cruz de la Sierra, Bolivia, where he exhorted the *Cartoneros* and the *Campesinos* to be protagonists of their growth and development. In this context, Pope Francis seems to favor cooperative forms of business, in which he places his hopes for the development of the weakest parts of society, especially unemployed youth.[15]

2. This brings us naturally to a further necessity underscored by

14. Francis, *Address at the Conferral of the Charlemagne Prize*, May 6, 2016, quoting Francis, Encyclical Letter *Laudato si'* (May 24, 2015), no. 127.

15. Francis, *Address to Representatives of the Confederation of Italian Cooperatives*, February 28, 2015.

Pope Francis, as previously emphasized by Pope Benedict XVI: ethics is an integral part of the economy and of economics, business research, and teaching at a business school, especially at those schools inspired by the Christian faith. Obviously, economics as a science possesses its own laws and autonomy. Nobody doubts that. However, we should not accept the reduction of all knowledge to efficient causality; we must also ask ourselves what things are for. Already at the beginning of the twentieth century, G. K. Chesterton wrote a book entitled *What's Wrong with the World*. And what's wrong with the world, he says, "is that we do not ask what is right."[16] He goes on to say, "When things go very wrong we need an unpractical man. Certainly, at least, we need a theorist." Only a theorist can go beyond the cult of efficiency and tell us what on earth the economy is here for.[17] Ethics tells us what things are here for. Pope Francis speaks along the same lines when he writes:

> The long-term measures that are designed to ensure an adequate legal framework for all economic actions, as well as the associated urgent measures to resolve the global economic crisis, must be guided by the ethics of truth. This includes, first and foremost, respect for the truth of man, who is not simply an additional economic factor, or a disposable good, but is equipped with a nature and a dignity that cannot be reduced to simple economic calculus.... The goal of economics and politics is to serve humanity, beginning with the poorest and most vulnerable wherever they may be, even in their mothers' wombs ... in the absence of such a vision, all economic activity is meaningless. In this sense, the various grave economic and political challenges facing today's world require a courageous change of attitude that will restore to the end (the human person) and to the means (economics and politics) their proper place. Money and other political and economic means must serve, not rule.[18]

In the former *Pontifical Council for Justice and Peace*,[19] we have tried to translate these thoughts into everyday business dealings: "For

16. G. K. Chesterton, *What's Wrong with the World* (Leipzig: Tauchnitz, 1910), 13.

17. Ibid., 16.

18. Francis, *Letter to H. E. Mr. David Cameron, British Prime Minister on the Occasion of the G8 Meeting (17–18 June 2013)*, June 15, 2013.

19. On August 17, 2016, Pope Francis merged this Pontifical Council with three other Vatican institutions, forming the Dicastery for Promoting Integral Human Development.

the business leader, this entails creating goods that are truly good and services that truly serve."[20]

3. Finally, a pressing moral concern brought up frequently by Pope Francis is the eradication of corruption. Already as archbishop of Buenos Aires, he spoke out against the cancer of society, which is corruption: corruption can only be forgiven if what was taken has been given back. As pope, Francis has raised his voice on many occasions to denounce corruption. Parents who feed their children on "unclean bread" earned through bribes and corruption are starving their children of dignity, because dishonest work robs us of our dignity.[21] Corruption is a worldwide problem that drains society of energy, discourages loyal competition, obstructs development, and ruins the free economy. An economy that is corrupt and unethical cannot be free in a Christian sense: it is in the hands of an oligarchy.

"Charity is at the heart of the Church's social doctrine," said Benedict XVI in his social encyclical *Caritas in veritate*.[22] Charity, though, is not a socioeconomic program that could be applied immediately without the mediation of philosophy and science, without economics and business education. It is therefore those of you who actually work in business who can bring about this momentous shift of paradigm in the economy. Neither Benedict XVI nor Francis has offered a technical solution or specific answer to these problems but has formulated his teachings as a challenge, as the challenge of charity: how do we insert charity into everyday business dealings and normal economics? Benedict XVI spoke of the logic of gift, gratuitousness, and fraternity.[23] Francis encourages us with the same aim in mind. His words on the economy are a prophetic cry against the anesthesia of well-being that reminds us that realities are more important than ideas; realities are greater than ideas. Ideas can also be ideologies or ineffective academic

20. Pontifical Council for Justice and Peace, *The Vocation of the Business Leader* (Vatican City: Pontifical Council for Justice and Peace, 2012), 80.

21. Francis, *Meditation: Dirty Bread of Corruption*, November 8, 2013.

22. Benedict XVI, *Caritas in veritate*, no. 2.

23. See ibid., 36.

debates that do not change anything.[24] The infinite word of God did not remain theory but became finite man. Francis wishes to provoke conversion as well as solidarity and inclusive economy: what am I going to do about the misery in the world? And when will I begin?

If this book contributes to such a provocation in its readers, then I think it has been worthwhile.

24. See Francis, *Evangelii gaudium*, nos. 231–33.

A Catholic Spirituality for Business

INTRODUCTION

MARTIN SCHLAG AND DOMÈNEC MELÉ

Spirituality is in fashion in many different contexts, among them business and organization studies. Topics such as spirituality at the workplace, spirituality management, spirituality in leadership, organizational spirituality, and other related topics are increasingly present in management literature. In this line, a vast body of literature on spirituality has appeared in the last two decades,[1] including many studies regarding spirituality in business[2] and workplace spirituality.[3] These include books,[4] handbooks,[5] and individual essays.[6] In addition, the Academy of Management—the largest association of professors and researchers in management globally—has an important interest group devoted to management spirituality and religion.

Most academic literature on spirituality in organizations and on leading organizations focuses on the connections between spiritual-

1. For a review, see Rajesh Ratnakar and Shreekumar Nair, "A Review of Scientific Research on Spirituality," *Business Perspectives and Research* 1, no. 1 (2012): 1–12.

2. Michael Bell, "Teaching of the Elders," in *The Palgrave Handbook of Spirituality and Business*, ed. Luk Bouckaert and László Zsolnai (Houndmills: Palgrave-Macmillan, 2011), 187–96.

3. See a review in Jeffery D. Houghton, Christopher P. Neck, and Sukumarakurup Krishnakumar, "The What, Why, and How of Spirituality in the Workplace Revisited: A 14-Year Update and Extension," *Journal of Management, Spirituality and Religion* 13 (2016): 177–205.

4. Elizabeth A. Denton and Ian I. Mitroff, *A Spiritual Audit of Corporate America: A Hard Look at Spirituality, Religion, and Values in the Workplace* (San Francisco: Jossey-Bass, 1999); Douglas A. Hicks, *Religion and the Workplace: Pluralism, Spirituality, Leadership* (Cambridge: Cambridge University Press, 2003); Joan Marques, Satinder Dhiman, and Richard King, *Spirituality in the Workplace: What It Is, Why It Matters, How to Make It Work for You* (Fawnskin, Calif.: Personhood, 2007); and Nancy R. Smith, *Workplace Spirituality: A Complete Guide for Business Leaders* (Lynn, Mass.: Axial Age, 2006).

5. Robert A. Giacalone and Carole L. Jurkiewicz, eds., *Handbook of Workplace Spirituality and Organizational Performance* (Armonk, N.Y.: M. E. Sharpe, 2010); Bouckaert and Zsolnai, *Palgrave Handbook of Spirituality and Business*; and Judi Neal, *Handbook of Faith and Spirituality in the Workplace: Emerging Research and Practice* (New York: Springer, 2013).

6. For a review, see David Geigle, "Workplace Spirituality Empirical Research: A Literature Review," *Business Management Review* 2, no. 10 (2012): 14–27.

ity and a wide range of organizational phenomena.[7] This comprises matters such as enhancing employee engagement,[8] employee job satisfaction and commitment to the organization,[9] and helping employees find meaning in their work,[10] among others. However, the interest in spirituality in management goes beyond empirical studies. Some scholars focus on ethical reasons for respecting employee identity,[11] while others consider the relationship between spirituality and ethics,[12] the relationship between spirituality and virtues,[13] spirituality in business education,[14] or the foundations of workplace spirituality.[15]

Spirituality has its origin in the Christian faith, although the development of Christian spiritual theology as a discipline has evolved over time and has been presented in different forms.[16] Of course, spirituality is not exclusive to the Christian faith. Spirituality is also an important part of other religions. Today spirituality is insistently presented

7. See a bibliographical review in Fahri Karakas, "Spirituality and Performance in Organizations: A Literature Review," *Journal of Business Ethics* 94, no. 1 (2010): 89–106.

8. Richard A. Roof, "The Association of Individual Spirituality on Employee Engagement: The Spirit at Work," *Journal of Business Ethics* 130, no. 3 (2015): 585–99.

9. John Milliman, Andrew J. Czaplewski, and Jeffery Ferguson, "Workplace Spirituality and Employee Work Attitudes: An Exploratory Empirical Assessment," *Journal of Organizational Change Management* 16, no. 4 (2003): 426–47; Arménio Rego and Miguel Pina E. Cunha, "Workplace Spirituality and Organizational Commitment: An Empirical Study," *Journal of Organizational Change Management* 21, no. 1 (2008): 53–75; and Alleah Crawford, Susan S. Hubbard, Steven R. Lonis-Shumate, and Martin O'Neill, "Workplace Spirituality and Employee Attitudes within the Lodging Environment," *Journal of Human Resources in Hospitality and Tourism* 8, no. 1 (2009): 64–81.

10. Gregory N. P. Konz and Francis X. Ryan, "Maintaining an Organizational Spirituality: No Easy Task," *Journal of Organizational Change Management* 12, no. 3 (1999): 200–210.

11. Hicks, *Religion*.

12. For instance, William C. Spohn, "Spirituality and Ethics: Exploring the Connections," *Theological Studies* 58, no. 1 (1997): 109–23.

13. Gerald F. Cavanagh and Mark R. Bandsuch, "Virtue as a Benchmark for Spirituality in Business," *Journal of Business Ethics* 38, no. 1 (2002): 109–17; Bruno Dyck, "Spirituality, Virtue, and Management: Theory and Evidence," in *Handbook of Virtue Ethics in Business and Management*, ed. Alejo J. G. Sison, Gregory R. Beabout, and Ignacio Ferrero (Dordrecht: Springer, 2017), 919–28.

14. Peter Williams and Stuart Allen, "Faculty Perspectives on the Inclusion of Spirituality Topics in Nonsectarian Leadership and Management Education Programs," *International Journal of Management Education* 12, no. 3 (2014): 293–303.

15. Richard Hudson, "The Question of Theoretical Foundations for the Spirituality at Work Movement," *Journal of Management, Spirituality and Religion* 11, no. 1 (2014): 27–44.

16. Virginia R. Azcuy, "La espiritualidad como disciplina teológica: Panorama histórico, consensos y perspectivas actuales" [Spirituality as a Theological Discipline: Historical Panoramic, Consensus and Current Perspectives], *Revista Teología* 47 (2011): 251–80.

as separate and disconnected from religion,[17] with some identifying themselves as "spiritual but not religious." This nonreligious-based spirituality is generally seen as a subjective experience of a sacred or transcendent dimension of the human being and the self-understanding of the deepest values and meanings by which people live.

Nonreligious spirituality is enormously present in organizational studies regarding spirituality in business and management. Marcic carried out a survey of about a hundred books related to spirituality in the workplace and found that only twenty of them referred to a higher power like God.[18] Developing perspectives and showing how Christian spirituality can be applied to organizations is a challenge for Christian scholars. Some work has been done in this regard, particularly from the Catholic perspective,[19] but much more seems necessary.

A second challenge is responding appropriately to those who have highlighted nonreligious spirituality as more appropriate than religion for organizations or scorn religion because of its institutional character, dogmas, and rituals. Certain scholars even contrast spirituality and religion. Along this line, it has been written, "While religions often direct people outward toward social rites and rituals, spirituality directs one inward toward the wealth of knowledge, sense, aspirations, feelings one harbors within."[20] This is a misunderstanding of religion, as spirituality is at the core of any genuine religion. This contrast between religion and spirituality may stem from those who experience or understand religion in legalistic terms, devoid of spirituality. However, a religion without spirituality is not a religion, but a cold sociological

17. However, sometimes nonreligious spiritual persons also accept some external manifestations, such as yoga or certain collective practices.

18. Dorothy Marcic, "God, Faith and Management Education," *Journal of Management Education* 24, no. 5 (2000): 628–49.

19. André L. Delbecq, "Christian Spirituality and Contemporary Business Leadership," *Journal of Organizational Change Management* 12, no. 4 (1999): 345–54; Domènec Melé and Claus Dierksmeier, eds., *Human Development in Business: Values and Humanistic Management in the Encyclical "Caritas in Veritate"* (New York: Palgrave-Macmillan, 2012); Dyck, *Management and the Gospel: Luke's Radical Message for the First and Twenty-First Centuries* (New York: Palgrave-Macmillan, 2013); Melé and Martin Schlag, eds., *Humanism in Economics and Business: Perspectives of the Catholic Social Tradition* (Dordrecht: Springer, 2015).

20. Marques, Dhiman, and King, *Spirituality*, 10.

phenomenon and an empty set of ceremonies. This is especially true for the Christian religion, in which faith in God, the fellowship of Jesus Christ, and the action of the Holy Spirit are at its heart. Liturgy and institutional aspects express and serve spirituality. The gospel, in fact, is rich with spirituality, as are the letters of the apostles. St. Paul repeatedly employed the Greek term *pneumatikos*, which equates to "spiritual." According to the apostle, the spirit is embedded completely in Christian life, and he stresses the necessity of living according to the spirit and not to the flesh.[21] Several fathers of the church presented interesting insights on spirituality,[22] and a rich multiform Christian spirituality has been developed within the Catholic Church.[23] The Second Vatican Council proposed a rich spirituality,[24] as has the more recent Magisterium, including the encyclical letters *Dominum et vivificantem*, by St. John Paul II (1986), *Deus caritas est*, by Benedict XVI (2009), and *Laudato si'*, by Francis (2015).

Jordan Aumann defined Christian spirituality as "a participation in the mystery of Christ through the interior life of grace, actuated by faith, charity and the other Christian virtues."[25] Spirituality informs the whole life of Christians—whatever the profession and state in life—and leads us to holiness. As the Second Vatican Council states, "All the faithful of Christ are invited to strive for the holiness and perfection of their own proper state.... Let all then have care that they guide aright their own deepest sentiments of soul."[26]

Some have tried to provide comprehensive definitions of spirituality, which can include the religious. Thus, Schneiders presented spirituality as "the experience of consciously striving to integrate one's life in terms not of isolation and self-absorption but of self-transcendence

21. See, for example, Gal 5:13–26; 1 Cor 2:12–16, 3:3, 16:9, 9:11, 14:1.

22. Manuel Diego Sánchez, *Historia de la espiritualidad patrística* [History of Patristic Spirituality] (Madrid: Editorial de espiritualidad, 1992).

23. Jordan Aumann, *Christian Spirituality in the Catholic Tradition* (London: Bloomsbury, 1985).

24. Pablo Martí, "La espiritualidad cristiana en el Concilio Vaticano II," *Scripta Theologica* 45, no. 1 (2013): 153–84.

25. Aumann, *Spiritual Theology* (London: Bloomsbury, 1991), 18.

26. Vatican Council II, Dogmatic Constitution *Lumen gentium* (November 21, 1964), no. 42.

toward the ultimate value one perceives. If the ultimate value is the Transcendent itself, the Deity, the spirituality is explicitly religious."[27] However, there are many definitions of spirituality; Karakas identified at least seventy different definitions.[28] Ratnakar and Nair observed that spirituality has acquired diverse meanings, which can conflict.[29] This issue is probably linked with the increasing acceptance of spirituality as a reality fully separated from religion.

The positive aspect of the current emphasis on spirituality is the recognition of the openness of the human being to transcendence and to the existence of certain values that transcend the individual. But what is the ultimate foundation of these values? What gives these values a compulsory moral character? Christian spirituality—like other theistic spiritualities—finds the answer in God. Pope Francis affirms, "Respect must also be shown for the various cultural riches of different peoples, their art and poetry, their interior life and spirituality."[30] However, not all spiritualities are equal. According to Francis, only God gives spirituality a full sense: "A spirituality which forgets God as all-powerful and Creator is not acceptable. That is how we end up worshipping earthly powers, or ourselves usurping the place of God, even to the point of claiming an unlimited right to trample his creation underfoot."[31]

The third and even more important challenge is to be aware that "the rich heritage of Christian spirituality, the fruit of twenty centuries of personal and communal experience, has a precious contribution to make to the renewal of humanity."[32] Being aware of spirituality brings about some interior impulse that encourages, motivates, nourishes, and gives meaning to our individual and communal activity,[33] and the

27. Sandra Schneiders, "Theology and Spirituality: Strangers, Rivals, or Partners?," *Horizons* 13, no. 2 (1986): 266–67.

28. Karakas, "Spirituality."

29. Ratnakar and Nair, "Review."

30. Francis, Encyclical Letter *Laudato si'* (May 24, 2015), no. 63.

31. Ibid., no. 75.

32. Ibid., no. 216.

33. See Francis, Apostolic Exhortation *Evangelii gaudium* (November 24, 2013), 261; see also Francis, *Laudato si'*, no. 216.

millennial history of Christianity shows that this is a reality for many Christians. Spirituality entails Christian values. Sometimes, older Christian cultures have these values. As Francis points out, "An evangelized popular culture contains values of faith and solidarity capable of encouraging the development of a more just and believing society, and possesses a particular wisdom which ought to be gratefully acknowledged."[34] However, in other cultural contexts the inculturation of the Christian faith is necessary. As St John Paul II affirmed, "A faith that does not become culture is a faith not fully received, not totally thought out, not faithfully lived."[35] Benedict XVI added that "adhering to the values of Christianity is not merely useful but essential for building a good society and for true integral human development."[36]

This book does not seek to provide a definitive answer to the aforementioned challenges, but to make a contribution to a better understanding of Christian spirituality and its connection with organizations. The authors in this book are convinced that markets can be ethical and social, that moral change toward ethical capitalism is possible. In order to reach this aim, the majority of moral, righteous businesspeople must form a network of virtuosity, spirituality, and gift. The path we choose focuses on the role of the individual virtuous entrepreneur. Markus Krienke in his chapter points out that the "first-person approach," centered on the entrepreneur, is a good way forward, rather than relying exclusively on "third-person approaches," which remain either extrinsic to business activity by imposing extraneous rules on business in a heteronomous way or evaporate without effect by confusing economic and ethical norms. Certainly, this does not make the "third-person perspective" redundant. Virtues need a normative guideline that clearly marks the limits of admissible behavior. Clemens Sedmak, in his chapter, presents a further nuance. He emphasizes not only a "first-person"

34. Francis, *Evangelii gaudium*, no. 68.

35. John Paul II, *Address to the Participants in the National Congress of the Ecclesial Movement for Cultural Commitment*, January 16, 1982; see John Paul II, *Foundation Letter of the Pontifical Council for Culture*, May 20, 1982.

36. Benedict XVI, Encyclical Letter *Caritas in veritate* (June 29, 2009), no. 4.

but also a "second-person perspective" and clearly affirms that the "central role of love is located not only on a personal micro-level, but also on the macro-level of structures," thus showing the "permeability" between the spheres of human life in society: "The same moral grammar permeates the different spheres of society." This is one of the core messages of Pope Benedict XVI's encyclical *Caritas in veritate*.

The first part of this book opens with two general reflections on Christian spirituality. Elizabeth Reichert analyzes its roots in Christ and the sacraments that unfold in the three *munera* of the baptized. From a different but nevertheless general perspective, Rafael Alvira considers the importance of spirituality and "presence" for business leaders. A U.S. American reader can find some unusual, even provocative, and thus innovative ideas in Alvira's contribution. Martin Schlag ends part 1 with a chapter on the central biblical message contained in the Sermon on the Mount and its implications for business and the economy.

Part 2 of the book focuses on the "logic of gift." This expression was introduced into official Catholic social teaching by the authority of Pope Benedict XVI, who presented it in association with the principle of gratuitousness, which in turn is an expression of fraternity.[37] However, before *Caritas in veritate* and ever since Marcel Mauss's groundbreaking work *The Gift*,[38] the importance of gift for human relationships and for the cohesion of society had been increasingly recognized. Alain Caillié and Jacques T. Godbout further fleshed out the implication of gift for contemporary society in the context of secular social sciences, striving to overcome utilitarianism.[39] It was the "civil economy" movement, however, that exercised greatest influence on Benedict XVI's encyclical *Caritas in veritate*. Authors like Luigino

37. Ibid., no. 34.

38. Marcel Mauss, *The Gift: The Form and Reason for Exchange in Archaic Societies* (London: Routledge, 1990). The original title was *Essai sur le don*, first published in 1925.

39. See, for example, Alain Caillé, *Critica della ragione utilitaria: Manifesto del Movimento antiutilitarista nelle scienze sociali* [Critique of Utilitarian Reason: Manifesto of the Anti-Utilitarian Movement in the Social Sciences] (Turin: Bollati Boringhieri, 1991), and Jacques T. Godbout, *Le langage du don* [The Language of Gift] (Montreal: Fides, 1996).

Bruni and Stefano Zamagni had been developing a specifically Christian and Catholic notion of gift, fraternity, reciprocity, and gratuitousness that was received in *Caritas in veritate* in 2009.[40] These notions are connected to one another, and they also nicely link parts 1 and 2 of this book.

Fraternity is a consequence of a particular view of the world, which sees all persons as members of the single human family with a common father, God. The "logic of gift" is also connected to the central Christian virtue *agape* (generous love for God and one's neighbors) or *charity* in Christian terminology, which requires giving what is one's own to others without expecting anything in return. The giving dimension of charity in turn connects gift with Christian spirituality, because the latter in essence "is an exercise of charity."[41]

The "logic of gift" begins by recognizing that prior to offering a gift we have already received great gifts as a consequence of God's love for us, since, according to the Christian faith, "in this is love: not that we have loved God, but that he loved us and sent his Son as expiation for our sins."[42] "Love is God's greatest gift to humanity,"[43] and "everything has its origin in God's love."[44] Benedict XVI argues that "it is the primordial truth of God's love, grace bestowed upon us, that opens our lives to gift."[45] Francis returns to the same thoughts repeatedly in his powerful and joyful proclamation of the gospel, filled with the gifts of the Holy Spirit.[46] Charity on the other hand requires truth—otherwise charity degenerates into sentimentality[47]—and so too does the logic of gift. It is precisely truth that makes the gift reasonable, and this has

40. See Luigino Bruni and Stefano Zamagni, *Civil Economy: Another Idea of the Market* (Newcastle upon Tyne: Agenda, 2016); Bruni and Zamagni, eds., *Dizionario di economia civile* [Dictionary of Civil Economy] (Rome: Città Nuova, 2009). For an attempt to implement the civil economy in an Anglo-Saxon context, see John Milbank and Adrian Pabst, *The Politics of Virtue: Post-Liberalism and the Human Future* (London: Rowman and Littlefield, 2016).

41. Francis, *Laudato si'*, no. 231.

42. See 1 Jn 4:10.

43. Benedict XVI, *Caritas in veritate*, no. 2.

44. Ibid.

45. Ibid., no. 8.

46. See Francis, *Evangelii gaudium*, nos. 112, 162, and many other passages.

47. See ibid., no. 3.

relevant consequences for organizations; in particular, it makes them human,[48] and it builds up a sense of community within them.[49]

The Christian faith, spirituality, generosity, gift, and virtues have had positive impact and continue to exercise a redeeming influence on business. The chapters in part 2 of this book develop some aspects of the logic of gift in the context of business and economic activity. As in part 1, in part 2 two general chapters are placed at the beginning. Both Domènec Melé and Germán Scalzo give an overall panoramic view of the importance of gift in social ethics, especially in business. Melé links parts 1 and 2 of the book by elaborating on the intrinsic nexus between gift and spirituality. Scalzo offers an important historic background and perspective to our topic. Clemens Sedmak argues in his chapter that religion and spirituality are not the servants of economic success. Good and virtuous behavior usually results in earthly success, but faith must not be instrumentalized as the steward or servant of earthly wealth. Juan Luis Martínez, José María Ortiz, and Martin Schlag close the book with an attempt to rethink business methodology and education, enriching them with spirituality and gift.

We hope that this volume will be useful both to university students and practitioners who wish to understand the recent popes' insistence on gift and spirituality in business and society. Ten years have passed since Benedict XVI published his social encyclical *Caritas in veritate*, and we especially wish to commemorate that pontifical document in our book. Pope Francis too ends each of his documents with a chapter on spirituality or contemplation. Far from being lifeless theory, such teachings are meant to be put into practice. This book is a contribution toward this aim.

We are grateful to the Catholic University of America Press for accepting this book for publication and the diligent publication process. We thank the anonymous peer reviewers for their valuable constructive criticism that has improved the volume. We acknowledge the

48. See ibid.
49. See ibid., no. 34.

untiring work of editing and correction by Elizabeth Reichert, without whom the manuscript would never have been accurately finished. We also thank Mary Catherine Adams for putting together the indexes.

BIBLIOGRAPHY

Aumann, Jordan. *Christian Spirituality in the Catholic Tradition*. London: Bloomsbury, 1985.

———. *Spiritual Theology*. London: Bloomsbury, 1991.

Azcuy, Virginia R. "La espiritualidad como disciplina teológica: Panorama histórico, consensos y perspectivas actuales" [Spirituality as a Theological Discipline: Historical Panoramic, Consensus and Current Perspectives]. *Revista Teología* 47 (2011): 251–80.

Bell, Michael. "Teaching of the Elders." In *The Palgrave Handbook of Spirituality and Business*, edited by Luk Bouckaert and László Zsolnai, 187–96. Houndmills: Palgrave Macmillan, 2011.

Benedict XVI. Encyclical Letter *Caritas in veritate*. June 29, 2009.

Bouckaert, Luk, and László Zsolnai, eds. *The Palgrave Handbook of Spirituality and Business*. Houndmills: Palgrave-Macmillan, 2011.

Bruni, Luigino, and Stefano Zamagni, eds. *Dizionario di economia civile* [Dictionary of Civil Economy]. Rome: Città Nuova, 2009.

———. *Civil Economy: Another Idea of the Market*. Newcastle upon Tyne: Agenda, 2016.

Caillé, Alain. *Critica della ragione utilitaria: Manifesto del Movimento antiutilitarista nelle scienze sociali* [Critique of Utilitarian Reason: Manifesto of the Anti-Utilitarian Movement in the Social Sciences]. Turin: Bollati Boringhieri, 1991.

Cavanagh, Gerald F., and Mark R. Bandsuch. "Virtue as a Benchmark for Spirituality in Business." *Journal of Business Ethics* 38, no. 1 (2002): 109–17.

Crawford, Alleah, Susan S. Hubbard, Steven R. Lonis-Shumate, and Martin O'Neill. "Workplace Spirituality and Employee Attitudes within the Lodging Environment." *Journal of Human Resources in Hospitality and Tourism* 8, no. 1 (2009): 64–81.

Delbecq, André L. "Christian Spirituality and Contemporary Business Leadership." *Journal of Organizational Change Management* 12, no. 4 (1999): 345–54.

Denton, Elizabeth A., and Ian I. Mitroff. *A Spiritual Audit of Corporate America: A Hard Look at Spirituality, Religion, and Values in the Workplace*. San Francisco: Jossey-Bass, 1999.

Dyck, Bruno. *Management and the Gospel: Luke's Radical Message for the First and Twenty-First Centuries*. New York: Palgrave-Macmillan, 2013.

———. "Spirituality, Virtue, and Management: Theory and Evidence." In *Handbook of Virtue Ethics in Business and Management*, edited by Alejo J. G. Sison, Gregory R. Beabout, and Ignacio Ferrero, 919–28. Dordrecht: Springer, 2017.

Francis. Apostolic Exhortation *Evangelii gaudium*. November 24, 2013.

———. Encyclical Letter *Laudato si'*. May 24, 2015.

Geigle, David. "Workplace Spirituality Empirical Research: A Literature Review." *Business Management Review* 2, no. 10 (2012): 14–27.

Giacalone, Robert A., and Carole L. Jurkiewicz, eds. *Handbook of Workplace Spirituality and Organizational Performance*. Armonk, N.Y.: M. E. Sharpe, 2010.

Godbout, Jacques T. *Le langage du don* [The Language of Gift]. Montreal: Fides, 1996.

Hicks, Douglas A. *Religion and the Workplace: Pluralism, Spirituality, Leadership*. Cambridge: Cambridge University Press, 2003.

Houghton, Jeffery D., Christopher P. Neck, and Sukumarakurup Krishnakumar. "The What, Why, and How of Spirituality in the Workplace Revisited: A 14-Year Update and Extension." *Journal of Management, Spirituality and Religion* 13 (2016): 177–205.

Hudson, Richard. "The Question of Theoretical Foundations for the Spirituality at Work Movement." *Journal of Management, Spirituality and Religion* 11, no. 1 (2014): 27–44.

John Paul II. *Address to the Participants in the National Congress of the Ecclesial Movement for Cultural Commitment*. January 16, 1982.

———. *Foundation Letter of the Pontifical Council for Culture*. May 20, 1982.

Karakas, Fahri. "Spirituality and Performance in Organizations: A Literature Review." *Journal of Business Ethics* 94, no. 1 (2010): 89–106.

Konz, Gregory N. P., and Francis X. Ryan. "Maintaining an Organizational Spirituality: No Easy Task." *Journal of Organizational Change Management* 12, no. 3 (1999): 200–210.

Marcic, Dorothy. "God, Faith and Management Education." *Journal of Management Education* 24, no. 5 (2000): 628–49.

Marques, Joan, Satinder Dhiman, and Richard King. *Spirituality in the Workplace: What It Is, Why It Matters, How to Make It Work for You*. Fawnskin, Calif.: Personhood, 2007.

Martí, Pablo. "La espiritualidad cristiana en el Concilio Vaticano II" [Christian Spirituality in Vatican Council II]. *Scripta Theologica* 45, no. 1 (2013): 153–84.

Mauss, Marcel. *The Gift: The Form and Reason for Exchange in Archaic Societies*. London: Routledge, 1990. Originally published in 1925 as *Essai sur le don*.

Melé, Domènec, and Claus Dierksmeier, eds. *Human Development in Business: Values and Humanistic Management in the Encyclical "Caritas in Veritate."* New York: Palgrave-MacMillan, 2012.

Melé, Domènec, and Martin Schlag, eds. *Humanism in Economics and Business: Perspectives of the Catholic Social Tradition*. Dordrecht: Springer, 2015.

Milbank, John, and Adrian Pabst. *The Politics of Virtue: Post-Liberalism and the Human Future*. London: Rowman and Littlefield, 2016.

Milliman, John, Andrew J. Czaplewski, and Jeffery Ferguson. "Workplace Spirituality and Employee Work Attitudes: An Exploratory Empirical Assessment." *Journal of Organizational Change Management* 16, no. 4 (2003): 426–47.

Neal, Judy. *Handbook of Faith and Spirituality in the Workplace: Emerging Research and Practice*. New York: Springer, 2013.

Ratnakar, Rajesh, and Shreekumar Nair. "A Review of Scientific Research on Spirituality." *Business Perspectives and Research* 1, no. 1 (2012): 1–12.

Rego, Arménio, and Miguel Pina E. Cunha. "Workplace Spirituality and Organizational Commitment: An Empirical Study." *Journal of Organizational Change Management* 21, no. 1 (2008): 53–75.

Roof, Richard A. "The Association of Individual Spirituality on Employee Engagement: The Spirit at Work." *Journal of Business Ethics* 130, no. 3 (2015): 585–99.

Sánchez, Manuel Diego. *Historia de la espiritualidad patrística* [History of Patristic Spirituality]. Madrid: Editorial de espiritualidad, 1992.

Schneiders, Sandra. "Theology and Spirituality: Strangers, Rivals, or Partners?" *Horizons* 13, no. 2 (1986): 266–67.

Smith, Nancy R. *Workplace Spirituality: A Complete Guide for Business Leaders*. Lynn, Mass.: Axial Age, 2006.

Spohn, William C. "Spirituality and Ethics: Exploring the Connections." *Theological Studies* 58, no. 1 (1997): 109–23.

Vatican Council II. Dogmatic Constitution *Lumen gentium*. November 21, 1964.

Williams, Peter, and Stuart Allen. "Faculty Perspectives on the Inclusion of Spirituality Topics in Nonsectarian Leadership and Management Education Programs." *International Journal of Management Education* 12, no. 3 (2014): 293–303.

PART 1

CHRISTIAN SPIRITUALITY IN LEADING BUSINESS

1

THEOLOGICAL FOUNDATIONS OF SPIRITUALITY IN THE WORKPLACE

The *Tria Munera Christi* and Its Implications for the Businessperson

ELIZABETH REICHERT

Spirituality in the workplace has stirred increasing interest among academics in recent decades. As outlined in the introduction to this volume, journals and conferences dedicated to the subject continue to grow in number, and some business schools are beginning to follow suit by taking steps to incorporate both spirituality and ethics into the curriculum. The phenomenon is crossing denominational and religious lines, also catching the attention of and garnering input from agnostic and nonreligious groups.

That being said, it has also been the target of critical reflection. Most notably, critics raise concerns about the vast array of definitions of spirituality in the workplace, a practically inevitable corollary of the diversity of contributors. In an attempt to encompass such diversity, some definitions have become so broad that they lose any real substance; they fall into a series of contradictions, with the ambiguities offering a certain insulation from critique.[1] Amid the myriad

1. See Dennis Tourish, *The Dark Side of Transformational Leadership: A Critical Perspective* (London: Routledge, 2013), 61–64; Dennis Tourish and Naheed Tourish, "Spirituality at Work, and Its Implications for Leadership and Followership: A Post-Structuralist Perspective," *Leadership* 6, no. 2 (2010): 210–11; Peter Case and Jonathan Gosling, "The Spiritual Organization: Critical Reflections on the Instrumentality of Workplace Spirituality," *Journal of Management, Spirituality and Religion* 7, no. 4 (2010): 261–63.

definitions, though, several critics have identified common threads in secular and religious proposals. These common threads can be summarized into three critical points:

1. *Spirituality in the workplace instrumentalizes employees and expands the business leader's control.* Spirituality in the workplace literature argues that employees want to find meaning in their work by connecting it to their inner life; it is thus assumed that the leaders of organizations are those who are obligated to provide this sense of meaning. While this holistic approach may be a welcome change from authoritarian models of leadership, at least it could be said of the authoritarian "that what he wanted primarily of you was your sweat. The new man *wants your soul*."[2] Spirituality becomes simply another control mechanism by which leaders get their employees to work harder. Setting themselves up as a sort of "priestly caste," these spiritual business leaders "are invited to exercise a colonizing influence on the deepest recesses of their employees' hitherto private belief and value systems."[3]

2. *Spirituality in the workplace appropriates authentic spirituality for economic ends.* A "thinly disguised performative intent" is "endemic" to spirituality in the workplace literature.[4] Scientific study of the matter must justify its utility, showing that it adds value, helps one to work more effectively, enhances competitiveness, and ultimately increases profits. In the end, spirituality is "*used* for profit making ends as opposed to its being *valued* for its own sake"; all the while "it is less clear that [these practices] confer unalloyed benefits to employees."[5]

2. William H. Whyte, *The Organization Man* (1956; repr. Philadelphia: University of Pennsylvania Press, 2002), 397, emphasis added, quoted in Case and Gosling, "Spiritual Organization," 267.

3. Tourish, *Dark Side*, 74, 61. See also Tourish and Tourish, "Spirituality at Work," 212–14; Case and Gosling, "Spiritual Organization," 267–69; Marjolein Lips-Wiesma, Kathy Lund Dean, and Charles J. Fornaciari, "Theorizing the Dark Side of the Workplace Spirituality Movement," *Journal of Management Inquiry* 18, no. 4 (2009): 288–300.

4. Tourish, *Dark Side*, 69.

5. Case and Gosling, "Spiritual Organization," 258; Tourish, *Dark Side*, 69. See also Robert A. Giacolone and Carole L. Jurkiewicz, "The Science of Workplace Spirituality," in *Handbook of Workplace Spirituality*, ed. Robert A. Giacalone and Carole L. Jurkiewicz (Armonk, N.Y.: M. E. Sharpe, 2010), 6–12.

Finally, then, these critics conclude that:

3. *Spirituality and business are incommensurable.* Business and spirituality are like oil and water, and no amount of mixing and shaking will manage to bring them together into a homogenous blend. Any overlap between the two spheres is merely incidental: "The workplace has no special relevance to spirituality; it is simply another site, amongst the multitude of transient phenomena within which subjective journeys may or may not be pursued."[6] This is not to denigrate the value of spirituality for the person working in business; rather, it is a recognition of the value of both work and spirituality for their own sake and not as mere means to one another.

Such pointed criticisms rightly call into question many of the underlying assumptions behind spirituality in the workplace literature. It would appear that it might be time to rethink the idea of spirituality in the workplace, or at least that a return to its philosophical and theological foundations is warranted. In agreement with the critics, a "neutral" response that pretends to incorporate all types of spiritualities is not likely to get us very far. Instead, this chapter intends to offer a specifically Christian response, understood as a proposal for Christians, not something to be imposed from on high on all members of the workplace regardless of creed. Furthermore, what follows is not an outline of a specific Christian spirituality in business, but a return to the foundations—that is, what it is about Christian spirituality—or better, the Christian person—that gives spirituality a place in the business sphere.

Spirituality in the workplace literature as well as the criticisms outlined previously assume that there must be something different about how the spiritual person—in our case, the Christian—goes about doing business. Thus, if we are following the Scholastic principle *agere sequitur esse* (action follows being), if there is something different about what a Christian businessperson *does*, then there must be something

6. Case and Gosling, "Spiritual Organization," 276. See also Tourish, *Dark Side*, 75–76.

different about who or what a Christian businessperson *is*. And at the heart of the Christian identity is our conformity to Christ: "Christ enables us to *live in him* all that he himself lived, and *he lives it in us*."[7] Through the grace of God we "come to share in the divine nature,"[8] so that with St. Paul we might say, "I live, no longer I, but Christ lives in me."[9] "For in him we live and move and have our being."[10] We become *alter Christus*—another Christ.

Our conformity to Christ, while it is something in which we are called to continually grow, is not something to be turned off and on as we pass through the various spheres of life. Nor is our spirituality: we are instructed to "pray without ceasing."[11] John Paul II does not mince his words when he confirms as much: "There cannot be two parallel lives in their existence: on the one hand, the so-called 'spiritual' life, with its values and demands; and on the other, the so-called 'secular' life, that is, life in a family, at work, in social relationships, in the responsibilities of public life and in culture."[12]

Spirituality in the workplace is not only possible for the follower of Christ; the alternative—checking one's faith at the office doors—implies a denial of what it means to be a Christian. John Paul II thus proclaims it a "*duty to form a spirituality of work* which will help all people to come closer, through work, to God."[13] But what does this mean, practically speaking? What can I gather from my being united to Christ that tells me something about how I conduct myself in the workplace? In the very same passage the Holy Father gives us a hint at where to look—that is, what aspect of our being *alter Christus* is key to

7. *Catechism of the Catholic Church* (Vatican City: Libreria Editrice Vaticana, 1993), no. 521. See also Jn 6:56 and 15:4–11.

8. 2 Pt 1:4.

9. Gal 2:20.

10. Acts 17:28.

11. 1 Thes 5:17.

12. John Paul II, Apostolic Exhortation *Christifideles laici* (December 30, 1988), no. 59. *Gaudium et spes* calls such a division "pernicious"; Vatican Council II, Pastoral Constitution *Gaudium et spes* (December 7, 1965), no. 43.

13. John Paul II, Encyclical Letter *Laborem exercens* (September 14, 1981), no. 24, emphasis added.

a spirituality of work. The Christian will live this particular spirituality, he says, "by accepting, through faith, *a living participation in* [*Christ's*] *threefold mission as Priest, Prophet and King*."[14]

THE *TRIA MUNERA*

The Christian's participation in this threefold mission as priest, prophet, and king—called the *tria munera*—is relatively new in the teaching of the Magisterium: it was explicitly stated for the first time in relation to the laity in the documents of the Second Vatican Council.[15] The concept, though, is latent in scripture and present already in the fathers of the church.[16] In synthesis, Jesus assumed and united in his one person the three offices of priest, prophet, and king, which were previously distinct roles in Israel, each playing a part in the mediation between God and his chosen people. Now every Christian, in virtue of his or her conformity to Christ in baptism, is made to participate in these *tria munera*.

This word *munera*, or *munus* in the singular, is often translated as "duty," "role," "task," "mission," "office," or "function." Correctly understood, the word *munus* carries with it all of the positive connotations of a privileged or special mission and none of the negative connotations of a burdensome "duty" or "task" imposed on a person.[17] In

14. Ibid., emphasis added. In a document entitled *Consilium de laicis, quid dicis de teipso?*, Cardinal Wojtyla follows the same line of thought outlined here. Reflecting on the nature of the newly established Council of the Laity, he says that if we are to understand the *operari* of the laity—and consequently the council—we must first understand their specific *esse*. Noting that the council must be "watchful to place this 'operari' on sound foundations," he immediately turns to their "participation in the threefold mission of Christ the Messiah" as definitive of their *esse*; Wojtyla, *Consilium de Laicis, quid dicis de teipso?*, December 3, 1968, no. 2, available at http://www.laici.va/content/laici/en/media/notizie/doc_wojtyla.html, accessed June 8, 2017.

15. Vatican Council II, Dogmatic Constitution *Lumen gentium* (November 21, 1964), no. 10–11, 31–36; Vatican Council II, Decree *Apostolicam actuositatem* (November 18, 1965), no. 2.

16. John Paul II says that "this aspect has never been forgotten in the living tradition of the Church" (John Paul II, *Christifideles laici*, no. 14). See also Cruz González-Ayesta, "Work as 'a Mass': Reflections on the Laity's Participation in the *Munus Sacerdotale* in the Writings of the Founder of Opus Dei," *Romana* 50 (2010): 192.

17. Janet E. Smith and Russell Hittinger both offer particular insight into the richness of meaning of the word *munus*; see Smith, "The Importance of the Concept of 'Munus' to Understanding *Humane*

classical Latin, as well as in scripture and Aquinas, *munus* is also translated as "gift," referring to both those gifts offered to God and those received from him.[18] We see, then, that the word brings together the concepts of both gift and mission. A *munus* is something entrusted to a person; "it is a responsibility that they have but a responsibility given to one as a kind of honor."[19] Furthermore, as the young Cardinal Wojtyla insisted in his book *Sources of Renewal: The Implementation of Vatican II*, a *munus* is less a matter of specific external actions tied to one's office than it is about one's internal dispositions, or "attitudes of participation," as he calls them. "The Christian bears witness to Christ not 'from the outside' but on the basis of participation, in him, in his mission."[20] So as not to impoverish the richness of meaning behind the word *munus*, it will be left in the Latin throughout this chapter.

Finally, the close relation among the three *munera* must be emphasized: "These attitudes interpenetrate and in a certain sense determine one another. They form, so to speak, an organic complex.... It is undoubtedly difficult to separate and distinguish with precision ... the individual powers and offices of Christ."[21] That being said, the Second Vatican Council and subsequent magisterial documents—as well as the nature of these *munera* in the Old and New Testaments—offer lines of distinction that will be followed here, always keeping in mind their interconnection. What follows is not an exhaustive study of the *tria munera*, but a painting in broad strokes from which one might draw insights and cues for applications in the workplace. The goal is to lay the theological foundations, showing that spirituality in the workplace is not only *possible* but *inherent* to the Christian identity properly

Vitae," in *"Humanae Vitae": 20 Anni Dopo* (Milan: Edizioni Ares, 1989), 677–90; and Hittinger, "Social Pluralism and Subsidiarity in Catholic Social Doctrine," *Annales Theologici* 16 (2002): 385–408.

18. Smith, "Importance of the Concept of 'Munus,'" 678.

19. Ibid., 680.

20. Wojtyla, *Sources of Renewal: The Implementation of Vatican II*, trans. P. S. Falla (1972; repr. San Francisco: Harper and Row, 1980), 219.

21. Wojtyla, *Sources of Renewal*, 221. He also insists on this point in his book *Sign of Contradiction*, basing his conclusion on *Lumen gentium* 10; see Wojtyla, *Sign of Contradiction* (1977; repr. New York: Seabury, 1979), 128.

understood, and that such a spirituality is not an appropriation of matters spiritual for economic ends, nor can its proper implementation lead to the instrumentalization of employees in the workplace.

ROYAL PRIESTS

Work is a given in the Christian life and "a fundamental dimension of man's existence on earth."[22] In the creation accounts in Genesis we read that God tells the first human couple to "be fertile and multiply; fill the earth and subdue it";[23] God places man in the garden "to cultivate and care for it."[24] As John Paul II confirms in his encyclical dedicated to the subject, *Laborem exercens*, "Even though these words do not refer directly and explicitly to work, beyond any doubt they indirectly indicate it as an activity for man to carry out in the world."[25] It is noteworthy that this command to work is given before the fall and therefore cannot be considered a punishment or curse; rather, it is a *munus*, carrying with it all the connotations outlined previously. And these commands to subdue, cultivate, and care for the earth are connected in particular to the kingly or royal *munus*.[26]

The human being is given the privileged responsibility of imitating God the Creator in working, and in this work each person shares in, continues, and develops the work of the Creator.[27] As the *Catechism* states, "Creation has its own goodness and proper perfection, but it did not spring forth complete from the hands of the Creator. The universe was created 'in a state of journeying' (*in statu viae*) toward an ultimate perfection yet to be attained, to which God has destined it."[28] Men and women, then, "can justly consider that by their labor they are unfolding the Creator's work ... and are contributing by their per-

22. John Paul II, *Laborem exercens*, no. 4.
23. Gn 1:28.
24. Gn 2:15.
25. John Paul II, *Laborem exercens*, no. 4.
26. Wojtyla, *Sources of Renewal*, 265.
27. John Paul II, *Laborem exercens*, no. 25.
28. *Catechism of the Catholic Church* (Vatican City: Libreria Editrice Vaticana, 1993), no. 302.

sonal industry to the realization in history of the divine plan."[29] This unfolding of the Creator's work, bringing it to perfection, says Wojtyla, "is the task and purpose of human labour.... The whole work of transforming the world and bringing it to man's level by means of science, technology and civilization—all this bears the imprint of man's kingship and his sharing in the *munus regale* of Christ."[30]

Work—when it is ordered to moral progress—is thus endowed with an extraordinary dignity. If the field of spirituality in the workplace is looking to find meaning in work, this is it. John Paul II, however, takes this yet another step further: not only is it the case that work is not a curse or punishment for sin, not only is it a privileged participation in the work of the Creator, but work can—and should—"*enter into the salvation process.*"[31] It is one thing to promote the idea of spirituality in the workplace understood in the sense that one might find deeper meaning in his or her work, or maybe even set aside time for prayer or meditation during the work day, but to say that our work itself enters into the very *process of salvation* is audacious, to say the least. But this is the Christian claim, and it gets at the core of the Christian understanding of spirituality in the workplace—that is, that spirituality is not something that is superimposed on the day-to-day of our nine-to-five; rather, it is the ordinary tasks of our day-to-day work that become the very landscape in which our salvation is played out and our spirituality is lived.

How is this possible? Because we are not only kings (and queens), but also *priests*. It is interesting that one of the strongest critics of spirituality in the workplace argues that spirituality has no business being in business, especially among managers and executives, because they are not "secular priests."[32] But this is *exactly what we are*, or at least

29. Vatican Council II, *Gaudium et spes*, no. 34, referencing John XXIII, Encyclical Letter *Pacem in terris* (April 11, 1963), no. 150.

30. Wojtyla, *Sources of Renewal*, 265, commenting on *Lumen gentium*, no. 36. See also John Paul II, *Laborem exercens*, no. 25, and Wojtyla, *Sign of Contradiction*, 138–39.

31. John Paul II, *Laborem exercens*, no. 24, emphasis added.

32. Tourish and Tourish, "Spirituality at Work," 219.

what the Christian is. And our work, which is closely tied to the royal *munus*, enters into the mysteries of redemption and salvation because the royal *munus* is closely connected to the *priestly*.

Sacred scripture and magisterial texts confirm this close relation, often mentioning the two *munera* as a single pair.[33] The command in Genesis mentioned previously to "cultivate and care" for the garden brings out this point even further. Also translated into English as "to till and to keep," the verse employs the Hebrew verbs *'abad* and *shamar*. In the Torah, these two verbs appear together again only in the book of Numbers and always in reference to the ministerial duties of the priests.[34] *'Abad*, often translated as "to serve," can refer to working the ground or working for someone as a servant, but also refers to serving God, specifically by offering sacrifice and completing cultic acts of worship. *Shamar*, meaning "to watch," "to guard," "to protect," likewise refers to both civic tasks (the guardian of a city, a gatekeeper, watching over animals) and cultic tasks (referring to the duties of the Levitical priests in the tabernacle).[35]

God's command to the man "to till and to keep"—which, as we have already seen, indicates man's royal *munus* and his vocation to work—therefore indicates also his *priestly munus*. In fact, the whole of Genesis 1–3 in its language and its sevenfold structure depicts the world as a "macro-temple"; the phrasing in the creation account closely parallels that of the construction of the tabernacle in Exodus.[36] Adam—and with him all of humanity—is thus presented as a royal

33. In scripture, see Ex 19:6; 1 Pt 2:9; Rv 5:9–10; in the Magisterium see, for example, Vatican Council II, *Lumen gentium*, no. 9–10, 13; Vatican Council II, Decree *Presbyterorum ordinis* (December 7, 1965), no. 2; John Paul II, *Christifideles laici*, no. 14; see also González-Ayesta, "Work as 'a Mass,'" 198–99, which says the two are connected based on their secular character.

34. Nm 3:7–8, 8:26, 18:5–6. See also Jeffrey Morrow, "Work as Worship in the Garden and the Workshop: Genesis 1–3, the Feast of St. Joseph the Worker, and Liturgical Hermeneutics," *Logos* 15, no. 4 (2012): 161.

35. See "עבד," ['abad], in *The Hebrew and Aramaic Lexicon of the Old Testament*, ed. Ludwig Koehler and Walter Baumgartner (Leiden: Brill, 1995), 2:773–74; and "שמר," [shamar], in Koehler and Baumgartner, *Hebrew and Aramaic Lexicon of the Old Testament* (Leiden: Brill, 1999), 4:1581–84; see also Scott Hahn, *Ordinary Work, Extraordinary Grace: My Spiritual Journey in Opus Dei* (New York: Doubleday, 2006), 27–29.

36. Morrow, "Work as Worship," 160–63.

priest, as created for work and worship, which, in the beginning, were not separate activities. "Adam enjoyed a unity of life; his work was ordered to worship and was itself an act of worship."[37]

Similarly, the word *leitourgia* chosen by the early Christians to describe their worship carries with it the dual connotation of work and worship. Literally translated as "public service" or "public work," it was used in ancient Greece to refer to a service to the community performed at one's own expense: this could take the form of military service or physical labor or, in the case of the wealthy, taxes paid in lieu of physical work.[38] Both the translators of the Septuagint and the authors of the New Testament took up the Greek *leitourgia*, using it primarily in reference to the worship of God, but also to work done as a service to the people.[39] The Latin equivalent, which is especially interesting for our discussion, in both sacred and secular usage, was not the transliterated *liturgia* but *munus*; and in Constantine's Rome, the priests were exempt from the obligation to perform public services (*munera*), meaning their work of worship was seen as work of public service.[40]

Without getting further bogged down in etymological excurses, it is clear that from the beginning, in the Jewish and Christian mentalities there has been a unity between work and worship. The Anglican New Testament scholar Charles F. D. Moule expresses this point beautifully:

The striking way in which what we might describe as "secular" words such as *leitourgein* (to render civic service) are applied also to "divine service" provides a very salutary reminder that worship, for a truly religious person, is the be all and end all of work; and that if worship and work are distinguished, that

37. Hahn, *Ordinary Work*, 28.

38. See "λειτουργέω," in *A Greek-English Lexicon*, ed. Henry George Liddell and Robert Scott (Oxford: Oxford, University Press, 1968), 1036–37; and Giorgio Agamben, *Opus Dei: An Archaeology of Duty* (Stanford, Calif.: Stanford University Press, 2013), 1–4.

39. See, for example, Ex 28:43, 29:30; 2 Chr 17:19; Lk 1:23; Rom 15:16; 2 Cor 9:12. See also John H. Miller, "The Nature and Definition of the Liturgy," *Theological Studies* 18, no. 3 (1957): 325–56, esp. 326–28.

40. Agamben, *Opus Dei*, 3; Miller, "Nature and Definition of the Liturgy," 328.

is only because of the frailty of human nature that cannot do more than one thing at a time. The necessary alternation between lifting up holy hands in prayer and swinging an axe in strong, dedicated hands for the glory of God is the human makeshift for that single, simultaneous, divine life in which work is worship and worship is the highest possible activity. And the single word "liturgy" in the New Testament, like "*abodah*," "work" or "service," in the Old Testament, covers both.[41]

In this light, one gleans a unitary reading of the Benedictine *ora et labora*: it is not the bringing together of two compartmentalized spheres, ensuring that both are penciled into a crowded daily schedule; rather, work and worship come to form a single reality. In the words of Josemaría Escrivá, we must work so that our "whole day will turn into an act of worship."[42]

Recapitulating, we have shown that each human person, in virtue of his or her royal *munus*, is called to work, and this work is endowed with the extraordinary dignity of participating in and continuing the work of the Creator. Furthermore, this work enters into the process of salvation, which is possible because of the unity of the royal and the priestly *munera*, the unity of work and worship. We must conclude this section, though, by saying more about the specificity of the priestly *munus*. In brief, the "attitude of participation" that characterizes the priestly *munus* is *sacrifice* or sacrificial offering, "whereby man commits himself and the world to God.... 'All the faithful ... offer spiritual sacrifices to God through Jesus Christ.'"[43]

Christ's death on the cross is the sacrifice *par excellence*. Yet, as the *Catechism* reminds us, "Christ's whole life is a mystery of *redemption*,"[44] including the work and the everyday tasks that comprised the thirty years of his hidden life.

41. Charles F. D. Moule, *The Birth of the New Testament* (1962; repr. London: Adam and Charles Black, 1981), 42–43, quoted in Hahn, *Ordinary Work*, 28–29.

42. Josemaría Escrivá, *The Forge* (1988; repr. New York: Scepter, 2011), no. 69.

43. Wojtyla, *Sources of Renewal*, 223, quoting Vatican Council II, *Presbyterorum ordinis*, no. 2. See also Rom 12:1.

44. *Catechism of the Catholic Church*, no. 517.

Jesus was always at work, and His work was one with His divine life and divine worship. He was always creating, redeeming, and sanctifying the world, and He was always united with His Father in the love of the Holy Spirit. All of the discrete, earthly actions of His life were earthly manifestations of that one, simple, eternal life, that serene yet dynamic heavenly activity. Thus, *everything* He did was redemptive—not just His suffering and death on the cross. His hours spent in the carpentry shop had a redeeming value, an atoning efficacy. He offered His work to God, and all these works worked to save the world.[45]

This is how work enters into the process of salvation; this is how work and worship are one. United to Christ, participating in his royal priesthood, every human act—whether eating or drinking, at work or at rest, in the office or the oratory—when done for the glory of God becomes sanctifying and salvific.[46]

Recognition of this reality calls us not only to work and to do so as a conscious offering to God, but also to work *well.* As Escrivá said, "'What use is it telling me that so and so is a good son of mine—a good Christian—but a bad shoemaker?' If he doesn't try to learn his trade well, or doesn't give his full attention to it, he won't be able to sanctify it or offer it to Our Lord."[47] The Law and the prophets of the Old Testament make it clear that a priest can give no less; they call for the *best* when it comes to sacrificial offerings.[48] This is not because *God* needs the best; rather, *we* need the best—that is, *we* need to make a sincere gift of ourselves if we are to flourish as human beings.[49] And this gift will be made—in part—by giving our best in our work, whether that be as a professional or in the day-to-day tasks of life. Thus the Second Vatican Council proclaimed, "By their competence in secular training

45. Hahn, *Ordinary Work*, 30.

46. See 1 Cor 10:31.

47. Escrivá, *Friends of God* (1977; repr. New York: Scepter, 2002), no. 61.

48. For example, in Genesis 4, the Lord favored Abel's offering over Cain's not because meat was more valuable than Cain's crops, but because Abel brought "the fatty portion of the firstlings of his flock" (v. 4)—that is, he brought the best of what he had, while Cain is said to have simply brought "from the fruit of the ground" (v. 3). Likewise, the Passover lamb sacrificed by the Israelites in Egypt had to be "without blemish" (Ex 12:5). See also Lv 22:20–24; Mal 1:7–9; and Hahn, *Ordinary Work*, 62–64.

49. Cf. Vatican Council II, *Gaudium et spes*, no. 24.

and by their activity, elevated from within by the grace of Christ, let [the faithful] vigorously contribute their effort, so that created goods may be perfected by human labor, technical skill and civic culture for the benefit of all men according to the design of the Creator and the light of His Word."[50]

PROPHETS OF TRUTH

Prophets are strange characters. Images of outsiders in funny clothing, harbingers of the future, and bizarre symbolic acts come to mind. While most are familiar with John the Baptist, his diet of locusts and honey, and his camel's hair garment,[51] the Old Testament prophets are even more outlandish—in fact, mental by today's standards: Jeremiah, for example, followed the Lord's instructions to purchase a loincloth only to subsequently be told to take it off, bury it, and then return later to find it rotted.[52] Isaiah, similarly, was told to remove his clothing and walk around naked.[53] And Ezekiel, possibly the most peculiar of them all, ate a scroll—which, he remarked, was pleasing to the palate—and lay down on the ground with an iron pan between him and his clay artwork of Jerusalem for 390 days, all the while eating barley cakes baked on cow manure (only because he convinced the Lord that human excrement was unfitting), after which he rolled over only to do the same thing for another forty days, and soon after was instructed to cut his hair and beard with a sword.[54]

The bizarre character of the Old Testament prophets does in fact touch upon a central element of the prophetic *munus*, but to reduce it to external appearances and actions would be a grave oversimplification. The mission of the prophet goes much deeper. The description of second-century Christians in "The Epistle to Diognetus" sheds light

50. Vatican Council II, *Lumen gentium*, no. 36.
51. Mt 3:4.
52. Jer 13.
53. Is 20.
54. Ez 2–5.

on this deeper meaning of the prophetic *munus* as it is lived out by followers of Christ in the world:

> Christians are indistinguishable from other men either by nationality, language or customs. They do not inhabit separate cities of their own, or speak a strange dialect, or follow some outlandish way of life. . . . With regard to dress, food and manner of life in general, they follow the customs of whatever city they happen to be living in, whether it is Greek or foreign.
>
> And yet there is something extraordinary about their lives. They live in their own countries as though they were only passing through. They play their full role as citizens, but labor under all the disabilities of aliens. . . . Like others, they marry and have children, but they do not expose them. They share their meals, but not their wives. They live in the flesh, but they are not governed by the desires of the flesh.[55]

Following in the same line, Karol Wojtyla identifies "the sign of contradiction" as the mark of a prophet: there is "something extraordinary" about the lives of the prophets—and Christians alike—not because they set themselves apart by outward appearance, but because they "*bear witness to the truth.*"[56] Just as the early Christians described previously, we are called to set ourselves apart in word and in deed by living and speaking the truth, particularly in regard to faith and morals.[57] And in a society that perceives itself to have moved beyond the restraints of archaic moral absolutes, the faithful Christian is prone to come across equally as "mental" as the Old Testament prophets. As Flannery O'Connor is said to have quipped, "You shall know the truth and the truth shall make you odd."[58]

The prophetic *munus* characterized by its witness to the truth is the antidote to the "health and wealth gospel" and the countermeasure to the appropriation of spirituality for profit-seeking ends. While

55. "The Epistle to Diognetus," in *Patres Apostolici*, ed. F. X. Funk (Tubingen: H. Laupp, 1901), vol. 1, ch. 5. The English translation of the quoted section can be found at http://www.vatican.va/spirit/documents/spirit_20010522_diogneto_en.html.

56. Wojtyla, *Sign of Contradiction*, 123, emphasis added.

57. Cf. *Catechism of the Catholic Church*, nos. 904–7.

58. Ralph C. Wood, *Flannery O'Connor and the Christ-Haunted South* (Grand Rapids, Mich.: William B. Eerdmans, 2004), 160.

the royal priesthood of the baptized calls the Christian to work—and to work *well*—offering it as a priestly sacrifice to God, the prophetic *munus* indicates that work done well cannot be equated with worldly success. It establishes limits; it is a calling to remind both ourselves and the world that morality and human dignity must guide and determine economic activity, not the other way around.[59] It is true that in many cases businesses that are guided by moral principles, that care for the impact they have on the environment and the communities in which they operate, and that are attentive to the social harmony of their workplaces will produce greater profits. This win-win scenario, however, will not always be the case, nor is it a reward promised to the faithful by some divine decree. There are times when the Christian will be compelled to be a sign of contradiction, to make difficult decisions, sometimes at great personal cost.

Two pairs of concepts, which are characteristic of the Old Testament prophets, will help to further delineate the prophetic *munus* of the baptized Christian and in particular the businessperson. The first pair of concepts is *theology–history*. This pairing is especially salient in the ordering of the Hebrew Bible: while the Christian Bible places the prophetic books at the end of the Old Testament underscoring Jesus as the fulfillment of the prophecies foretold of him, the Tanakh places these books immediately after the Torah and the first of what Christian scholars refer to as the historical books (Joshua, Judges, 1 and 2 Samuel, 1 and 2 Kings). In doing so, they emphasize not the prophet's capacity to foretell a distant future, but to speak the will of God to the present situation.

The prophets, of course, do not speak into a vacuum. They are not spouting vague words of wisdom into the sky but are speaking

59. Similarly, Pope Francis asks those in business "to ensure that humanity is served by wealth and not ruled by it"; Francis, *Message to the Executive Chairman of the World Economic Forum on the Occasion of the Annual Meeting at Davos-Klosters (Switzerland)*, January 17, 2014. Elsewhere he decries the injustices that occur "when the deity of money is at the centre of an economic system rather than man, the human person"; Francis, *Address to the Participants in the World Meeting of Popular Movements*, October 28, 2014.

to a particular history during the rise and fall of the monarchy (and, removed from the context of this story as it unfolds in the historical books, the words and actions of the prophets will be incomprehensible).[60] And though the emphases and styles may differ among them, when they evaluate and speak to the moral issues of their day, the prophets always do so in view of the Torah. Their messages are not a matter of personal commentary or opinion; they are steeped in their religious tradition.[61] So too, in virtue of our prophetic *munus*, the Christian is called to scrutinize the "signs of the times," always using right reason under the guidance of the Holy Spirit and the teaching of the church, accepting "that which is not just the word of men but truly the word of God."[62]

The second pair of concepts is *dismantling–energizing*.[63] The public prophets of Israel arise in the midst of grave spiritual and moral decline; their primary mission is to call the Hebrew people back to the Lord in a time when faith in the one true God was being undermined.[64] Likewise, the Christian faithful are called to proclaim the gospel "without hesitating to courageously identify and denounce evil."[65] At the same time, though, the prophets did not simply cast judgments and proclaim death sentences: there was "another thing which made the prophets' proclamation something absolutely new and hitherto unheard-of in Israel ... even in the very act of proclaiming judgment, they made known the beginnings of a new movement

60. See Gerhard von Rad, *The Message of the Prophets* (1967; repr. London: SCM, 1969), 100.

61. See ibid., 11, and Alberto Ferreiro, "Introduction to the Twelve Prophets," in *Ancient Christian Commentary on Scripture*, ed. Thomas C. Oden, vol 14, *The Twelve Prophets*, ed. Alberto Ferreiro (Downers Grove, Ill.: InterVarsity, 2003), xix.

62. Vatican Council II, *Lumen gentium*, no. 12, which references 1 Thes 2:13. See also Vatican Council II, *Gaudium et spes*, nos. 4, 11. In this line, the words of Martin Schlag serve as a sort of examination of conscience: "More than a few Catholics and non-Catholics who praise the pope actually praise their own ideas, measuring the pope's ideas against theirs. They obey selectively, when it suits them, and on the points that fit with their personal agendas"; Schlag, *The Business Francis Means* (Washington, D.C.: The Catholic University of America Press, 2017), 113.

63. This pairing of concepts is taken from Walter Brueggemann, *The Prophetic Imagination* (1978; repr. Philadelphia: Fortress, 1985), 109.

64. See, for example, Zec 1:3.

65. John Paul II, *Christifideles laici*, no. 14.

towards salvation."[66] Moreover, the prophets' strongest messages of hope were proclaimed during the exile, precisely when all was thought to be lost. The prophet "seeks to penetrate despair so that new futures can be believed in and embraced by us."[67] The prophet always speaks the voice of truth, translating it into life's various situations: denouncing injustice in times of moral decline and emitting a beacon of hope in times of despair.

Pope Francis in particular has raised a prophetic voice scrutinizing the signs of the times, and his example should serve as an impetus, sparking our own prophetic imagination. Like the Holy Father, we must call out corruption and unjust inequalities where we see them, and we must dismantle the driving attitudes and assumptions behind the self-centered throwaway culture.[68] But businesspersons must also energize, primarily in their example, by being innovators and "artisans of development for the common good,"[69] by "creating goods which are truly good and services which truly serve,"[70] and by respecting human dignity and seeking to include the marginalized on the peripheries.[71] As John Paul II wrote, the laity—in virtue of their prophetic *munus*—have a particular responsibility "to testify how the Christian faith constitutes the only fully valid response ... to the problems and hopes that life poses to every person and society.... *Open wide the doors to Christ!* Open to his saving power the confines of states, and systems political and economic, as well as the vast fields of culture, civilization, and development. Do not be afraid!"[72]

66. Von Rad, *Message*, 12.

67. Brueggemann, *Prophetic Imagination*, 111.

68. See, for example, Francis, Encyclical Letter *Laudato si'* (May 24, 2015), nos. 20–22, 162; Francis, *Meditation: Dirty Bread of Corruption*, November 8, 2013. For a more in-depth overview of these and other points Pope Francis has underscored in his message to those in the business world, see Schlag, *Business*, 127–48.

69. Francis, *Address to the Christian Union of Business Executives (UCID)*, October 31, 2015.

70. Pontifical Council for Justice and Peace, *The Vocation of the Business Leader* (Vatican City: Pontifical Council for Justice and Peace, 2012), no. 40.

71. See, among others, Francis, Apostolic Exhortation *Evangelii gaudium* (November 24, 2013), no. 20.

72. John Paul II, *Christifideles laici*, no. 34, quoting John Paul II, *Homily for the Inauguration of His Pontificate* (October 22, 1978), no. 5.

SERVANT KINGS AND QUEENS

Thus far we have bypassed the assumption—held both by many proponents of spirituality in the workplace and by its critics—that if spirituality has a place in the world of work, giving it greater meaning, then it is up to business leaders to provide it. As was made clear at the beginning of the chapter, what is being proposed here is not something to be imposed from on high by managers and executives. Christian spirituality in the workplace is "personal," not in a privatized or compartmentalized sense, as though it had no bearing on one's public work life or cannot be shared, but in the sense that it is not something meant to be incorporated structurally in a top-down model, turning business leaders into pseudo-spiritual directors.

The question nevertheless begs to be answered: what of spirituality among business leaders? How do "spiritual business leaders" avoid setting themselves up as a sort of "priestly caste," or worse—as has been accused of them—using spirituality as just another control mechanism to get employees to work harder, "exercising influence on the deepest recesses" of their lives? Without by any means attempting to offer an exhaustive picture of a spirituality of the business leader, we will return to the kingly or royal *munus* to at least begin to answer these questions. The royal *munus* is especially interesting in the context of business leaders because understood poorly it falls into the very traps outlined previously, but understood properly it is the corrective to an authoritarian hierarchical understanding that would allow an elite, enlightened few to wield an (un)godly amount of power over their subordinates.[73]

The name *munus regendi* certainly does not help matters; a cursory reading might even leave one with the disturbing idea that this *munus* implies the baptized ruling over the nonbelievers of the world by some divine right. Karol Wojtyla, however, strongly insists that the

73. Tourish, for example, analyzes transformational and spiritual leadership alongside that of cults; see *Dark Side*, esp. 29–39.

royal *munus* "is not the right to exercise dominion over others; it is a manifestation of the 'kingly character' of man."[74] In order to properly understand what this "kingly character" means for business leaders in positive terms, we need to first delineate what we might call two "expressions" of the royal *munus*: the personal expression and the social expression.

In regard to the former, business leader or not, Christian or atheist, *every* human being participates in the royal *munus*. As Russell Hittinger notes, John Paul II makes this point implicitly in connecting the royal *munus* to conscience, praxis, and human dignity; this *munus*, says the pope, is "embedded within the structure of the human personality."[75] And this *munus*, which characterizes every human being, is expressed in a plurality of *munera* or gifts, as the *Catechism* states: "God has not willed to reserve to himself all exercise of power. He entrusts to every creature the functions"—*munera* in the Latin text—"it is capable of performing."[76]

At first, this understanding of the personal expression of the royal *munus* would seem to solve the problem of any despotic vision of a leadership of the baptized, given that every person participates in the royal *munus*. On the other hand, it gives rise to another problem, as we would appear to have an anarchical clash of the titans on our hands with so many kings and queens running around. We must therefore delineate its social expression: while the royal *munus* is something "natural," embedded in and an articulation of the basic dignity of all human beings, it is Christ who reveals to us its proper form in relation to other persons—that is, servant leadership. For "the Son of Man did not come to be served but to serve."[77] "Christ, the 'Servant of the Lord,' will show all people the royal dignity of service, the dignity which is

74. Wojtyla, *Sign of Contradiction*, 138. In a similar fashion, Pope Francis says we must "forcefully reject the notion" that the dominion of Genesis 1:28—which is connected to our kingly *munus*—"justifies absolute domination over other creatures"; see Francis, *Laudato si'*, 64.

75. Wojtyla, *Sign of Contradiction*, 137–41; quotation on 138. See also John Paul II, Encyclical Letter *Redemptor hominis* (March 4, 1979), no. 21; and Hittinger, "Social Pluralism," 399–400.

76. *Catechism of the Catholic Church*, no. 1884. See Hittinger, "Social Pluralism," 407.

77. Mt 20:28.

joined in the closest possible way to the vocation of every person."[78] "To serve is to reign."[79]

An analogy might help to elucidate the interplay between the personal and social expressions of the royal *munus*. I once heard a professor explain the controversial Pauline verses about a wife's subordination to her husband by comparing their relationship to a dance.[80] A husband's leadership parallels that of the leader of a ballroom dance: he is not a puppeteer pulling the strings of his passive and pretty marionette doll; rather, his task as leader is to enable her to dance her part well—in other words, to flourish or to shine. Whether or not one agrees with the professor's interpretation, it offers interesting insight into the points we are considering here and their application to business.

In fact, we can draw out the analogy even further (understanding, of course, that, despite the references to "him" and "her," we are no longer considering the male-female relation): at a social dance, dancers continually swap partners throughout the night; the leader will thus find himself coupled with partners of varying levels and abilities. In these pairings, the difference between a good *dancer* and a good *leader* becomes manifest. When a good dancer but poor leader is paired with a beginner partner, fearing she might bring him down he throws out every move in his playbook, regardless of whether or not his partner can follow. He shines, and she is left feeling incapable, though both ultimately suffer because the beauty of this kind of dance lies in the coordination of the two. The good leader, on the other hand, dances at the level of his partner; feeling out her capabilities, he begins with what she knows and moves on from there, leading her with subtle yet clear cues for each step she should take. The *great* leader can lead even the untrained dancer, unlocking a talent she didn't know she had.

It is to be hoped the parallels to management are obvious. And the insights therein are nothing novel; they are simply good management

78. John Paul II, Encylical Letter *Mulieris dignitatem* (August 15, 1988), no. 5.
79. Vatican Council II, *Lumen gentium*, no. 36.
80. See Eph 5:21–33; Col 3:18. I thank Dr. John Bergsma for this example.

practice, which—moreover—means that good management, in part, is nothing other than the proper interplay between the personal and social expressions of the royal *munus*. In theological and philosophical terms, this interplay is expressed in the related concepts *logic of gift* and *subsidiarity*. "The human being is made for gift."[81] And the "logic of gift," which Benedict XVI says must find its place in economic activity,[82] presupposes what the kingly *munus* affirms, that each person has gifts to give and *must* give—we cannot forget that a *munus* is both gift and mission—and the gifts we are speaking of here are not only or even primarily material, but talents and skills and the offering of one's whole self.

Subsidiarity, in turn, is the principle that articulates the social expression of the royal *munus* and its proper relation to the personal expression and the logic of gift. This principle tells us that when any *subsidium*—meaning support or reinforcement—be given to another, "the plurality of functions or *munera* should not be destroyed or absorbed."[83] Moreover, these *munera* should be *enabled*. One of the roles of the business leader, then—as servant leader or royal steward—is to insert the logic of gift into the workspace by enabling those under his or her charge to exercise their own personal royal *munus* in the development of their individual *munera*. Long before writing his social encyclicals, the young Fr. Karol Wojtyla beautifully expressed this idea in a letter to a friend: "The greatest achievement is always to *see* values that others don't see and to *affirm* them. The even greater achievement is to *bring out* of people the values that would perish without us."[84]

Finally, a word of caution must be spoken: while all that we have

81. Benedict XVI, Encyclical Letter *Caritas in veritate* (June 29, 2009), no. 34.

82. Ibid., no. 36.

83. Hittinger, "Social Pluralism," 394. Pope Benedict makes the connection between subsidiarity and the logic of gift explicit in *Caritas in veritate*, no. 57: "Subsidiarity respects personal dignity by recognizing in the person a subject who is always capable of giving something to others."

84. Cited in George Weigel, *Witness to Hope: The Biography of Pope John Paul II* (New York: HarperCollins, 1999), 102. For a more thorough development of the principle of subsidiarity as gift-recognition, see Hittinger, "Social Pluralism"; and for more on its connection to the logic of gift and its applications to business, see Michael Naughton et al., *Respect in Action: Applying Subsidiarity in Business* (St. Paul, Minn.: University of St. Thomas, 2015).

just outlined, when applied to business leadership, may very well be good management practice, it cannot be *just* that, lest the logic of gift fall prey to the logic of power. These principles and practices will not survive on utility alone; they must be morally and spiritually grounded.[85] Morally speaking, we must be attentive to our own self-governance—that is, to the cultivation of virtue. Ruling is hardwired into our nature, but its proper expression is threatened by sin: the person who refuses to govern him- or herself will instead inevitably turn that rule toward others, and it will be what we can rightly call an "unruly rule." Spiritually speaking, cut off from the transcendent, closed off to our creator, it is easy to forget that our lives are gift. When this happens, the *munus* is bankrupt of its richness: the ties between gift and mission are cut, distorting both in the process. Our *munera* become rights without responsibilities: rights dwindle into mere immunities—which, Hittinger points out, "etymologically implies the absence of a *munus*"[86]—and responsibilities become onerous chores. We must, therefore, heed the words of Benedict XVI, who summarizes the importance of a morally and spiritually grounded logic of gift when he writes, "Without truth, without trust and love for what is true, there is no social conscience and responsibility, and social action ends up serving private interests and the logic of power, resulting in social fragmentation, especially in a globalized society at difficult times like the present."[87]

BUSINESS, CONTEMPLATION, AND THE EUCHARIST

We would be remiss to conclude without considering a very important point, without which our *work as worship* runs the risk of falling into *worship of work*. It was noted earlier that the human person is called

85. On this note, see Naughton et al., *Respect in Action*, esp. 22–27, nn. 48–54.
86. Hittinger, "Social Pluralism," 393.
87. Benedict XVI, *Caritas in veritate*, no. 5.

to imitate the Creator in his work, and much of this chapter was dedicated to drawing out this point and its consequences for the Christian—who is priest, prophet, and king—in his or her daily work life. It is important to remember, though, that the human person is also called to imitate the Creator in his *rest*—so important it was included among the Ten Commandments.

The Sabbath rest to which God calls us is not to be confused with idleness. God is not commanding us to "do nothing," be it a common temptation for the workaholic who finally manages to step away from the office. In fact, Thomas Aquinas identifies both sloth and idleness as *opposed* to the third commandment.[88] What, then, positively speaking, is this rest we are called to? It is the rest of the *soul*. "For just as the tired body desires rest, so also does the soul. But the soul's proper rest is in God."[89] That is, we are called to contemplation, to ponder and gaze upon the divine; he tells us, "Be still and know that I am God!"[90]

This rest—or leisure, as Josef Pieper describes it—"is the power to step beyond the working world and win contact with those superhuman, life-giving forces that can send us, renewed and alive again, into the busy world of work."[91] And here emerges a sort of paradox: rest, understood as leisure or contemplation, can have extraordinarily fruitful consequences for one's work, but it cannot be *for* one's work. Experience attests to the fact that rest allows one to return refreshed to work, accomplishing more in less time than those who work continuously. Yet we cannot confuse the means with the end: our work is ordered to worship, not the other way around. When the means and end are confused, when rest becomes ordered to work, both suffer: as Pieper notes, "When separated from worship, leisure becomes toil-

88. See Thomas Aquinas, *Collationes de decem praeceptis*, a. 5, in *The Catechetical Instructions of St. Thomas*, trans. Joseph B. Collins (New York: Wagner, 1939), 69–116, available online at http://dhspriory.org/thomas/TenCommandments.htm#5, accessed June 21, 2017, and *Summa theologiae* II-II q. 35, a. 3, ad 1 (Cambridge: Cambridge University Press, 2006).

89. Aquinas, *Collationes de decem praeceptis*, a. 5.

90. Ps 46.

91. Josef Pieper, *Leisure: The Basis of Culture*, trans. Gerald Malsbary (1948; repr. South Bend, Ind.: St. Augustine's Press, 1998), 54.

some, and work becomes inhuman."[92] And elsewhere he rightly observes, "Nobody who wants leisure merely for the sake of 'refreshment' will experience its authentic fruit."[93]

Escrivá diagnosed this disorder as "professionalitis," what we today call "workaholism": "You should put your professional interests in their place: they are only means to an end; they can never be regarded—in any way—as if they were the basic thing. These attacks of 'professionalitis' stop you being united with God."[94] The cure? We have to be willing to "waste time" for God (and what a glorious waste it is!); we have to set aside time for mental prayer. Yes, our work is a prayer—after all, one of the aims of this chapter was to show just that—but it cannot be the only form of prayer. The man who claims to go to work out of love for his family but never spends time with them—that is, undivided time, fully present, free from distractions—is fooling himself. The same is true in relation to God. "If we do not learn how to stop completely from time to time, how to make a space in which we do nothing except think about God, we will find it very difficult to remain in God's presence while working."[95]

In addition to mental prayer—undivided time in the presence of God—the Eucharist is an essential part of our rest or leisure. While baptism is the *foundation* of a spirituality of work, allowing us to participate in the priestly, prophetic, and kingly *munera* of Christ, the Eucharist is its *source* and *summit*. It is summit because all our activity is directed toward it; we offer our entire lives as a living sacrifice in union with that of Christ, which is re-presented on the altar in the Eucharist. And it is source because it is the fuel that allows us to make such an offering: "It spurs us on our journey through history and plants a seed of living hope in our daily commitment to the work before us."[96] Like the sunflower with its gaze ever directed to its life-giving source in a

92. Ibid., 72.

93. Ibid., 54.

94. Escrivá, *Furrow* (1986; repr. New York: Scepter, 2011), no. 502.

95. Jacques Philippe, *Time for God* (1992; repr. New York: Scepter, 2008), 29–30.

96. John Paul II, Encyclical Letter *Ecclesia de Eucharistia* (April 17, 2003), no. 20.

continuous ebb and flow of movement and rest, day in and day out, so too "all of the works of man are done as if on an altar, and each of you, in that union of contemplative souls which is your day, in some way says 'his Mass,' which lasts twenty-four hours in expectation of the Mass to follow, which will last another twenty-four hours, and so on until the end of our life."[97]

BIBLIOGRAPHY

Agamben, Giorgio. *Opus Dei: An Archaeology of Duty*. Stanford: Stanford University Press, 2013.

Aquinas, Thomas. "Collationes de decem praeceptis." In *The Catechetical Instructions of St. Thomas*, translated by Joseph B. Collins, 69–116. New York: Wagner, 1939. Available online at http://dhspriory.org/thomas/TenCommandments.htm#5. Accessed June 21, 2017.

———. *Summa theologiae*. Cambridge: Cambridge University Press, 2006.

Benedict XVI. Encyclical Letter *Caritas in veritate*. June 29, 2009.

Brueggemann, Walter. *The Prophetic Imagination*. Philadelphia: Fortress Press, 1985. Originally published in 1978.

Case, Peter, Robert French, and Peter Simpson. "From *Theoria* to Theory: Leadership without Contemplation." *Organization* 19, no. 3 (2012): 345–61.

Case, Peter, and Jonathan Gosling. "The Spiritual Organization: Critical Reflections on the Instrumentality of Workplace Spirituality." *Journal of Management, Spirituality and Religion* 7, no. 4 (2010): 257–282.

Catechism of the Catholic Church. Vatican City: Libreria Editrice Vaticana, 1993.

Echevarría, Javier. *Vivir la Santa Misa* [Living the Holy Mass]. Madrid: Rialp, 2010.

Escrivá, Josemaría. *Friends of God*. New York: Scepter, 2002. Originally published in 1977.

———. *Furrow*. New York: Scepter, 2011. Originally published in 1986.

———. *The Forge*. New York: Scepter, 2011. Originally published in 1988.

"The Epistle to Diognetus." In Vol. 1, *Patres Apostolici*, edited by F. X. Funk. Tubingen: H. Laupp, 1901.

Ferreiro, Alberto. "Introduction to the Twelve Prophets." In *Ancient Christian Commentary on Scripture*, edited by Thomas C. Oden, vol. 14, *The Twelve Prophets*, edited by Alberto Ferreiro, xvii–xxv. Downers Grove, Ill.: InterVarsity Press, 2003.

97. Escrivá, notes taken during a meditation, March 19, 1968; cited in Javier Echevarría, *Vivir la Santa Misa* [Living the Holy Mass] (Madrid: Rialp, 2010), 17.

Francis. *Meditation: Dirty Bread of Corruption*. November 8, 2013.

———. Apostolic Exhortation *Evangelii gaudium*. November 24, 2013.

———. *Message to the Executive Chairman of the World Economic Forum on the Occasion of the Annual Meeting at Davos-Klosters (Switzerland)*. January 17, 2014.

———. *Address to the Participants in the World Meeting of Popular Movements*. October 28, 2014.

———. Encyclical Letter *Laudato Si'*. May 24, 2015.

———. *Address to the Christian Union of Business Executives (UCID)*. October 31, 2015.

Giacalone, Robert A., and Carole L. Jurkiewicz. "The Science of Workplace Spirituality." In *Handbook of Workplace Spirituality*, edited by Robert A. Giacalone and Carole L. Jurkiewicz, 3–26. Armonk, NY: M.E. Sharpe, 2010.

González-Ayesta, Cruz. "Work as 'a Mass': Reflections on the Laity's Participation in the *Munus Sacerdotale* in the Writings of the Founder of Opus Dei." *Romana* 50 (2010): 192–206.

Hahn, Scott. *Ordinary Work, Extraordinary Grace: My Spiritual Journey in Opus Dei*. New York: Doubleday, 2006.

Hittinger, Russell. "Social Pluralism and Subsidiarity in Catholic Social Doctrine." *Annales Theologici* 16 (2002): 385–408.

John XXIII. Encyclical Letter *Pacem in terris*. April 11, 1963.

John Paul II. *Homily for the Inauguration of His Pontificate*. October 22, 1978.

———. Encyclical Letter *Redemptor hominis*. March 4, 1979.

———. Encyclical Letter *Laborem exercens*. September 14, 1981.

———. Encyclical Letter *Mulieris dignitatem*. August 15, 1988.

———. Apostolic Exhortation *Christifideles laici*. December 30, 1988.

———. Encyclical Letter *Ecclesia de Eucharistia*. April 17, 2003.

Koehler, Ludwig, and Walter Baumgartner, eds. *The Hebrew and Aramaic Lexicon of the Old Testament*. 5 Vols. Leiden: Brill, 1995–2000.

Liddell, Henry George, and Robert Scott, eds. *A Greek-English Lexicon*. Oxford: Oxford, University Press, 1968.

Miller, John H. "The Nature and Definition of the Liturgy." *Theological Studies* 18, no. 3 (1957): 325–56.

Morrow, Jeffrey. "Work as Worship in the Garden and the Workshop: Genesis 1–3, the Feast of St. Joseph the Worker, and Liturgical Hermeneutics." *Logos* 15, no. 4 (2012): 159–78.

Moule, Charles F. D. *The Birth of the New Testament*. London: Adam and Charles Black, 1981. Originally published in 1962.

Naughton, Michael J., Jeanne G. Buckeye, Kenneth E. Goodpaster, and T. Dean Maines. *Respect in Action: Applying Subsidiarity in Business*. St. Paul, Minn.: University of St. Thomas, 2015.

Philippe, Jacques. *Time for God*. New York: Scepter, 2008. Originally published in 1992.

Pieper, Josef. *Leisure: The Basis of Culture*. Translated by Gerald Malsbary. South Bend, Ind.: St. Augustine's Press, 1998. Originally published in 1948.

Pontifical Council for Justice and Peace. *The Vocation of the Business Leader*. Vatican City: Pontifical Council for Justice and Peace, 2012.

Schlag, Martin. *The Business Francis Means*. Washington, D.C.: The Catholic University of America Press, 2017.

Smith, Janet E. "The Importance of the Concept of 'Munus' to Understanding *Humane Vitae*." In *"Humanae Vitae": 20 Anni Dopo*, 677–90. Milan: Edizioni Ares, 1989.

Tourish, Dennis. *The Dark Side of Transformational Leadership: A Critical Perspective*. London: Routledge, 2013.

Tourish, Dennis, and Naheed Tourish. "Spirituality at Work, and Its Implications for Leadership and Followership: A Post-Structuralist Perspective." *Leadership* 6, no. 2 (2010): 207–24.

Vatican Council II. Dogmatic Constitution *Lumen gentium*. November 21, 1964.

———. Decree *Apostolicam actuositatem*. November 18, 1965.

———. Pastoral Constitution *Gaudium et spes*. December 7, 1965.

———. Decree *Presbyterorum ordinis*. December 7, 1965.

Von Rad, Gerhard. *The Message of the Prophets*. London: SCM, 1969. Originally published in 1967.

Weigel, George. *Witness to Hope: The Biography of Pope John Paul II*. New York: HarperCollins, 1999.

Whyte, William H. *The Organization Man*. Philadelphia: University of Pennsylvania Press, 2002. Originally published in 1956.

Wojtyla, Karol. *Consilium de Laicis, quid dicis de teipso?* December 3, 1968. http://www.laici.va/content/laici/en/media/notizie/doc_wojtyla.html. Accessed June 8, 2017.

———. *Sources of Renewal: The Implementation of Vatican II*. Translated by P. S. Falla. San Francisco: Harper and Row, 1980. Originally published in 1972.

———. *Sign of Contradiction*. New York: Seabury, 1979. Originally published in 1977.

Wood, Ralph C. *Flannery O'Connor and the Christ-Haunted South*. Grand Rapids: William B. Eerdmans, 2004.

2

DOES SPIRITUALITY MATTER IN LEADING ENTERPRISES?

RAFAEL ALVIRA

The idea of a possible relevance of spirituality for business, and even more so for leaders, would appear senseless to most. Spirituality is usually conceived as something proper to men and women belonging to religious orders or religious institutions, or perhaps also as an interior human state similar to that of the mystic. Spirituality is not seen as having any relation to the world of business, at least in two senses: on the one hand, because business is a typically "worldly" activity, and from this point of view the person belonging to a religious institution may live "in the world," but is usually not dedicated to "worldly" activities; on the other hand, because what is proper to the "religious realm" is "contemplation," and this is an activity normally linked to a peaceful and calm way of life. Even taking care of the poor and the sick—typical activities of "religious people"—presupposes a style of life very different from that of business. In the Christian tradition until the Reformation and in Catholic countries even longer, religion in its purest form was conceived as a peaceful life of contemplation and a certain "retirement" from the world or, for lay people, as a peaceful family life.

The author is deeply indebted to Prof. Dr. Martin Schlag and Dr. David Thunder for the revision of the text.

At the same time, the deep relation between religion, politics, and ethics was at that time a normal assumption, and therefore, as the development of trade and business began to grow remarkably, the question of the ethics of the new commercial or business society arose. The question was treated philosophically in France, but even more so in Scotland. The great Scottish thinkers of the seventeenth and eighteenth centuries—Hutcheson, Reid, Smith, Ferguson—studied the question accurately and defended the ethical constitution of the commercial society—and thus also the legitimacy of a commercial society—with excellent arguments. The whole question was about ethics, civil society, and in some cases also explicitly the respect of God and religion, but not about "spiritual" or "mystic" or "ecclesial" dimensions.

The history after the Enlightenment gave its verdict on the separation of religion and ethics. Already Machiavelli had separated ethics and politics in the political realm, defending the autonomy of the latter. Later Adam Smith, in a reaction against a quasi-Jansenist spirit (which had misguided Bernard Mandeville), paved the way for separating ethics and economics through his system of descriptive and thus fake normativity. Finally, in the twentieth century, Hans Kelsen pleaded for a pure positivist right without ethical foundation. As a whole, it is clear that the total "disentanglement" of ethics from religion has led ethics to a secondary and purely individualistic attitude, a kind of contradiction, because ethics in the classical sense was the most profound and most socially effective dimension of human life.

The problem of ethics is that, being an interior and universal disposition of the human spirit, it is at the same time practice, but practice means life. It is very difficult to habitually act in a just, non-self-centered manner if nothing awaits us after this life on earth—that is, if there is no future punishment or reward for our ethical behavior. The result of the separation of ethics and religion has therefore led to not only the insignificance of ethics, but also its practical diminution across the Western world.

The point on which the weakness of the modern position is clearest is at the same time the most important new "discovery" in the business world: trust. It is difficult to organize commerce and business in general if you cannot trust the persons with whom you are in contact—that is, with the so-called stakeholders. The flourishing of "business ethics" is easy to understand even if today it is still more a fashion than a reality. Indeed, in business so-called ethical codes are in vogue, but a code is still merely a juridical instrument. In the sphere of theory, there are many good publications; some of them, inspired by the classical Aristotelian or even Thomist doctrines, discuss mainly the theory of virtue. Others, who in my opinion are perhaps less profound, are inspired by the modern Scottish ethical tradition. Both currents are often dedicated more to the study of ethical cases than to the inclusion of those cases in a general ethical and political framework.

In this respect it is also interesting to observe that the development of "business ethics" has not had a parallel in the development of a "political ethics" or a "juridical ethics" and that religion has in recent years been increasingly marginalized in the public sphere.

When ethics and religion are excluded from the life of a society, the unavoidable consequence is its collapse in a system of totalitarian or tyrannical power, even if this power not surprisingly tries to hide itself by means of rhetorical skill. Indeed, today public discourse takes for granted the assumption that we live in the freest and most perfect political world in all of history, but closer scrutiny cannot support this appearance.

There is no valid substitute for religion—in spite of Habermas's attempt to find one—nor for ethics—notwithstanding modernity's pretensions to the contrary. This is so from a theoretical point of view because, in order to be accepted as valid, any substitute would have to be so similar to ethics and religion as to be virtually identical with them. And it is also so from a practical point of view because the historical verdict is clear: a religion like deism, in which God is far away—neither in contact with the realities of this world nor a person with whom you can talk—cannot be the solution. Moreover, it is not even a true religion, as the so-called counterrevolutionary thinkers immediately pointed out. Louis de Bonald, for instance, emphasized that a God who does not govern the world through his providence is necessarily condemned to disappear from human life, irrelevant. History has fully vindicated this view. In this manner, then, we have made our main point: we must take religion seriously again, and "spiritual" and "spirituality" are precisely the concepts connected to a religion and a God that are truly involved in our lives.

WHAT DOES SPIRITUALITY MEAN?

In the following considerations I will avoid the temptation to simply list the virtues that may be embraced within the so-called spiritual realm and the errors and faults that each person and every society commits when they lack them (of which there is ample evidence in cases and statistics). Of course, on principle, I agree with this approach as a useful way to tackle the question, but here I wish rather to give some foundation for the thesis—that leaders need spiritual formation. I will begin by reflecting upon the concept of spirituality.

What does spirituality mean? It means the form of life of the human spirit. And what does spirit mean? Is it a synonym for soul, or mind, intelligence and will? In the history of philosophy and in the Christian tradition there have been two principal references to the spirit: the neo-Platonist and Pauline one, which explains the structure of the human being as a compound of body, "psychic" soul, and spirit; and the Aristotelian and Thomist one, which sustains that the structure of the human being is a compound of body and soul, the soul having two functions: the "vivification" of the body and the relation to the transcendent reality. This latter relationship is the spiritual function of the soul.

In this chapter it is not possible to enter into technical philosophical discussions about this topic. All that matters here is that by spirit we usually understand some dimension of the human being that in a certain sense transcends the physical level, linking us to a world or reality that transcends also the psychic level.

The human experience of knowing, reflecting on, and even transforming the physical and psychic world makes it impossible to deny this complex structure, which allows us in a certain sense to be "over ourselves." Even Karl Marx, who only accepted the reality of the material world, wrote about the human spirit (*Geist*) quite frequently.

It is strange that a material spirit could distance itself from a material world, but, in any case, the point here is that we experience two different kinds of material world: the exterior one, the nature surrounding us, including in a certain sense our body; and the interior world, our psychological life. And the question is whether the spirit has as a function only to observe and eventually transform our "psyche" and our surrounding world, or if it also has a relation to a real existent superior world.

We must put aside for the time being the question of what "materiality" means, a concept usually taken for granted and also believed to truly correspond to "the true reality"; meanwhile, the truth is that—as Aristotle saw—it is an indefinable "reality." The point on which our study must concentrate now is that of the possible twofold structure of the spirit (be it material or not): is it only able to become aware of being an "ego" and observing itself from this "ego," or is it also capable of "looking" into a transcendent world?

According to the first possibility, human interiority is equal to the experience of our psychic and physical life, and as a consequence the study of the character and temperament of a person should be a relevant task for research on the figure of a leader. However, being a human person means essentially living in a society; it is therefore not sufficient to know our "interior reality," but at the same time we must learn what relating to the others and the sense of living in society mean.

We are then constrained to take a step forward and to open the door to the ethical sphere, distinguishing first of all between ethology and ethics. A mere ethological point of view would content itself with accurately describing the conditions and the different forms of behavior of a person, while an ethical point of view affirms the possibility of improving the psychic conditions—and above all the behavior—of a person through learning—that is, by acquiring virtues. It is important here to keep in mind that for ethics the concept of striving for personal perfection through a virtuous life is absolutely central, which is not the case in ethology. Ethology lacks the idea of final perfection of human life.

Both psychological insight and ethical behavior belong to what we have called "spirit." Nevertheless, the idea of an ethic of the "perfection of the human person" presupposes on the one hand an affirmation of the existence of a superior limit to our spirit, because without limit there is no perfection; this limit of the spirit is what we usually call "God." On the other hand, the perfection of the human person presupposes the affirmation of the existence of a real element that is not dependent on his or her psychic and bodily conditions but is able to control them. This is liberty.

SPIRITUALITY AND THE PROBLEM OF LIBERTY

Liberty is no doubt a core dimension of spirituality. The concept and the reality of liberty, however, suffer a plight similar to many other concepts of common usage: they are taken for granted and are therefore very often misunderstood.

Liberty may be understood as a weak force, unable to direct human life or, as Nietzsche thought, a blind force, striving always to achieve its random desires. It can also be understood as a force capable of seeking the greatest utility for ourselves in all circumstances or as a seeing force pointing out and helping us to achieve our human perfection. This last interpretation is the only one that clearly includes the existence of a transcendent world because it implies perfection and, as a consequence, transcendence. The others reduce liberty to a special kind of inner-world element, thus simultaneously rendering the human person an unavoidably imperfect being, unable to know him- or herself because in this world self-knowledge is only possible for a being that transcends itself. In other words, only a being that exists in this world and at the same time is free in relation to it can truly know him- or herself. An essentially imperfect person would not be able to conduct his or her own life. This, however, clearly contradicts human experience. Such a contradiction or absurdity is only overcome by accepting a form of ethics based on the possibility of truly knowing and achieving the perfection of the human being. The classic theory of virtue is precisely such an ethics: it acknowledges the real possibility of this perfection and describes the method to reach it—namely, learning and acquiring the ethical virtues.

The classic theory was substantially developed in two steps. The first is represented by the School of Athens in the classical Greek period: it maintained that the perfection of the human person could be reached only by relating to others in the right manner: a purely individualistic and monological life was not human. Being part of a human community was seen as a material requisite of human nature. The consequence of this insight was that justice was considered to be the virtue par excellence, and the other virtues were seen as helping us to be just. Not being tempered or courageous or prudent sooner or later detracts from our ability to achieve justice.

The second step was achieved by the Christian tradition: it points to the relevance of a particular human being, who is viewed as representative of human perfection, in order to found ethics definitively. Indeed, it is one thing to respond to our natural social inclination as a "material" requisite for human flourishing and something else to believe that striving for human perfection—that is, aspiring to realize the "essential" requisites of being human—is sensible because human perfection actually exists in Jesus Christ.

Both steps are necessarily linked. On the one hand, not being virtuous—that is, just—it is impossible to work for and with others; on the other hand, to reach human perfection you need virtue, but only if perfection is real are we convinced of the relevance to strive for it.

We see then, that we are free to achieve justice or not, but, if we are to reach our perfection we must be just. In other words, we discover that we are *obliged*, that we ought to do something. The obligations are not—as they are today so often understood—external pressures or impositions. The obligations are, first of all, interior "free constraints." If you follow the law because it could be very inconvenient to you if you do otherwise, you are nevertheless acting freely.

LIBERTY AND THE QUESTION OF OBLIGATION

What does obligation mean? It means discovering the necessity to respond to some requirement in a precise manner and knowing at the same time that it is possible not to respond. To put it in another way: an obligation is an inwardly necessary but outwardly free requirement for a given person. Obligation is not what people usually think it is. Quite often people consider that the main "constraint" of an obligation is external—the law and the police, for instance—when, on the contrary, it is interior. Even if I am subject to no exterior constraint I will never stop caring for my mother; by contrast, I may well try to find a way to avoid fulfilling a law I don't like. The biggest and greatest obligations are always the obligations of love and friendship. This implies that the separation between the ethics of *Sollen* (duties) and *Tugend* (virtues) is wrong.

Keeping this in mind, we can instead follow the thesis of my unforgettable master—Prof. Millán-Puelles—who refused to accept the dichotomy of "ought ethics" and "virtue ethics" so widely affirmed in the twentieth century, insisting that the virtues are precisely the fulfillment of our obligations.

And so the point is, how far does our obligation extend? That is, is there an empirical line showing the limits of our obligation? We fulfill an obligation by answering—*responding*—to the gift we have received and by serving the gift-giver in an adequate manner. This is the meaning of *responsibility*. So the question is, are we universally responsible, or do we only have responsibilities toward the concrete "empirical" persons from whom we have received some gift—for instance, our parents, teachers, friends, and so on? For a pure "virtue ethics," which—in the words of its defenders—aims at happiness (*eudaimonia*), it may perhaps be sufficient to achieve justice toward the concrete empirical persons to whom we are indebted. However, if this were sufficient, then our acts would not respond to the universality of our own nature and that of the virtues. We are indeed individuals, but being human is only possible as a real participation in the universality of human nature. And this means that every action of an individual person is measured by its degree of humanity as a consequence of its unavoidable implication in the life of humankind. In other words, we are obliged—of course, in very different degrees of intensity—to all people of all times, because they belong to humankind just as we do. Furthermore, there is a concrete obligation to take care of—according to our possibilities—all of our contemporary fellow human beings. Finally, we are also obligated to take care of the necessary *conditions* for life on earth, the home of humankind, which implies responsibility toward the social and the material world in which we live. This is the ecological commandment.

CONCRETE OBLIGATIONS, UNIVERSAL ETHICS

Of course, these last considerations seem to go too far. Who has strength to occupy him- or herself with the whole of humanity? Here we come to a crucial point, and its peculiar difficulty can be solved only through the accurate distinction between the material conditions and the interior disposition of our soul. We cannot address every problem of the world, and as a consequence, we cannot be praised for justice or accused of injustice in those cases in which we have not been involved or implicated in some way. This, however, is only the empirical, external side of the question. The interior side is never purely individual: on the contrary, it is always universal: every right, correct, and just deed is just because it reflects justice or, as Kant said, because it can be used as a maxim for every similar case. And this means in every action we work in favor of or against humanity, and that also affects my own condition as a human being. In other words, the "extensive" (quantitative) and the "intensive" (qualitative) dimensions of humanity must not be separated. It is impossible to act qualitatively in a human or inhuman manner, even in the smallest actions, without implicitly or explicitly affecting the whole of humanity in a quantitative sense. As Louis de Bonald emphasized, every person even by her or his apparently insignificant acts either builds up or destroys society.

IS THERE A "PARTICULAR ETHICS" OR AN "APPLIED ETHICS"?

Therefore, properly speaking, there is no such thing as "particular ethics," either in a qualitative or in a quantitative sense. The obligations are concrete and particular, but ethics is always universal. The obligations in business are concrete and particular, but business ethics is simply ethics. Its "material" reference and its obligations are different from sports ethics or political ethics, for instance, but its "soul" is always the same, otherwise it would not be ethics. The denomination "applied ethics" therefore seems to be more precise.

One consequence of this insight is that there is no point in educating a business leader by merely giving her or him a collection of good recipes or formulae to be applied in specific situations. Learning ethics presupposes a deeper formation of the soul, practical first of all, and theoretical later, to reinforce practical learning. In other fields of human knowledge, one can first learn the theory and then learn its technical application, but in ethics—as Aristotle pointed out—it works the other way around: who has not learned to behave ethically—which is only possible through the example of parents and teachers, etc.—cannot understand the theory of ethics properly, whose practical aim is to help to improve ethical behavior.

Thus business ethics lectures in a business school can have counterproductive consequences on the education of the students if the teachers themselves do not behave well and promote ethically correct practical theories in their lectures. Lectures on business ethics, though, when properly conducted, are very important for a business school, because the intellectual and human level of its students is usually high, and such people usually need to understand why it is appropriate or fitting to do this or that in order to act well. Therefore, for their ethical education it would not be sufficient for students just to witness the good behavior of their teachers: they also require the theoretical underpinnings.

IS IT POSSIBLE TO BEHAVE ETHICALLY?

Coming back to the previous question: do we have the interior strength to behave ethically in such a bad and complicated world? Or, in other words, do we have the interior strength to universalize our practical maxims? The answer should be, in principle, yes, because we have the power of our liberty, which lifts us up over the empirical world. However, why should we always behave ethically if we will all die, and there is no life after death? Certainly, it might be more beautiful to behave well, and it will probably give us much greater interior satisfaction, but we also realize that life is short and difficult, and the easiest solution in many cases would not seem to be the ethical one; in some cases we even fear being cheated as a consequence of our "goodness."

It is here that spirituality is required. The finitude of this world steadily threatens good ethical behavior. Our nature longs for goodness, perfection, and happiness, which are impossible to reach if there is no other real transcendent world that awaits us after death and that at the same time gives us the conviction and the strength to behave ethically in this world. Socrates was right: only the ethics of obligation and virtue—that is, of perfection—conforms to the constitution of the human being, but ethics is practical and needs to acted on, and without religion—without spirituality—ethics would remain a beautiful theoretical proposal that cannot possibly be fulfilled.

In other words, if the human being is constituted as someone who longs for perfection but is unable to reach it, then she or he is a contradictory being, and ethics is also a contradictory discipline, asking for what we cannot have, attempting what cannot be fulfilled. Peace and joy are substituted then by tricks and entertainment. We must live and forget our condition—which is a new contradiction—instead of "memorizing" it, as Plato said. This means not forgetting that we will die but reflecting upon the meaning of death. In forgetting God, modern Western civilization has also forgotten the human person, who seeks survival through entertainment, drugs, and hope in the new god—that is, in the reality that can provide us with security—namely, the state.

A "reasonable and peaceful society and state" may be organized, for a time, exclusively around the good feelings of its members or the high level of wealth they enjoy, even if few people in such a society believe in the transcendent condition of the human being. Nevertheless, reasonableness and peace disappear quickly when difficulties arise, and this will inevitably happen sooner or later. Furthermore, this kind of society can never cure the deep bitterness of despair in the souls of its people.

As a consequence, I think it is a difficult task to be a leader in business without being truly ethical—that is, without enacting justice. This implies learning practically to be just and includes being prudent, courageous, and temperate. It is not easy to be just without believing in the transcendent condition of the human being—that is, in his or her spirituality. We are all convinced that justice is much more than "quantitative" relations, at least when we ourselves are affected. To be just toward others implies the effort to put oneself in the "place" of the other and to try to treat her or him the same way that one would have wanted to be treated. And this is impossible without spirituality, because spirituality helps to achieve something that is very difficult yet indispensable in order to act ethically: the sense and the reality of *presence*.

"BEING PRESENT" AS A NECESSARY CONDITION FOR ETHICAL BEHAVIOR

This is indeed difficult because it demands a large amount of presence. In order to understand what is meant here, it can help to reflect on the relationship between the verbs "to be," "to have," and "to be able." "To be" means to exist in a determinate form; "to have" adds a reality to the being itself; "to be able" also means to have something, specifically to have a possibility—that is, to have power.

"To have" and "to be able" are the verbs that reveal the relation of the human being to the past and the future. Indeed, the past is what we have and the future what we can do. Both—to have and to be able—are verbs, and as such indicate "energy." You need energy to retain the past and to face the future. From this point of view we must emphasize the difference between human beings and the other beings of this world: there is a "part" of the human being that is determined neither toward the past nor toward the future. We are not only capable of forgetting, we can also refuse to retain—that is, to learn, and for us humans the future is not solely a consequence of instinct. Indeed, the human being does not have instincts in the determinate form of irrational animals.

Being free in relation to our past and to our future implies that we are in a "place" from which we can observe the past and the future, and this is the present. The present is nothing trivial; on the contrary, it is not an easy task to understand the present. On the one hand, the "chronological" present is the *moment* or the *instant*, which is a pure limit between past and future, and it is the paradox of the permanent "passing away" of something—the instant—that is "fixed" but is a time without extension as time, and this can be understood only through the idea of "qualitative" time. If the instant is a time that neither passes nor has an "extension" as time, then it must necessarily be qualitative. And indeed, a limit falls under the category of quality. This means that the instant or moment is the "presentation" of the limit, and it is the human being who produces the limit: we "create" the instant making us present in time. Without the human soul there is no present in time, there is no chronological present.

The instant is *produced* in two different cases: when the human soul is "surprised" or feels itself "claimed" by something moving in time or when the human being makes a *decision*. Indeed, a decision from the point of view of time separates past and future, and this is precisely one of its distinguishing features. It is proper to the human decision—as human—that it always requires study in advance, which means looking at the experience of the past and at the open possibilities of the future before deciding. Such study "takes time," but the act of deciding as such happens in an instant, in a moment.

In the moment of surprise, our liberty is influenced by the surrounding world; in the moment of decision we strive to influence the surrounding world. The surprise is related to the past (and therefore this kind of instant is more "passive"), while the decision is related to the future (and therefore this kind of instant is more "active"). Admiration is the continuation of the surprise; work is the continuation of the decision. But in both cases—surprise and decision—the present is the transitory presence of the spirit in the "passing away" of time: the "chronological" present in an instant of our life.

On the other hand, the human soul is capable of being present beyond time or transcending it. This kind of presence in the classical Platonic and neo-Platonist philosophy is called *eternity*. Platonism sustains that the ideas do not change. Consequently, by contemplating them we transcend time from an *objective* point of view. Contemplating the ideas, we live in a continuous—not only transitory—permanent present, because we face something that does not change. An idea can be understood more profoundly, but as such is not subject to time.

There is, however, also the *subjective* side of eternity. True love is not subject to time, and therefore it is correct to affirm that a love that finishes never actually existed. This kind of love is eternal because it is always young: it cannot fade; it cannot become old, it is always new; it constantly maintains what it has, and at the same time increases it; it can never come to an end because it has not yet begun. Indeed, the experience that a person has of true love—or of true friendship—is that she or he has *discovered* the love or the friendship, not that it has begun. In contrast, sympathies or passions may at any time change, begin, or end.

True love or true friendship has two special and characteristic dimensions: it is the force that provides us with the possibility of springing from time into eternity, and it is the force—the only one—that produces the wonder of *presence*. Love takes us out of time, and this is exactly the same thing as making the present appear to us, to put us in the present. The "passing away" of time is not able to do that, and a purely temporal being could never "be present." This is why Aristotle says that time is impossible and incomprehensible without eternity, and this also explains why the measure of the degree of humanization of each person is her or his capacity to "be present."

Nietzsche affirms—against Plato—that the human being is plain temporality. If this thesis were true the consequence would be—as Deleuze has rightly commented—that the person would unavoidably be *dispersed*. Alternatively, if it is not true, then it is possible to be present.

The point here is that it is totally impossible to be a leader, to govern an organization, without a deep incorporation of this capacity. You need a lot of love to be truly present: without spirituality a leader is dispersed, has no sense of reality. Even worse—which is very often the case—he or she misunderstands the real situation, driven this way and that by his or her imaginations, interests, or passions. In such cases the leader is present to him- or herself, not to the "real reality," as Plato would have said. Therefore, the interest of classical learning was to develop and reinforce the capacities of the intellect and the will with a precise aim: to increase the reality of "being present" in the human person. A person without strength of intellect and will is always "dispersed"—that is, not truly present in the different "moments" of her or his life. It is a person "lost" in the past through melancholy or desire of revenge, or "lost" in the future through foolish imaginations, or lost in the particular interests that prevent him or her from adequately appreciating reality. Only learning the ethical, theoretical, and artistic or technical virtues helps people to span the bridge between time and eternity—that is, moving from being dispersed in time to being truly present. This is a fundamental condition for being a leader. Whether directly or indirectly, physically or spiritually, the leader must be present, otherwise this absence immediately shows its face in the form of dysfunctions appearing in the organization. To be truly and steadily present is a difficult endeavor, because an organization has many dimensions and often many persons. To be a true leader is incompatible with dispersion, lack of memory, or foolish imagination. Presence implies a great amount of intellectual attention and reflection and of true friendship to the persons and love to the organization and its work; and it implies understanding the deep order of the organization, which is impossible without having a clear insight into its ultimate purpose.

GOODS ARE PRESENT, MONEY IS NOT

Contrary to a widespread conviction, this last purpose cannot be earning money, because money is essentially a means and not an end. There are means that under certain circumstances are necessary, and in a commercial society money is necessary, but a necessity is not an end.

Here it is important to recall the distinction between "goods" and "money." Some material and, even more so, immaterial "goods" are absolutely necessary to live in this world, but money is only necessary in a commercial society. That is because commerce in principle has the function of providing some goods that a person is not able to produce by her- or himself. The problem is the quantitative amount of material goods that you need and that you want to possess. It is often the case that you have sufficient space to conserve the goods you need for a short time, but you never have sufficient space for a longer time and for guarding against possible contingencies. For that and for the virtual infinity of the desired goods the only solution is *money*. Money exists to try to solve this problem. It is absurd to try to possess a huge amount or even "infinity" of goods, but it is possible, and it makes sense to save money. The possession of money and its increase as an end of one's endeavors can be interpreted in different manners.

One possibility is poverty and the fear of the future: living in a commercial society one seeks money if one does not have sufficient resources to survive; one desperately needs money, and one is quite prepared to do anything for it. In this case the end is not money, but survival. Another possibility is the foolish desire of having ever more money, even if one already has enough to live well. In this case money seems to be the end, but again it is not. It makes no sense simply to have a great amount of money or to increase it, because as such money is virtually nothing: it is coins, bank notes, or numbers written in a bank. The acting person in such a scenario is not fully aware of her or his true aim. This aim in reality is the desire to convert life on earth into a pleasant and endless one. This of course is foolish: already in the classical Greek period it was very clear that an endless temporal life is the worst thinkable hypothesis. Nevertheless, such moral corruption exists and has been profoundly described by Nicolas Grimaldi with the term "frenzy of money."

It is an old piece of wisdom that true love is life in the most profound sense and that the highest form of life is love. As a consequence, love is something that gives me *satisfaction*, but at the same time, as life, it gives me the desire for *growth*. And this is the reason money imitates or mimics love: the possession of money gives a certain sense of sufficiency, but, on the other hand, the desire of having more never ends. The decisive difference is that love is interior and money exterior. In love, we live in the presence of a good. When one "loves money" one is in the presence of nothing; one is only dispersed and lost.

Love and money are compatible when love is the end and money the means; otherwise they are incompatible. You cannot *serve* God and wealth. The essential exterior infinity of money makes it incapable of providing the human being with interior peace. Therefore, Plato saw perfectly that if someone asserts that her or his last end is money, she or he is looking for a substitute for peace—namely, pure pleasure. We may add power, but as Aquinas emphasized, power is a principle and not an end and therefore cannot satisfy a person. Indeed, one seeks power with a longing for pleasure, either in a "hedonistic" sense (as means to acquire pleasant goods or services) or simply by having the pleasure one experiences in power as such. "Power society," "money society," and "hedonistic society" are three variations of the same kind of society. Of course, every person needs power and pleasure; we cannot live without a certain amount of them, but they are necessary as means. If we take them as ends we destroy our life and we damage the lives of the others.

A frequent excuse to justify that money can be a last end is to place the question in the sphere of "pure business" and not in the personal one. Earning money would be the end of the company, not the last end of the persons involved in the company. One may imagine an organization created to make money, but in which the owners know very well that money is only a means. It can be a very good company, because the purpose of the business is to *use* the money for some end: their endeavor is generating means for some ends. What is morally wrong is to truly aim at earning money as the last end and treating the stakeholders of a company as pure instruments to achieve this aim, because you should not do anything in society without having in mind and promoting the common good.

COMMON GOOD

Speaking of the common good: nowadays *common* and *public* are frequently confused. They are not synonymous concepts. *Public* is something at the free disposal of individual users, while *common* is not at our individual disposal: if I try to avail of it privately I will destroy it.

There are two immaterial forms of the common, which are its proper forms, and one material one. The immaterial forms refer to the intellect and the will. In the realm of the intellect, only truth is common: I may affirm that two plus two makes five, but I am wasting time. This is not at my disposal. Truth is common. So are friendship and love, which are rooted in our will: they are radically common. I cannot "use" my friendship with another person whimsically without destroying it, because true friendship, like true love, is not at our individual disposal if we want to maintain them.

Material forms of the common are common in a wide sense: the air and the water are common. They are common as "universal instruments" for humanity, whereas truth and love are "universal mediations," not instruments in the proper sense of the word. If a truth or a true love is used as an instrument, it is no longer truth or love. In this context, it is important to distinguish between instrument and means. Using truth and friendship as instruments is tantamount to destroying them, but truth and friendship are necessary means for the development of our spirit and at the same time of society. True community is a necessary means for the human being to be a human being, but never an instrument.

The most difficult task of a leader is to try to transform her or his company into a true community or at least to approach this goal as much as possible. It may seem an impossible or even an "old romantic" endeavor; nevertheless, not trying to reach this goal is equivalent to accepting defeat from the very beginning. Indeed, every self-proclaimed human society—and a business or a company in general is a kind of society—that totally lacks a common ground is not a society. A society without anything interior in common is a social lie.

THE TRUE LEADER

One may try to design a good world "*etsi Deus non daretur*"—as if God did not exist. And you may deem possible a world that would exist even "*etsi veritas, amicitia et amor non darentur*"—as if truth, friendship, and love did not exist. The latter is indeed the modern political and economic design of the world. It is true that if someone seeks the truth, friendship, and love in the private sphere, she or he is not officially hindered, but truth, friendship, and love are not elements of the political and economic system today. The system only has rules and coercion for maintaining the rules. In other words, it is a sophistic system. Indeed, everything seems to indicate quite clearly that we live in a sophistic system. There is nothing true or good; there only exists the force of language (rhetorical power) and political and economic power. That is all. Such a system, however, is below the human level, which includes spirit, and spirit means the real possibility of incorporating truth, friendship, and love into one's life and to communicate these to others.

It is hard to conceive the figure of a true leader without virtues, without a deep respect for the truth and a fundamental friendship with her or his stakeholders. A leader who presents him- or herself as a pure defender of rules is no leader, even if he or she has a high level of emotional intelligence, because emotions are not acts of friendship: I trust a friend, not an emotional specialist. Hitler, for instance, was a specialist in creating emotions, and he called himself *Führer*—that is, "leader." There are many purely emotional leaders today both in politics and in business. To be a true leader inside a system that structurally is hardly spiritual is of course a difficult task. But if one is not prepared to pay the price, he or she should not try to play the role.

Paying the price means something very characteristic of the spirit: renunciation. One must often renounce the "easy solutions," "easy success," short-term solutions—in a word, the easy life. It is very difficult—almost impossible—to change or to improve a society if the leaders are not an example and a mirror for the society. Undoubtedly what is needed is to educate a large group of leaders with spirituality as soon as possible. We already have sufficient experience of a world organized and governed by leaders educated for maximizing profit.

BIBLIOGRAPHY

Alvira, Rafael. "Work, Social Structure and Leadership: Spirituality and the Problem of Employment." Paper presented at the Third International Symposium on Catholic Social Thought and Management Education: Rethinking the Spiritual and Social Life within Business. Goa, India. January 10–12, 1999.

———. "Social Justice and the Common Good within and between Different Spheres of Society." In *Pursuing the Common Good: How Solidarity and Subsidiarity Can Work Together*, edited by Margaret S. Archer and Pierpaolo Donati, 605–17. Vatican City: Pontifical Academy of Social Sciences, 2008.

DeBonald, Louis. *Théorie du pouvoir politique et réligeux* [Theory of Political and Religious Power] [1796]. Paris: Libraire D'Adrien Le Clere, 1854.

Deleuze, Gilles. *Nietzsche and Philosophy*. New York: Columbia University Press, 1983. Originally published in 1962.

Fukuyama, Francis. *Trust: The Social Virtues and the Creation of Prosperity*. New York: Free Press, 1966.

Grimaldi, Nicolas. *Introducción a la filosofía de la historia de Carlos Marx* [Introduction to the Philosophy and History of Karl Marx]. Madrid: Dossat, 1986.

Habermas, Jürgen. "Religion in the Public Sphere." *European Journal of Philsophy* 14, no. 1 (2006): 1–25.

Kelsen, Hans. *The Essence and Value of Democracy*. Lanham, Md.: Rowman and Littlefield, 2013. Originally published in 1920.

———. *Pure Theory of Law*. Clark, N.J.: Lawbook Exchange, 2005. Originally published in 1934.

Lázaro, Raquel. *La sociedad comercial en Adam Smith: Método, moral y religión* [Commercial Society in Adam Smith: Method, Morality and Religion]. Pamplona: Eunsa, 2002.

———. "Adam Smith: Anthropology and Moral Philosophy." *Revista Empresa y Humanismo* 13, no. 1 (2010): 145–84.

Machiavelli, Niccolò. *The Prince: With Related documents* [1513]. Boston: Bedford and St. Martin's, 2016.

Millán-Puelles, Antonio. *La libre afirmación de nuestro ser: Una fundamentación de la ética realista* [The Free Affirmation of Our Being: A Foundation of Realist Ethics]. Madrid: Rialp, 1994.

Múgica, Luis Fernando. *Tradición y Revolución: Filosofía y sociedad en el pensamiento de Louis de Bonald* [Tradition and Revolution: Philosophy and Society in the Thought of Louis de Bonald]. Pamplona: Eunsa, 1988.

Rodríguez Lluesma, Carlos. *Los modales de la pasión: Adam Smith y la sociedad comercial* [Domesticated Passions: Adam Smith and the Commercial Society]. Pamplona: Eunsa, 1997.

Sison, Alejo José G. *Happiness and Virtue Ethics in Business.* Cambridge: Cambridge University Press, 2015.

Smith, Adam. *An Inquiry into the Nature and Causes of the Wealth of Nations* [1776]. London: Dent, 1910.

3

SPIRITUALITY IN BUSINESS AND WORK BEYOND THE DISTINCTION BETWEEN SYSTEM AND EVERYDAY LIFE

Regenerating the Principles of Liberalism in Late Modernity

MARKUS KRIENKE

It won't be difficult to show, as others have already done, that virtue is the mother of wealth and vice the mother of poverty.

—Antonio Rosmini, *Opere inedite di politica* [Unpublished Works on Politics]

If the external, material part of society does not reflect something internal and spiritual, the society's appearance is only a chimera; it cannot last.

—Antonio Rosmini, *The Philosophy of Politics*, vol. 2

INTRODUCTION

The general problem in business ethics is to find a certain synthesis between the economic and the moral imperatives; wherever this synthesis is considered possible, it often remains a mere regulative idea, with tragically unstable results. This discipline therefore reflects the modern division of the world into two worlds: that of the public sphere and the economic system on the one hand, and that of the private sphere with its face-to-face relationships of everyday life on the other. As is immediately evident, this conflict creates not only economic costs, but first of all moral costs for the individual entrepreneur and for the worker. It seems the businessperson is torn between two conflicting modes of reasoning and action: should he or she act according to the economic or the moral imperative? Kant resolves this question—in all its drama—with the intransigence of the categorical imperative. Indeed, it was only with Hegel that modernity attempted a theoretical solution that does not leave the individual struggling with this conflict, but resolves it on the level of public morality, where certain institutions like corporations and the state preestablish a synthesis. As a result, the Hegelian idea is not so different from the neo-Thomistic vision of a corporativistic order: in both models, the common good of social institutions integrates the conflict of individual interests into a higher social synthesis. While the neo-Thomists argue for the Aristotelian primacy of the common good over individual interests, in the Hegelian view only institutions, though based on the affirmation of individual rights and freedom, can realize the idea of a common good that is shared, recognized freedom. Another common aspect of both concepts—which are nevertheless more dissimilar than they are alike—is that this synthesis is realized as a juridical synthesis of natural law or of public law, which gives individual rights their moral basis.

Both ideas suggest the Kantian approach, which implies that the distinction between the extrinsic sphere of constitutional order and intrinsic moral motivation is ethically deficient because it founds public morality on the postulation of the coincidence between extrinsic incentives (in the form of rules and laws) and the interior voice of duty. If, as occurs in late modern societies, this harmony stabilized by the three postulates of practical reason is no longer given, the Kantian approach loses any possibility of being socially effective. Probably the function of a strong state in the ordoliberal approach of the Freiburg School is the modern secular memory of this rational postulate in Kant's system: the dialectics between system and everyday life. As for Kant, religion is the dimension in which morality finds its justification; the question of spirituality in business ethics emerges just at this point:

spirituality is an individual religious experience, a sort of first-person religious approach. As such, it interacts with the unresolved antinomies of the world and its social structures in a third-person mode. In other words, without the experience of the still insufficient coordination between the economic and the ethical aspects, no spiritual experience would be of any relevance for the sphere of business. Therefore, the main problem of the Hegelian or neo-Thomist approaches is that, in a kind of "economic theology" (in analogy to the conceptions of political theology) or "social theodicy," they resolve a priori the tension between the economic and the moral aspects *without* considering the space of the first-person experiences, which are first of all experience of businesspeople.

But not only Hegelian or neo-Thomist approaches resolve the "unresolvable" between economics and morals in a metaphysical perspective. Without recourse to metaphysics, there are significant recent approaches that reduce the one aspect to the other: on the one hand thinkers like Friedman and Homann consider business as the specific way of realizing morals in modern, diversified societies, and on the other hand authors like Ulrich and Zamagni aim to interpret markets as a way of interpersonal or civic relationships with moral significance.

THE PROVOCATION: BUSINESS AS A BETTER MORAL?

Milton Friedman in the United States and Karl Homann in Germany have presented—independently of each other and each in his own way—the radicalization of an approach that releases the economic reality from every extrinsic moral imperative. For Friedman and Homann, business in a free economy is the specifically modern way of realizing morality, which, contrary to premodern notions, is compatible with the dimension of individual freedom. For the realization of freedom, a morality based on religion is no longer necessary; illuminated self-interest through economic agency is sufficient—that is, morality would better be realized through self-interested rational choices. For Homann, the market economy is the realization of morality itself. He wants to overcome the gap between individual morality and systemic imperatives: economic incentives are socially more reliable than moral intentions. In other words, moral aims should be realized without moralizing the market for the sake of morality itself. Central for this reasoning is the insight that "it is impossible to enforce morality against the functional correlations of modern society but only within and through them. For that reason it is indispensable to transform regulative moral ideas in strategic motivation to action."[1] In the same way business and managerial activities are regulated by the rules of competition and not by moral appeals. In this sense entrepreneurship is a "rare means" that is optimized by the free market.[2] Friedman underlines "the great virtue of private competitive enterprise—it forces people to be responsible for their own actions and makes it difficult for them to 'exploit' other people for either selfish or unselfish purposes. They can do good—but only at their own expense."[3]

In these approaches the figure of the entrepreneur is interpreted by the market imperative: the Kantian dimension of morality that commands strictly and without any conditions is no longer taken into consideration because it is deemed to be already included—and in a better way—in the rules of free market. The entrepreneur's moral and religious convictions do not influence his agent rationality: for Homann and Friedman only a society regulated by the market creates the space and the possibilities for their realization. This model, however, is no longer convincing in the postsecular age of social systems.

The critique of the *homo oeconomicus* model is not due to any doubts about the objective results of economic analyses of neoclassi-

1. Karl Homann, *Vorteile und Anreize* [Advantages and Incentives], 2nd ed. (Tübingen: Mohr Siebeck, 2002), 19, author's translation.

2. See Homann, *Ethik in der Marktwirtschaft: Position Nr. 3* (Munich: Deutscher Instituts Verlag, 2007), 34.

3. Milton Friedman, "The Social Responsibility of Business Is to Increase Its Profits," in *An Introduction to Business Ethics*, ed. George D. Chryssides and John H. Kaler (1970; repr. London: Thomson Learning, 2006), 252.

cal economics, but rather the discomfort with the rational "solution" of the dialectics between moral convictions in private life and in a rationalist Weberian view of the functionalities of social systems. And this doubt has been expressed first by placing the entrepreneur and the worker at the center of attention as the principal agents of business.

The question that arises is whether this approach can overcome the distinction between system and everyday life without the described Hegelian, neo-Thomistic, or ordoliberal consequences. The dimension that each of these approaches fails to consider is that in the entrepreneur's perspective the solution lies in a third dimension, which is the personalistic dimension of spirit, which is not to be identified with a metaphysical perspective or the rational calculus of economicism. While the Hegelian and the neo-Thomistic approaches have the problematic consequence of becoming an "economic theology," which implies a corporativistic solution of the contradictions of the economic reality in a metaphysical order, the ordoliberal idea fails because it works only on the idealistic premise that we can foresee and be fully informed about all consequences of an action. But the core values of business, which include creativity, innovation, and new ideas, are not to limited to this logic of economic calculus.[4] They are central outcomes of the spiritual dimension of a person and his or her interpersonal relationships. A possible point of departure for resolving this problem would be not to think about the entrepreneur's relationships from the viewpoint of the market, but the other way around: to think about the market from the viewpoint of the relationships that form concrete business realities.[5] The question that has to be raised, however, is whether these relationships have to be considered "civic" in Zamagni's sense: whose consideration risks too closely identifying

4. See Thomas Beschorner, "Unternehmensethiken: Eine theoretische Einführung," in *Integritäts- und Umweltmanagement in der Beratungspraxis* [Business Ethics: A Theoretical Introduction], ed. Thomas Beschorner and Matthias Schmidt (Munich: Mering, 2004), 157; and Michael Novak, *Business as a Calling* (New York: Free Press, 1996), 120.

5. See Stefano Zamagni, *Impresa responsabile e mercato civile* [Responsible Business and Civil Market] (Bologna: Il mulino, 2013), 79.

the business reality with the politic realm of the *homo ethicus*.[6] Zamagni's radical contraposition of egoistic self-interest and the moral value of reciprocity shows more similarities to the Rousseauian distinction between *volonté particulière* and *volonté générale* than to the Italian Enlightenment to which he refers.[7] Against this ethical politicization of the business reality it seems much more sober and realistic to identify business relationships first of all as communicative. Indeed, Ulrich's approach refers to Habermas's strategy of communicative relationships and has precisely this advantage. Today a large part of business practice is communication: markets and business can be thought of as a continuous communicative process. Competition and cooperation can be seen as two contemporary aspects in a communicative structure that has to presuppose the truth and reliability of the actors as a communicative a priori. Without truthfulness and reliability there is neither communication nor community, nor, therefore, is there success in business. But if we have communicative structures, as the business reality presupposes, we have eo ipso cooperative structures. The conditions for communication are thus the openness to cooperation itself in the a priori of the economic reality. People cooperate not only in an ideal ethical situation, but simply by nature. Therefore, the focus on the business reality of today's economy points to the dimensions of liability and fidelity of communication structures more than the civic dimensions of an economic reality of the end of eighteenth-century Europe. But, because it presents an ideal model, the cognitive structure of communication faces two specific limits in the business reality. On the one hand, it is impossible to have full information, which would be a condition for an ideal communicative structure. On the other hand, in the economic reality there remains the temptation to supply wrong information for one's own advantage. In this perspective it is easy to see that the individual moral dimension

6. See Zamagni, "Introduction," in *The Economics of Altruism*, ed. Stefano Zamagni (Aldershot: Edward Elgar, 1995), xvii.

7. See Luigino Bruni and Stefano Zamagni, *Civil Economy: Efficiency, Equity and Public Happiness* (2004; repr. Frankfurt: Peter Lang, 2007), 170.

will always be the Achilles heel of any economic system. Therefore, the individual person and economic "preferences" will always have to be considered in light of their higher "values," and in this dimension the reduction of economics to utilitarian structures and selfish preferences is overcome because now the individual must cast judgment on these very preferences and structures: these judgments are indeed part of the moral domain whether something is "good" or not.[8] That is why it is also valid to consider the ethical contribution to economy in terms of economic outcome, and it is precisely this dimension that is rejected by the approaches of Zamagni and Ulrich. For a spiritual view of business ethics it is no problem to instead also positively affirm this dimension: that ethical strategies may help the economy in cutting costs and optimizing transactions. Therefore, the observation that "when another experience or need appears, the spirituality is often set aside" may indeed reflect a determinate cultural configuration of Western society but not the relationship between economics and morals or religion in itself.[9]

"CIVILIZING" THE MARKET ECONOMY?

To better identify the contribution of spirituality for the problem of the gap between system and everyday life in the entrepreneur's reality, it is worth first analyzing the approaches that, in contraposition to the institutional model of ordoliberalism, place the economic reality within the social ethical relationships in society. With this method, the authors try to express that if prosperity for all is a central issue of business, then business ethics cannot be the operation that places business in the "outskirts" of the society.[10] Two approaches, whose in-

8. Hans Joas, *Die Entstehung der Werte* [The Genesis of Values], 2nd ed. (Frankfurt: Suhrkamp, 1999), 31.

9. Gerald F. Cavanagh and Mark R. Bandsuch, "Virtue as a Benchmark for Spirituality in Business," *Journal of Business Ethics* 38, no. 1 (2002): 111.

10. See Robert C. Solomon, *Ethics and Excellence: Cooperation and Integrity in Business* (New York: Oxford University Press, 1993), 21.

tention is to overcome the modern dichotomy between state and market through an embedding of economic processes into the dimension of civil society, are developed by Ulrich and Zamagni. The question, thus, seems to be whether the market economy has to be civilized, and both authors would answer affirmatively. In other words, they try to diminish the modern differentiation of economy and society. At the end of the day, both do criticize the *preference* that the market de facto realizes for entrepreneurship or business activity.[11] The fundamental problem of the liberal social market economy would be to divide the logic of market from social logic and social politics and to conceive social politics as only a posteriori corrections of inequalities produced by the market. Both would not stand exclusively in competition but would have to be seen as compatible and reciprocally dependent.

Indeed, the idea of the late modern integration of free markets in civil society is mainly developed by the integrative economic ethics of Peter Ulrich and the civil economy approach of Stefano Zamagni. In order to avoid the aforementioned "moral costs," each attempts to integrate the modern idea of free markets with a specific moral dimension: discourse ethics in the first case and the classic virtue approach in the latter. Indeed, for Ulrich the economic order is located in a political context of discursive structures. Without any consensus of the latter one, the former could never concretely take shape.[12] Ulrich contradicts Homann, stressing that economic rationality can never replace moral rationality; it is, rather, the other way around: the first can only be legitimized in that wider sense of rationality that is the moral one. The ethical dimension of the discourse has the primacy over economy. Also, the political sphere of the rule-giver is no longer so

11. See Peter Ulrich, "Zivilgesellschaft: Dritter Sektor oder Dritter Weg? Zur wirtschaftsethischen Bedeutung des Bürgerengagements" [Civil Society: Third Sector or Third Path? The Relevance of Civic Involvement for Business Ethics], *Zeitschrift für Wirtschafts- und Unternehmensethik* 9, no. 3 (2008): 332; Zamagni, *Non profit come economia civile* [Non-Profit as Civil Economy] (Bologna: Il mulino, 1999).

12. See Ulrich, "Integrative Wirtschaftsethik: Grundlagenreflexion der ökonomischen Vernunft" [Integrative Business Ethics: Foundational Reflections on Economic Rationality], *Ethik und Sozialwissenschaft* 11, no. 4 (2000): 7.

presumably neutral as the modern Kantian and Hegelian idea suggested. In this perspective, every economic interest is per se an individualistic and presumptively egoistic interest, because in the case of doubt, this interest must be ordered according to the compromises of the political discourse. This latter one has the lexicological prevalence over the first one: this is the "primacy of ethics."[13] The problem is that this ethical premise of the concrete business agency remains abstract, and a wide critique asks Ulrich to concretize the ways in which it could be realized.[14] "It tries to challenge the quasi-scientific methodology of economics and widen the economic horizon to its non-economic prerequisites and the normative though often forgotten philosophical and social roots, rudiments, and foundations in the history of economic and social thought."[15] As for the normative ethical approach in economy, for Ulrich economic agency is also according to general and ideal norms.[16]

In these attempts to re-embed the economic reality in something like the context of everyday life, both choose different strategies: for Ulrich, as well as for Jürgen Habermas, whom he references, everyday life remains clearly distinguished from the economic system, and their synthesis remains a regulative idea that depends on the realization of the discursive principle in the economic reality. Zamagni seeks to challenge this distinction and to rethink the idea of economic reality out of individual virtues. In this way, both authors react emblematically to the *impasse* of the recent discussion, which faces the necessity to rethink economic discourse as a moral discourse. Both are convinced that the neoliberal ideas about the morality of free markets in a spontaneous (Hayek) or constitutional *ordo* (Eucken) are no longer

13. Ibid., 13.

14. See Beschorner, "Unternehmensethiken," 166f.

15. Martin Büscher, "Economic Systems and Normative Fundaments: A Social Market Economy in the Light of Economic Ethics," *Journal of Socio-Economics* 22, no. 4 (1993): 314.

16. See Ulrich, "Auf der Suche nach der ganzen ökonomischen Vernunft: Der St. Galler Ansatz der integrativen Wirtschaftsethik" [In Search of the Whole of Economic Rationality: The St. Gallen Approach to Integrative Business Ethics], in *Moral und Kapital: Grundfragen der Wirtschafts- und Unternehmensethik*, ed. Wolfgang Kersting (Paderborn: Mentis, 2008), 239ff.

adequate to face the challenge of the recent economic crisis. Zamagni goes back to the early modern idea, developed particularly in Italy, of the responsibility of every entrepreneur toward the whole society (*civitas*), which is based on the "public dimension of the company."[17] The question of happiness in this model is treated only through the civil dimension of the enterprise.[18] Relations of fairness are seen as the real social bonds of enterprises.[19]

According to Zamagni, the various social roles of entrepreneur, worker, and consumer have to be rethought as social roles and realizations of citizenship. In this way every company would contribute to the "democratization of the market."[20] His conception is to educate businesspeople, through a system of "good enterprises"—in the sense of nonprofit enterprises—to become "good people." However, this approach does not sufficiently distinguish the level of institutional norms and individual freedom. It tries to think the economic relationship as completely free from power: even economic incentives are interpreted as exercises of power and as belonging to the modern vision of the Taylorian labor society with passive, noncritical consumers. In this way, Zamagni tries to substitute in the economic sphere the motivation of self-interest with the motivation of virtue, counting on the utopian dynamic of relationships of gratuity; but, even for the classical approach, these are supererogatory actions and not relationships of justice. Only the latter can be required by institutional norms, while the former follow the logic of liberty. That is why Zamagni's theory is ultimately a sort of Rousseauian utopia.

Both approaches criticize the liberal market approach in a radical, external way. The economic logic would exclude any moral argument—say Ulrich and Zamagni against approaches like Homann's. They criticize the ordoliberalist approach for not considering the relational aspect, and they try to avoid the negative consequences of

17. Zamagni, *Impresa responsabile*, 8.
18. See ibid., 18.
19. See ibid., 26f.
20. Ibid., 119f.

economic competition by embedding it in a political concept of public relationships. In other words, the ones who are not willing to cooperate reciprocally should be "educated" by a better social configuration of markets and enterprises to become "better" participants in the economic exchange. A central element for both Ulrich and Zamagni is the proposal to consider the third sector as equivalent to the business sector and therefore formulate a radical critique of economics as business economics.[21] They are opposed to any understanding of the market as a civilizing institution: civilization is to be realized despite the market economy. Only reciprocity as a noncapitalist virtue allowed the market to be a civil institution.[22] Without any doubt, both thinkers indicate an important dimension to integrate into our modern understanding of economy; but, instead of integration in the ordoliberal approach, they propose a radical political-moral alternative that, in Ulrich's case, leads back to ordoliberal solutions and in Zamagni's case to a utopian vision. Where these visions do not end with ordoliberal affirmations, Hegel's question from the end of the chapter "Morality" in his *Philosophy of Right* remains: does this not lead to the consequence that every subject tries to legitimate as good and benevolent all his economic actions, even if they are motivated by nothing but subjective, selfish interests? And further, Zamagni's approach does not establish any limits for good ends and intentions, which "sanctify" any means to reach them. This leads, as Hegel analyzed, to the "vanity" of the "beautiful soul."[23] In this vision, the economic question of why profit should not be a justified end, and therefore one of the legitimate ends of business activity, remains unanswered.[24]

21. See Ulrich, "Zivilgesellschaft," 335; Zamagni, *Non profit*.

22. See Bruni and Zamagni, *Civil Economy*.

23. Georg Wilhelm Friedrich Hegel, *Elements of the Philosophy of Right* [1820], ed. Allen W. Wood (Cambridge: Cambridge University Press, 1991), n. 140, supplement.

24. See Andrew V. Abela, "Profit and More: Catholic Social Teaching and the Purpose of the Firm," *Journal of Business Ethics* 31, no. 2 (2001): 111; Domènec Melé, "Integrating Personalism into Virtue-Based Business Ethics: The Personalist and the Common Good Principles," *Journal of Business Ethics* 88, no. 1 (2009): 239.

FROM VIRTUE TO INSTITUTION

Ulrich and Zamagni are right when they underline that extrinsic motivations alone—like prohibitions and incentives—do not lead to socially qualified actions.[25] However, their radical integration of economy into an ethical approach—which is for Ulrich the general ethics of the universal communicative structure with its fundamental values of justice and fairness and for Zamagni the sphere of supererogatory actions like gratuity and love—fails to determine the institutional aspect of economy because it considers the individual interest of profit *already* and *always* tempered by moral virtues. It is clear that the institutional frame needs the integration of individual virtues. This was already known to Kant and is a central topic of the ordoliberals. Recently Wieland insisted on this aspect.[26] The question is whether this realization needs, as the Aristotelian and Thomistic theory would stress, a civic sphere of common good, excluding methodological individualism as a reductive way.[27] Here, "the telos represents the goal, the fulsome meaning of life. While it can be said that we advance toward that end through the virtues, the movement implied is not a change of place but a change of person. To Aristotle, a person moves toward the telos by being changed according to it."[28] Maritain specifically insisted on this perspective of common good for the realization of Thomistic ethics. But in this Aristotelian perspective, the "virtues of the market" cannot be realized, because the whole of economic activity is subordinated to the logic of specific communities, like the family or the polis. It is this communitarian logic that does not consider that every type of community that is centered on a concept of common good has to

25. See Zamagni, *Impresa responsabile*, 131.

26. See Josef Wieland, *Die Ethik der Governance* [The Ethics of Governance] (Marburg: Metropolis, 1999), 71ff.

27. See Helen Alford, "The Influence of Thomistic Thought in Contemporary Business Ethics," in *Handbook of the Philosophical Foundations of Business Ethics*, ed. Christoph Luetge (Dordrecht: Springer, 2013), 232.

28. Paul J. Wadell, *Friendship and the Moral Life* (Notre Dame, Ind.: University of Notre Dame Press, 1989), 42f.

be thought of not already as the solution, but as part of the problem, because the dimension of "egoism" can characterize not only individuals but also every type of community. Therefore, in Rosmini and Hegel "society" as the *topos* of economy is structurally different for the communities of family or church, because it is based on the idea of the individual, not of community.

Now, at this point it becomes clear how business can be understood as the "missing link" between the individualist approach of modern societies and the moral need for social bonds. In this perspective, the Italian term *economia aziendale* is especially interesting: it is a concept that considers business an institution with its "capacity . . . to be durable, or to survive over time in order to satisfy human needs by linking the social and human dimensions with monetary and economic aspects."[29] In this perspective, it would be the institutional dimension of the enterprise and not directly individual virtue that inserts into the market the long-term perspective of sustainability instead of short-term outcome. Therefore, it is not primarily the reduction of the modern separation of the economy from the political sphere, but the introduction of the communicative structure of modern business that guarantees the consideration of social relationships within the economy. The result is not the social relationships of premodern common good conceptions or those of a communitarian political perspective that place family, religious community, or voluntary associations at the center. The institutional concept of *economia aziendale*, instead, stresses two dimensions in a specific synthesis: "The first is more *internal* and applies to the common interest of the participants in the *azienda* whereas the second is more *external* and refers to the *azienda* as a system of relationships with other organizations and envisages the role that it covers in society."[30] In this institutional perspective, the sum of the individual interests is no longer simply a "bad" form of

29. Ericka Costa and Tommaso Ramus, "Italian Economia Aziendale as a Model Inspired by Catholic Humanism," in *Humanism in Economics and Business: Perspectives of the Catholic Social Tradition*, ed. Domènec Melé and Martin Schlag (Dordrecht: Springer, 2015), 152.

30. Ibid., 153.

common good; it is a concrete subsidiary interpretation that holds that the common good is also realized in other spheres, and only in the final political perspective can it be evaluated objectively. In this sense, this concept realizes the Rosminian insight that it is always "subjective love generating an objective love."[31] Every economic action, for Rosmini, is the "mediator"[32] between "one's own utility" and "the force of truth and justice."[33] In consequence, "no one institution, including the state, can embody the fullness of the common good"; rather, this is constructed only by the plurality of institutions.[34] But, the other way around, every institution can be considered in its direction toward the common good and therefore as situated within such a social constitution. As Costa and Ramus stress, in this perspective there is not such a deep gap between for-profit and not-for-profit organizations or enterprises as Zamagni's approach claims. Both of these can be valued in their contribution to the common good. "In a word, businesspeople are constantly on all sides, involved in building community. Immediately at hand, in their own firm, they must build a community of work. A great deal depends on the level of creativity, teamwork, and high morale a firm's leaders can inspire."[35] In this perspective, profit is understood in a broader perspective. If, as Rawls asserts, justice is the first virtue of institutions, then it seems that an enterprise is to be understood as an "association of individuals," that of course continually aims to become more a "community of persons."[36]

Through economic action fundamental values must be realized by the virtues, and this requires an obvious focus on the businessperson. To center this perspective, the first condition is to rethink liberty as

31. Rosmini, *Philosophy of Politics*, 2:31.

32. Carlos Hoevel, *The Economy of Recognition: Person, Market and Society in Antonio Rosmini* (Dordrecht: Springer, 2013), 69.

33. Rosmini, *The Philosophy of Right*, ed. Denis Cleary and Terence Watson (Durham: Rosmini House, 1993), 1:84.

34. See Michael Naughton, "Thinking Institutionally about Business: Seeing Its Nature as a Community of Persons and Its Purpose as the Common Good," in Melé *and* Schlag, *Humanism in Economics and Business*, 191.

35. Novak, *Business as a Calling*, 126.

36. See this distinction in Naughton, "Thinking Institutionally," 182.

not exclusively focused on private property, even if property is one of its fundamental dimensions. Liberty defines instead an intersubjective space and interaction, which distinguishes the subject from its property. Personhood realizes itself not through private property and thus through the business sphere, but in relationships that require the virtue of moderation, which was stressed by the central thinkers of ordoliberal thought. From Rosmini to Röpke, "moderation" (*Maßhalten*) is the fundamental virtue of a businessman.[37] At this point it really becomes clear that business ethics is not an ethics of imperatives but needs social rules and frameworks: this virtue of *moderation*, which expresses the freedom of the individual from her property, opens the sphere of recognition. Indeed, it is not the property of the other that is recognized, but his or her personality and freedom. Only because this latter dimension is separated from private property are recognition of the other and its accompanying juridical guarantees ethically possible. Economics can be developed when it is founded on recognition for the other. Present-day consumerism that devours the virtue of moderation at its very root at the same time eliminates the effective recognition of the other in society.

The difference between recognition and reciprocity is that in the act of recognition the subject is individual and active: the social interaction is not the passive *donum*, but is based on the constitution of the individual as a free and self-determining subject:[38] "It is contradictory to say that something is useful to society and it is not useful to individuals."[39] We could indeed verify that the rise of recognition in the modern age went hand in hand with the development of modern economics. This recognitive structure can be properly understood as the

37. See Wilhelm Röpke, "Ethik und Wirtschaftsleben" [1955], in *Wilhelm Röpke: Marktwirtschaft ist nicht genug; Gesammelte Aufsätze*, ed. Hans-Jörg Hennecke (Leipzig: Waltrop, 2009), 286; Rosmini, "Esame delle opinioni di Melchiorre Gioia in favor della moda" [Examination of the Fashionable Opinions of Melchiorre Gioia], in *Opere edite e inedite di Antonio Rosmini*, vol. 49, *Frammenti di una Storia della empietà e scritti vari*, ed. Rinaldo Orecchia (Padova: Cedam, 1977), 111f.

38. See Rosmini, *Philosophy of Right*, 1:66.

39. Rosmini, *Saggi di Scienza Politica: Scritti inedita* [Essays on Political Science: Unpublished Works], ed. Giovanni Battista Nicola (Turin: Paravia, 1933), 22.

"connective capital,"[40] because it means the right integration of the individual dimension of recognition, as Hegel theorized.[41] The more the economic paradigm characterized society, the more the category of recognition advanced to its core meaning. In Early Christianity private property, business, and economic success were not seen as something positive per se:[42] on the one hand, it "has its roots in sin" and therefore "cannot be unconditional," but "can be put to good uses."[43] The "business and work ethics of Benedict" (*ora et labora*), which is one of the principal references for the development of the modern liberal order, found its subjective form only through its integration with the Franciscan behavior of the biblical "possessing as if they did not."[44] Indeed, only in medieval times do we find for the first time the affirmation of private property, and in the medieval disputes it became clear that this spiritual Franciscan principle did not substitute the ethical reality of individual personhood and private property,[45] but, to the contrary, provided the spiritual foundation for the affirmation of the dimension of personhood in economic discourse. Indeed, with the Reformation the accumulation of wealth became socially acceptable, because it was a question of moral judgment, and that was a purely individual and personal affair. Such a development, however, was only possible because of the role of individual conscience.[46] Maybe it could be argued that the development of the spiritual perspec-

40. See Casey Ichniowski and Kathryn L. Shaw, "Connective Capital as Social Capital: The Value of Problem-Solving Networks for Team Players in Firms," Working paper n. 15619, National Bureau of Economic Research, December 2009, http://www.nber.org/papers/w15619.

41. See Albena Neschen, "Hegel on Modern Economics and Business," in *Handbook of the Philosophical Foundations of Business Ethics*, ed. Christoph Luetge (Dordrecht: Springer, 2013), 419f.

42. See Darlene Bay, Kim McKeage, and Jeffrey McKeage, "An Historical Perspective on the Interplay of Christian Thought and Business Ethics," *Business and Society* 49, no. 4 (2010): 659.

43. Robert W. Dyson, *The Pilgrim City: Social and Political Ideas in the Writings of St. Augustine of Hippo* (Woodbridge: Boydell, 2001), 107.

44. "I tell you, brothers, the time is running out. From now on, let those having wives act as not having them, those weeping as not weeping, those rejoicing as not rejoicing, those buying as not owning, those using the world as not using it fully. For the world in its present form is passing away"; 1 Cor 7:29–31.

45. As it was interpreted by Giorgio Agamben, *The Time That Remains: A Commentary on the Letter to the Romans*, ed. Patricia Dailey (Stanford, Calif.: Stanford University Press, 2005).

46. See Bay, McKeage and McKeage, "An Historical Perspective," 670.

tive in the business reality created one of the ideal presuppositions for the development of modern economy. In this sense, Ulrich's and Zamagni's interpretations of methodological individualism would be reductive because it failed to consider that this individualism requires the spiritual dimension of the "possessing as if they did not." If it is historically true that at least in some degree it is not only the case that religion has formed economic ideas, but that the economic reality as secular realization of human individuality has also helped religion to affirm its fundamental religious principles,[47] then the actual juridical framework of business reality does not suggest a radical contraposition between two imperatives, the economic and the moral one, but rather a historical synthesis. Does this framework, in its modifications due to the globalization process, modify or alter the individual moral decisions in economic reality?

RATIONALITY BETWEEN CALCULUS AND LIBERTY

Melé argued that the virtue approach has to be integrated with the dimension of principles, and this would be the fundamental message of Thomistic ethics in business.[48] Therefore, it does not seem true that in contrast to deontological or utilitarian ethics, the virtue approach is not expression of a determinate culture, but a notion that is present in every culture.[49] On the one hand, utilitarian motivations are present all over the world, otherwise globalization would have never occurred. Further, if the deontological model is a sort of secularization of religious commandments, it is simply impossible to negate its intercultural capacity. On the other hand, if it is also true that the idea of virtue is a core element of all cultures, the concretization of the "lists" of virtues can differ, and only if we reduce virtues and values to the most general ones is it possible to identify effective coincidences. And it is rather

47. See ibid., 672.
48. See Melé, "Integrating Personalism."
49. See Zamagni, *Impresa responsabile*, 105f.

this general sphere that can find corresponding institutional arrangements in every culture. Melé therefore stressed this systematic cooperation between the aspects of virtue and principles against the idea of reducing the economic reality to a moral civic basis. In this sense, the ordoliberal approach always stressed that the just and fair relationships in the economy are not only ensured by individual virtues but have to be institutionally ensured.[50] This dimension is effectively the only way to stabilize an international minimum consensus of rules and institutions. The problem of the major interpretations of free market economy is that rationality is seen to be reduced to pure maximization of individual outcome. To the contrary, in the modern tradition, this is what liberty *is not*. For Kant, for example, the businessperson who takes the just price according to purely economic calculations is not free, but only when she takes the just price for moral motivations, which is, for Kant, practical rationality. To act only for the economic and not the moral imperative for Kant simply would *not* be rational. In this sense, a methodological individualism that is not contrary to the affirmation of the dignity of every individual, but rather its condition, and therefore indispensable for the fundamental dimension of recognition, is also be stressed by Rosmini: society is the *means* and individuals are the end.[51] Rosmini takes an argument from Kant and rethinks it in an Augustinian way: freedom is not having options but means the will itself. If in Kant the Augustinian *libertas ipsa voluntas* is realized, then the problem of the relationship between business and morals is the specific manner in which the problem of liberty is formed in modern society. If morality is realized in concrete choices because it is impossible not to choose, then every social system that negates this choice is morally deficient.

In this perspective, every theory that reduces the economic option to the moral one or vice versa is morally problematic. It is true

50. See Walter Eucken, *Grundsätze zur Wirtschaftspolitik* [Principles of Economic Policy], ed. Edith Eucken and K. Paul Hensel (1952; repr. Tübingen: Mohr Siebeck, 2004), 254.

51. See Rosmini, *Philosophy of Right*, 6:37f.

that Zamagni and Ulrich claim to reduce the individual disadvantages that result from the moral choice. But if this eliminates that economic logic that offers only the possibility of self-realization of the spiritual dimension of the person, then an important dimension for moral self-realization is eliminated. In this sense, Rosmini stresses clearly, "I do not know how public happiness can exist unless it results from the happiness of individual persons."[52] The point, therefore, is not the problem of the relation between economy and morals, but the question of which institution guarantees practical rationality in everyday life, in maintaining contracts and rules. For precisely this reason the ordoliberals deal with the state, and this institution is completely lacking in Ulrich's and Zamagni's approaches.

Therefore, the ordoliberal reasoning does not agree with metaphysic syntheses as in Hegel or the neo-Thomists, nor with the reductions of Homann or Ulrich and Zamagni, but returns rather to a fundamental Kantian insight: Koslowski remembers that for Kant the gap between rational-moral actions and self-interest actions and the resulting moral costs can be faced only with the postulates of practical reason, first being the existence of God—that is, with religion. "Religion here is a postulate guaranteeing the exigency of being moral. It helps build up a social capital on which trust can be founded."[53] In this sense, with Kant it can be argued that ethics of markets can be compatible with religion.

This late modern context requires the integration of the liberal framework of *ordo* with the fundamental personalistic structures of entrepreneurs' and workers' self-realization. In this sense, it seems erroneous to reduce the ordoliberal approach to the same principles and problematics that characterize the thought of Adam Smith.[54] But the

52. Rosmini, *Saggi di Scienza Politica*, 22.

53. Peter Koslowski, "Ethical Economy as the Economy of Ethics and as the Ethics of the Market Economy," in *Corporate Citizenship, Contractarianism and Ethical Theory: On Philosophical Foundations of Business Ethics*, ed. Jesús Conill Sancho, Christoph Luetge, and Tatjana Schönwälder-Kuntze (Farnham: Ashgate, 2008), 161.

54. As affirmed for example by Büscher, "Economic Systems," 312.

social market economy, which is based on ordoliberal reasoning, does not mean to affirm only the authorities of families, churches, communities, and traditions against a liberal market.[55] The very core of the idea of social market economy is the interpersonal dimension of recognition. Therefore, spirituality in business does not only mean to run one's own business in the right way but to do it "for the benefit of others."[56] In this sense the Lutheran interpretation of work as a *calling* fundamentally reflected on its relational dimension. And this is a process of becoming persons. Therefore, Mahoney characterizes business ethics in four circles of interpersonal relationships: the relationships between the members of a business organization, with the customers, between companies (that is, with the members of other companies), and with society in a broad sense.[57] This is the ethical perspective at which the characterization of a company as communicative structure aims. According to Rosmini, indeed, human providence extends to the sphere of family as well as to the sphere of economics: "The most sacred, moral stimulus of one's own duty, which foresees and provides for the future necessities of domestic and civil society [is] in a way more helpful than any other duty."[58] In contrast to the domestic society, in the civil society and therefore in the economic sphere the concept of reciprocity is realized by individual fundamental rights,[59] because "what is *lawful* . . . , such as rights, must whenever required give way to the cause of virtue and of the moral perfection of the world."[60] This means that the economic concepts are not to be understood primarily as utilitarian (and this is ultimately the problem in Ulrich and Zamagni), but as rights.[61] Again, the realization of moral values with-

55. See Rainer Kreuzhof and Wolfgang Ockenfels, "On the Proper Essence of Christian Economic Ethics," *Management Revue* 21, no. 1 (2010): 90.

56. Vivian Ligo, "Configuring a Christian Spirituality of Work," *Theology Today* 67, no. 4 (2011): 444.

57. See John Mahoney, "Christian Perspectives on Business Ethics," *Studies in Christian Ethics* 2, no. 1 (1989): 28.

58. Rosmini, *Philosophy of Politics*, 2:342.

59. See ibid., 2:93; Rosmini, *Philosophy of Right*, 2:100.

60. Rosmini, *Philosophy of Right*, 2:467.

61. See ibid., 2:237.

out a juridical framework is simply impossible in human societies. In this sense, it is unreasonable to think about a civil economic order without the juridical guarantee of individual liberal rights.

The delta between economic reality and moral imperative that in Kant remained open finds in Rosmini an institutional correspondence: universal benevolence in its social aspect is realized—at least in a sacramental way—in the supernatural society that is the church.[62] This means that the maximum of sociality can never be external and economic (this material point of view is the misunderstanding in Ulrich and Zamagni) but internal and leading to the spiritual sphere.[63]

FROM *CARITAS IN VERITATE* TO RECENT CHALLENGES

Melé doubts the conclusion of De George that only philosophers can provide ethical principles for a business that is not only made up of Christians.[64] He notes that philosophers too base their individual proposals on relatively diverging presuppositions; not everyone would accept a deontological or a utilitarian or a virtue-based approach. Furthermore, considering the anthropological implications of Catholic Social Teaching, he asks whether it might not contain spiritual guidelines valid for all the people, not only for Christians.[65]

The preceding considerations have tried to show how the perspective of Christian spirituality can make an important contribution in interpreting the significance of business and entrepreneurship. The encyclical *Caritas in veritate* aims precisely at this point: the dimension of gift, gratuity, and forgiveness does not affirm a logic against ordoliberal structures but achieves their necessary integration and therefore

62. See ibid., 4:8–11; Rosmini, *Philosophy of Politics*, 2:314–16.

63. See Rosmini, *Philosophy of Politics*, 2:57, 71, 88f.

64. See Richard T. De George, "Theological Ethics and Business Ethics," *Journal of Business Ethics* 5, no. 6 (1986): 424.

65. See Domènec Melé, "Scholastic Thought and Business Ethics: An Overview," in *Handbook of the Philosophical Foundations of Business Ethics*, ed. Christoph Luetge (Dordrecht: Springer, 2013), 152f.

their late modern foundation, in the same way as we have seen in the case of the Franciscan's spiritual attitude toward private property. They see every actor in the economic dynamic as someone who has part in a diverse dimension of "time": the eschatological sphere that provides the foundation for property-based economic action of the individual in the measure in which it detracts it from him and creates the sphere of personal relationships. Relationships based on reciprocal recognition give economic actions a new quality if in their specific communicative structures a different time structure is realized, not only in a quantitative but also in a qualitative sense. The specific change that we are facing in the communicative structure clearly consists in a lack of quality time: while the information exchanged and the number of contacts increase, the quality is reduced to the superficial level of bare information. The qualitative experience of time in the spiritual dimension "decelerates" the economic rhythm, and not from an extrinsic but an intrinsic point of view, and thus not against the economic "logic," but refounding the principles of liberal order. In this way, an interreligious dialogue on the spiritual principles of economy that are focused on the dimension of the person in an "absolute" dimension is not a threat, but a new possibility for the affirmation of the principles of the free market with respect to the human person. In this way, the relative chapters of the social encyclicals also acquire significance beyond mere decoration.

Further, Ulrich thinks that an economic action can be justified when all who are implied in or affected by the action would accept it in an objective, third-person point of view. The spiritual dimension insists instead on the first-person perspective: the diverse moral quality of economic action is the new time dimension of spiritual experience. In this perspective, the high quantitative potentials of the modern economy and the rapidity of globalized economic processes become clear as the immanent realization of the human tendency to overcome the limitedness of human nature and its mortal destiny. If human life is ontologically limited, only through the acceleration of social processes can life become longer, and therefore the human desire of immortality is partially realized. In other words, if life is too short, by accelerating life through economic perfection, a multiplicity of lives can be lived at the same time. The spiritual perspective, in contrast, interprets economic activity in a limited space of time.

Finally, in the quantitative perspective the dimension of the future becomes the optimistic perspective of the realization of desires: everything seems possible, under the condition that there is enough time.[66] But the same acceleration and optimistic vision of the future also cause panic, because despite all the technological progress, not everything can be realized, and modern man lives with the existential panic of missing out on many things. For this reason, the economic logic—even in its acceleration—does not achieve the acceptance of human existence. Therefore, the temporality of economic processes, and thus the effect of spirituality in business against the perfectionist acceleration of it, constrain economic actors—first of all the entrepreneur—to rational agency: "Time forces us to want not all that is possible, but only what is rational."[67] In other words, spirituality in business aids in the discovery of this rationality. Again, it becomes clear that economic rationality can be affirmed on the basis of spiritual experience, and this perspective casts a critical light on any conception that aims to resolve the difference of economics and ethics with superficial ordo-economic or civil-economic approaches.

BIBLIOGRAPHY

Abela, Andrew V. "Profit and More: Catholic Social Teaching and the Purpose of the Firm." *Journal of Business Ethics* 31, no. 2 (2001): 107–16.

Agamben, Giorgio. *The Time That Remains: A Commentary on the Letter to the Romans*. Edited by Patricia Dailey. Stanford, Calif.: Stanford University Press, 2005.

66. See Hans-Joachim Höhn, *Zeit und Sinn: Religionsphilosophie postsäkular* [Time and Meaning: Post-Secular Philosophy of Religion] (Paderborn: Schöningh, 2010), 196.

67. Ibid., 199, author's translation.

Alford, Helen. "The Influence of Thomistic Thought in Contemporary Business Ethics." In *Handbook of the Philosophical Foundations of Business Ethics*, edited by Christoph Luetge, 227–50. Dordrecht: Springer, 2013.

Bay, Darlene, Kim McKeage, and Jeffrey McKeage. "An Historical Perspective on the Interplay of Christian Thought and Business Ethics." *Business and Society* 49, no. 4 (2010): 652–76.

Beschorner, Thomas. "Unternehmensethiken: Eine theoretische Einführung" [Business Ethics: A Theoretical Introduction]. In *Integritäts- und Umweltmanagement in der Beratungspraxis*, edited by Thomas Beschorner and Matthias Schmidt, 151–78. Munich: Mering, 2004.

Bruni, Luigino, and Stefano Zamagni. *Civil Economy: Efficiency, Equity and Public Happiness*. Frankfurt: Peter Lang, 2007. Originally published in 2004.

Büscher, Martin. "Economic Systems and Normative Fundaments: A Social Market Economy in the Light of Economic Ethics." *Journal of Socio-Economics* 22, no. 4 (1993): 311–22.

Cavanagh, Gerald F., and Mark R. Bandsuch. "Virtue as a Benchmark for Spirituality in Business." *Journal of Business Ethics* 38, no. 1 (2002): 109–17.

Costa, Ericka, and Tommaso Ramus. "Italian Economia Aziendale as a Model Inspired by Catholic Humanism." In *Humanism in Economics and Business: Perspectives of the Catholic Social Tradition*, edited by Domènec Melé and Martin Schlag, 147–62. Dordrecht: Springer, 2015.

De George, Richard T. "Theological Ethics and Business Ethics." *Journal of Business Ethics* 5, no. 6 (1986): 421–32.

Dyson, Robert W. *The Pilgrim City: Social and Political Ideas in the Writings of St. Augustine of Hippo*. Woodbridge: Boydell, 2001.

Eucken, Walter. *Grundsätze zur Wirtschaftspolitik* [Principles of Economic Policy]. Edited by Edith Eucken and K. Paul Hensel. Tübingen: Mohr Siebeck, 2004. Originally published in 1952.

Friedman, Milton. "The Social Responsibility of Business Is to Increase Its Profits." In *An Introduction to Business Ethics*, edited by George D. Chryssides and John H. Kaler, 249–54. London: Thomson Learning, 2006. Originally published in 1970.

Hegel, Georg Wilhelm Friedrich. *Elements of the Philosophy of Right* [1820]. Edited by Allen W. Wood. Cambridge: Cambridge University Press, 1991.

Hoevel, Carlos. *The Economy of Recognition: Person, Market and Society in Antonio Rosmini*. Dordrecht: Springer, 2013.

Höhn, Hans-Joachim. *Zeit und Sinn: Religionsphilosophie postsäkular* [Time and Meaning: Post-Secular Philosophy of Religion]. Paderborn: Schöningh, 2010.

Homann, Karl. *Vorteile und Anreize* [Advantages and Incentives]. 2nd ed. Tübingen: Mohr Siebeck, 2002.

———. *Ethik in der Marktwirtschaft: Position Nr. 3* [Ethics in the Market Economy: Position No. 3]. Munich: Deutscher Instituts Verlag, 2007.

Ichniowski, Casey, and Kathryn L. Shaw. "Connective Capital as Social Capital: The Value of Problem-Solving Networks for Team Players in Firms." Working Paper no. 15619. National Bureau of Economic Research. December 2009. http://www.nber.org/papers/w15619.

Joas, Hans. *Die Entstehung der Werte* [The Genesis of Values]. 2nd ed. Frankfurt: Suhrkamp, 1999.

Koslowski, Peter. "Ethical Economy as the Economy of Ethics and as the Ethics of the Market Economy." In *Corporate Citizenship, Contractarianism and Ethical Theory: On Philosophical Foundations of Business Ethics*, edited by Jesús Conill Sancho, Christoph Luetge, and Tatjana Schönwälder-Kuntze, 149–68. Farnham: Ashgate, 2008.

Kreuzhof, Rainer, and Wolfgang Ockenfels. "On the Proper Essence of Christian Economic Ethics." *Management Revue* 21, no. 1 (2010): 82–94.

Ligo, Vivian. "Configuring a Christian Spirituality of Work." *Theology Today* 67, no. 4 (2011): 441–66.

Mahoney, John. "Christian Perspectives on Business Ethics." *Studies in Christian Ethics* 2, no. 1 (1989): 20–40.

Melé, Domènec. "Integrating Personalism into Virtue-Based Business Ethics: The Personalist and the Common Good Principles." *Journal of Business Ethics* 88, no. 1 (2009): 227–44.

———. "Scholastic Thought and Business Ethics: An Overview." In *Handbook of the Philosophical Foundations of Business Ethics*, edited by Christoph Luetge, 133–58. Dordrecht: Springer, 2013.

Naughton, Michael. "Thinking Institutionally about Business: Seeing Its Nature as a Community of Persons and Its Purpose as the Common Good." In *Humanism in Economics and Business: Perspectives of the Catholic Social Tradition*, edited by Domènec Melé and Martin Schlag, 179–99. Dordrecht: Springer, 2015.

Neschen, Albena. "Hegel on Modern Economics and Business." In *Handbook of the Philosophical Foundations of Business Ethics*, edited by Christoph Luetge, 415–29. Dordrecht: Springer, 2013.

Novak, Michael. *Business as a Calling*. New York: Free Press, 1996.

Röpke, Wilhelm. "Ethik und Wirtschaftsleben" [Ethics and Economic Life] [1955]. In *Wilhelm Röpke: Marktwirtschaft ist nicht genug; Gesammelte Aufsätze*, edited by Hans-Jörg Hennecke, 270–88. Leipzig: Waltrop, 2009.

Rosmini, Antonio. *Opere inedite di politica* [Unpublished Works on Politics]. Edited by Giovanni Battista Nicola. Milan: Tenconi, 1923.

———. *Saggi di Scienza Politica. Scritti inediti* [Essays on Political Science: Unpublished Works]. Edited by Giovanni Battista Nicola. Torino: Paravia, 1933.

———. "Esame delle opinioni di Melchiorre Gioia in favor della moda" [Examination of the Fashionable Opinions of Melchiorre Gioia]. In *Opere edite e inedite di Antonio Rosmini*, vol. 49, *Frammenti di una Storia della empietà e scritti vari*, edited by Rinaldo Orecchia, 97–145. Padova: Cedam, 1977.

———. *The Philosophy of Right*. 6 vols. Edited by Denis Cleary and Terence Watson. Durham: Rosmini House, 1993–96.

———. *The Philosophy of Politics*. 2 vols. Edited by Denis Cleary and Terence Watson. Durham: Rosmini House, 1994.

Solomon, Robert C. *Ethics and Excellence: Cooperation and Integrity in Business*. New York: Oxford University Press, 1993.

Ulrich, Peter. "Integrative Wirtschaftsethik: Grundlagenreflexion der ökonomischen Vernunft" [Integrative Business Ethics: Foundational Reflections on Economic Rationality]. *Ethik und Sozialwissenschaft* 11, no. 4 (2000): 555–66.

———. "Auf der Suche nach der ganzen ökonomischen Vernunft: Der St. Galler Ansatz der integrativen Wirtschaftsethik" [In Search of the Whole of Economic Rationality: The St. Gallen Approach to Integrative Business Ethics]. In *Moral und Kapital: Grundfragen der Wirtschafts- und Unternehmensethik*, edited by Wolfgang Kersting, 61–75. Paderborn: Mentis, 2008.

———. "Zivilgesellschaft: Dritter Sektor oder Dritter Weg? Zur wirtschaftsethischen Bedeutung des Bürgerengagements" [Civil Society: Third Sector or Third Path? The Relevance of Civic Involvement for Business Ethics]. *Zeitschrift für Wirtschafts- und Unternehmensethik* 9, no. 3 (2008): 331–36.

Wadell, Paul J. *Friendship and the Moral Life*. Notre Dame, Ind.: University of Notre Dame Press, 1989.

Wieland, Josef. *Die Ethik der Governance* [The Ethics of Governance]. Marburg: Metropolis, 1999.

Zamagni, Stefano. "Introduction." In *The Economics of Altruism*, edited by Stefano Zamagni, xv–xxii. Aldershot: Edward Elgar, 1995.

———. *Non profit come economia civile* [Non-Profit as Civil Economy]. Bologna: Il mulino, 1999.

———. *Impresa responsabile e mercato civile* [Responsible Business and Civil Market]. Bologna: Il mulino, 2013.

4

WHAT DOES THE SERMON ON THE MOUNT MEAN FOR CHRISTIANS IN BUSINESS?

MARTIN SCHLAG

> Jesus himself offers a "manual" for this strategy of peacemaking in the Sermon on the Mount. The eight Beatitudes (cf. Mt 5: 3–10) provide a portrait of the person we could describe as blessed, good and authentic.
>
> —Pope Francis, Peace Message, January 1, 2017

There is no such thing as "Christian economics." God has not revealed the scientific laws of economic reality, nor has he revealed the laws of biology or those of natural science in general, nor of astronomy, of secular history, of political science, and so forth. That being said, can we with the same degree of certainty affirm that there is no such thing as a "Christian economy"? Christianity has in general resisted the temptation to create theocratic polities because the Bible does not contain a revealed civil law. The Bible is not a socioeconomic codebook or an immediately applicable system of social ethics. Consequently, at least in the Catholic tradition, the church has stressed the need of human reason to apply the revealed principles of morality to the specific problems of each age and has called the resulting norms "natural law." Natural law is not revealed except for its general principles contained in the Ten Commandments, and these too are universal rules of moral common sense. Thus, there are no specifically Christian traffic rules, nor Christian laws on finance, nor even specifically Christian codes of business ethics. All these different moral norms work the same for and can be recognized by people with or without the Christian faith or any other religious faith.

On the other hand, believing Christians feel that their faith makes a difference. They experience their profession as a vocation; they know that God is present everywhere, that the world is the arena for their personal sanctification. So Christian faith at least functions as an inspiring motivation for ethical and moral compliance. Christians have additional reasons for behaving well because they believe that their deeds decide their eternal life. There is, in other words, a Christian way of life in the world of business.

In this essay I want to show how one of the core texts of Christianity, the Sermon on the Mount, can influence the business dealings of a Christian. Right from the beginning it is important to keep in mind that a tension toward a fuller realization of the Sermon on the Mount in the economy and in business will always remain. The Sermon on the Mount cannot be domesticated and perpetually challenges us all to improve personally and as a community.

WHY THE SERMON ON THE MOUNT?

I have chosen the Sermon on the Mount because no other text of holy scripture has been commented on as much as the Sermon on the Mount.[1] Certainly, Allison is right to point out that the Sermon on the Mount cannot be the quintessence of Christianity because it does not proclaim the redemption of Christ:[2] the Sermon on the Mount must not and cannot be isolated from the death and resurrection of Christ. However, the Sermon on the Mount contains an ethical program that can be described as characteristically Christian and new, even in comparison with the high standards of Jewish rabbinic teaching. Dumais has convincingly argued that even though there are many

1. See Marcel Dumais, *Il Discorso della Montagna: Stato della ricerca, Interpretazione, Bibliografia* (Turin: Elledici, 1999), 23–44.

2. See Dale C. Allison, *The Sermon on the Mount: Inspiring the Moral Imagination* (New York: Crossroad, 1999), xi.

elements in the Sermon on the Mount that are clearly rooted in the Jewish faith and in rabbinic teachings, on the whole the Sermon on the Mount constitutes a "new ethics" because it contains new elements and content, like love for one's enemies and the formulations of the Our Father and the Golden Rule. The composition of the Sermon on the Mount as a whole represents an original and unique project of life that we identify as specifically Christian. Furthermore, the motives for this new life are new in comparison with the Old Testament: the Sermon on the Mount is proclaimed in the eschatological context of the coming of the Kingdom of God and motivated by it; the Sermon on the Mount is intrinsically connected to the person of Jesus also as the risen Lord (Mt 28:1, 28:8–20); through our loving and merciful actions we should imitate God Father and become similar to him.[3]

This specificity of the Sermon on the Mount has been appreciated also by non-Christians. Mahatma Gandhi, for instance, famously said, "The message of Jesus is contained in the Sermon on the Mount, unadulterated and taken as a whole."[4] Unfortunately, what the Jewish scholar Pinchas Lapide wrote is also true: the history of the interpretation of the Sermon on the Mount is a long attempt to "tame it," to remove its challenging bite and rough edges, to dull its tip, while at the same time eschewing a guilty conscience about such a reductive interpretation.[5] Some interpretations of the nineteenth and twentieth centuries have especially tried to neutralize the Sermon on the Mount, insinuating that Jesus was not able to say what he really wanted to; or that what he said was not meant for his time or that it was meant for a different world. In contrast, the two most renowned and oft-cited interpretations—those of Tolstoy[6] and Bonhoeffer[7]—took the Ser-

3. See Dumais, *Il Discorso,* 128; of a different opinion there is Pinchas Lapide, *Il discorso della montagna: Utopia o programma?* [The Sermon on the Mount: Utopia or Program for Action?] (Brescia: Paideia, 2003), 34–36.

4. Mahatma Gandhi, as quoted in Jeremy Holtom, "Gandhi's Interpretation of the Sermon on the Mount," in *The Oxford Handbook of the Reception History of the Bible,* ed. Michael Lieb, Emma Mason, and Jonathan Roberts (Oxford: Oxford University Press, 2013), 546, who in turn cites Charles F. Andrews, *Mahatma Gandhi: His Life and Ideas* (Woodstock, Vt.: Skylight Paths, 2003), 54.

5. Lapide, *Il discorso,* 9ff.

6. See Leo Tolstoy, *The Kingdom of God Is within You* (Doylestown, Pa.: Wildside, 2005).

7. See Dietrich Bonhoeffer, *The Cost of Discipleship* (New York: Macmillan, 1979).

mon on the Mount literally. These seem to be the ones that attract us, and this fact proves that the Sermon on the Mount cannot be "domesticated."[8] The Sermon on the Mount is a constant challenge for the church and for our Christian conscience. It must be taken seriously.

THE PRACTICABILITY OF THE SERMON ON THE MOUNT

The difficulty that immediately crops up is the practicability of the Sermon on the Mount. Is it really possible to fulfill its commandments? How can one live in such a way and still be successful in the competitive world of business? Following Joachim Jeremias's seminal work,[9] we can distinguish three different types of interpretation in the course of history, which all share the conviction that the Sermon on the Mount is impossible to fulfill: the perfectionist, the pedagogical, and the interpretation of the Sermon on the Mount as an interim ethics.

1. The perfectionist interpretation interprets the Sermon on the Mount as a series of very difficult ethical injunctions that only few people, a spiritual elite, but not all Christians, can fulfill. Such an interpretation can be traced back to the Didache. This early first- or second-century Christian document made a distinction between those who are perfect and can carry the whole yoke of Christ and the imperfect who should carry as much as they can.[10] This division into perfect and imperfect Christians was the interpretation of the Sermon on the Mount adopted by Catholic scholasticism. It was reinforced by the institution of a special "state of perfection" of the religious orders whose members strive not only to fulfill the moral precepts that bind all Christians but also the "counsels" Jesus gave in the gospel. Contemporary Catholic exegesis does not maintain this division into

8. See Dumais, *Il Discorso*, 42–43.

9. Joachim Jeremias, *Die Bergpredigt* [The Sermon on the Mount] (Stuttgart: Calwer, 1965), 7–15.

10. See "Didache," in *The Apostolic Fathers*, book 6, chapter 2, trans. Francis X. Glimm, Joseph M.-F. Marique, SJ, and Gerald G. Walsh, SJ (Washington, D.C.: The Catholic University of America Press, 1947), 176.

two classes of Christians. We have returned to the vision of the early church fathers who applied the Sermon on the Mount to all Christians as the "perfect standard of the Christian life."[11] Dumais is right in saying that the interpretation of the Sermon on the Mount as a model of demanding perfection for elite groups has had a highly positive, stimulating effect on the whole church.[12]

2. The pedagogical interpretation or theory of impossibility (*Unerfüllbarkeitstheorie*) is the point of view of Lutheran orthodoxy. Luther himself held a series of sermons on the Sermon on the Mount: the Sermon on the Mount should be an inner attitude of the heart even when the Christian as soldier or magistrate must act in a way that contradicts the word of the gospel and suffers interiorly for having to do so—for example, when using power to enforce law instead of offering the other cheek. Luther distinguished between the Christian person and his function and in so doing was influenced by his conception of the "two regiments." This leads to a conception of the Sermon on the Mount as individual and of no direct normativity for social ethics, as is generally the case in the Protestant tradition.[13] There are some allusions in Luther to the function of the Sermon on the Mount to make us grasp our sinfulness;[14] this function of biblical law as condemnatory is called *usus elenchticus legis*.[15] It implies that it is impossible to fulfill the Sermon on the Mount. This interpretation was developed after Luther by the "Lutheran orthodoxy," which read Matthew from St. Paul.[16] For Lutheran orthodoxy Matthew 5–7 was law opposed to the gospel and to grace. The Sermon on the Mount therefore was mere

11. See Augustine, "Commentary on the Lord's Sermon on the Mount," in *Commentary on the Lord's Sermon on the Mount with Seventeen Related Sermons*, trans. Denis J. Kavanagh, OSA (Washington, D.C.: The Catholic University of America Press, 1951), Book 1, ch. 1, p. 19.

12. See Dumais, *Il Discorso*, 50–53.

13. The phrase attributed to Otto von Bismarck, for example, is characteristic of this line of thought: "*Mit der Bergpredigt kann man keinen Staat regieren*" (No state can be ruled by the Sermon on the Mount).

14. Martin Luther, *D. Martin Luthers Werke: Kritische Gesammtausgabe* [D. Martin Luther's Works: Complete Critical Edition] (Weimar: Hermann Böhlaus Nachfolger, 1883), 1:32, 359, 17ff; see also Dumais, *Il Discorso*, 31.

15. From the Greek verb *elencho*, which means "to prove guilty."

16. See Dumais, *Il Discorso*, 33.

praeparatio evangelica. Jeremias rejected this theory: it is not exegesis but *eisegesis*, because it reads Paul into Matthew. We should read Paul from Jesus, not the other way around. In the text itself there is no reflection on the incapability of man to fulfill God's commandments; Jesus expects his disciples to fulfill his words.[17] The correct intuition in this interpretation is the necessity of grace for Christian life.

3. The third strand of interpretation is based on the assumption of eschatological immediacy or the conception of an interim ethics. It places the Sermon on the Mount in the context of an assumed eschatological urgency of Jesus as an apocalyptical preacher. The exhortations of the Sermon on the Mount are held to be unfeasible for normal times and are justified as a sort of provisional normative ordering in the case of an emergency. The words of the Sermon on the Mount appeal to the followers of Christ to make a last extreme effort at the end of time. Everything must be cast aside, even law. Jeremias rightly rejected this interpretation: Jesus does not focus on some catastrophic end-times scenario but on the presence of salvation.[18]

Is it possible to comply with the moral standards enshrined in the Sermon on the Mount? The answer to this question is yes, but not with our own strength or abilities. Contemporary interpretations have sought to reconcile the objective difficulty of fulfillment with the serious commitment to literal interpretation. The following three points offer particular insight into the possibility of living out the serious demands of the Sermon on the Mount:

1. God's grace comes first. As Jeremias put it, the moral injunctions in the Sermon on the Mount are always consequences. Jesus' words are the consequences of his life, death, redemption, and teaching as Christ. The Sermon on the Mount is preached to people who are already infused with enthusiasm for the Kingdom of God. It is really God who is at work in his kingdom: with his help and in his love the moral

17. Jeremias, *Die Bergpredigt*, 11–13.
18. Ibid., 13–15.

program of the Sermon on the Mount is possible.[19] It is no coincidence that chapters 5–7 of Matthew are followed by the series of miracles in chapters 8–9: the words and deeds of Jesus belong together. He reveals with his healing power, showing that he can make us whole again and give us the strength we need for a holy life. What Jesus presupposes in the Sermon on the Mount is the whole of the rest of the gospel and salvation. He describes what a life of divine filiation means, what life looks like in the new Christian era. The Sermon on the Mount is a sovereign gift of forgiveness and at the same time the holy will of our Father God. In other words, living up to the standards of the Sermon on the Mount is an answer to a gift we have already received.[20] God's grace always precedes our ethical life. God is not a reward at the end of the struggle, but he is there at the outset. Before Jesus talks to us and gives us his moral program, he talks about God, the Father. In the Sermon on the Mount divine filiation is presented as the foundation of Christian ethical life. By following Jesus' teaching, we show that God's grace has become effective in us and that we are children of our heavenly father.

2. From the Lutheran tradition we can take the idea that we must never feel perfect and justified before God's infinite love and the never-ending needs of our fellow men. Therefore, the poverty of spirit of the first beatitude is the right attitude with which to start. A spiritually poor person is not self-sufficient but expects all help from God and can thus receive the gift of the Kingdom of God. We thus also become similar to Jesus who, though he was God, "offered prayers and supplications with loud cries and tears to the one who was able to save him from death, and he was heard because of his reverence" (Heb 5:7).

3. The Sermon on the Mount contains a program of spiritual growth in the Holy Spirit. On our own, we are incapable of fulfilling the moral program of the Sermon on the Mount. This program is a vocation to live as children of God and to behave like the Father does, who is love and mercy, and as such, it exceeds any exclusively human-

19. See ibid., 28ff; Dumais, *Il Discorso*, 396–98.

20. Eberhard Schockenhoff, *Die Bergpredigt: Aufruf zum Christsein* [The Sermon on the Mount: A Call to Being a Christian] (Freiburg: Herder, 2014), 108–13.

istic ethics. In his parables of growth, Jesus reveals that the new Law he teaches is a life project. More than being, the Sermon on the Mount expresses a "becoming": our gradual becoming children of God is reflected in a gradual change of our actions. We never fully live our identity as children of God such that we no longer have to grow. The future tense in Matthew 5:48—"you will be perfect"—could express this idea.[21] The Sermon on the Mount is an ethics of grace, but of "costly grace" in the sense of Bonhoeffer—that is, grace that requires a lot of effort, that costs us our lives.[22]

GENERAL STRUCTURE OF THE SERMON ON THE MOUNT

Many things have been and could be said about the Sermon on the Mount in general and about each of its parts. For our purposes here, we are trying to gain an overall view and grasp some of its important implications for daily work in business. Two reflections on the general structure of the Sermon on the Mount give special insights:

1. The first stems from Joachim Jeremias. According to this theologian the Sermon on the Mount seen in its entirety was an early Christian catechesis: it gave the Christian community an outline of what their lifestyle was to look like in contrast to that of their Jewish contemporaries. In this sense Matthew 5:20 seems to be central: "I tell you, unless your righteousness surpasses that of the scribes and Pharisees, you will not enter into the kingdom of heaven." Here Matthew

21. Even though there are various translations that use the imperative "be perfect" in this verse, the Greek original "*esesthe*" expresses the future tense.

22. "Cheap grace is the deadly enemy of our Church.... That is what we mean by cheap grace, the grace which amounts to the justification of sin without the justification of the repentant sinner who departs from sin and from whom sin departs. Cheap grace is not the kind of forgiveness of sin which frees us from the toils of sin. Cheap grace is the grace we bestow on ourselves. Cheap grace is the preaching of forgiveness without requiring repentance, baptism without church discipline, Communion without confession, absolution without personal confession. Cheap grace is grace without discipleship, grace without the cross, grace without Jesus Christ, living and incarnate. Costly grace is ... the call of Jesus Christ at which the disciple leaves his nets and follows him.... It is costly because it costs a man his life, and it is grace because it gives a man the only true life"; Bonhoeffer, *Cost*, 45–47. See also Dumais, *Il Discorso*, 51–52, 398–99.

Our Father who art in heaven; Hallowed be thy name.	Treasure in heaven: Mt 6:19–21 The light of the body: Mt 6:22–23
Thy Kingdom come, thy will be done. Give us this day our daily bread.	God and Mammon: Mt 6:24 Care and anxiety, the Kingdom of God and its justice: Mt 6:25–34
And forgive us our trespasses as we forgive those who trespass against us.	Judging others: Mt 7:1–6
And lead us not into temptation,	No pearls to the dogs: Mt 7:7 (The pearls are the Christians themselves, the dogs the temptation.)
But deliver us from evil.	Ask, seek, knock: Mt 7:7–11

addresses two groups in Jewish society that had distinct characteristics: the scribes were the theologians of the time, the Pharisees the pious lay Jews. The followers of Christ were supposed to surpass their conceptions of justice. The Sermon on the Mount reflects this program in its three parts: Matthew 5:21–48 refers to the theologians, with Jesus explaining the insufficiencies in their conceptions; then follows Matthew 6:1–18, dedicated to the typical expressions of Pharisaical piety (prayer, fasting, alms), where Jesus again shows how his followers should differ; finally, Matthew 6:19–7:27 unfolds the particulars of the greater righteousness demanded of a disciple of Christ.[23]

This interpretation can be integrated with Bornkamm's proposal, which is quoted by many exegetes, some of whom endorse it, while others accept it partially.[24] Bornkamm explains the otherwise unconnected verses Matthew 6:19–7:11 as comments on and unfolding of the Our Father. Personally, I think there is a correspondence between Our Lord's prayer and these verses. The order of the topics would otherwise be just too great a coincidence. The single verses of Matthew 6:19–7:11 and the lines of the Our Father can be correlated as above.[25]

23. See Jeremias, *Die Bergpredigt*, 19–23.

24. Guelich, for example, endorses this interpretation; see Robert A. Guelich, *The Sermon on the Mount: A Foundation for Understanding* (Waco: Word, 1982), 324–25; while Lambrecht and Dumais accept it in part; see Jan Lambrecht, *The Sermon on the Mount: Proclamation and Exhortation* (Wilmington, Del.: Michael Glazier, 1985), 155–64, and Dumais, *Il Discorso*, 107–12.

25. The ordering in the table is mine, though the idea stems from Bornkamm, "Der Aufbau der Bergpredigt." *New Testament Studies* 24, no. 4 (1978): 419–32.

- Introduction: Jesus sits as sign of his teaching authority, and the disciples come
  - Beatitudes
    - Salt and light of the world
      - Antitheses: Decision for a greater justice
        - Piety: Almsgiving
          - Our Father
        - Piety: Fasting
      - Treasure in heaven, God and mammon, care and anxiety: decision for the Kingdom of God and its (greater) justice
    - Judging others, generosity with others
  - The narrow gate, tree known by its fruit, deeds not words, house on solid rock
- End: reaction of the multitudes impressed by Jesus' authority

Whatever one may think of this attribution, it is clear that the ethics of the Sermon on the Mount are inseparable from spirituality and prayer. A life according to the new ethics of Jesus is impossible without prayer as its inner source of strength.

2. The second interpretation likewise arrives at the centrality of prayer, without, however, attributing certain passages to the Our Father.[26] Considering the contents of the Sermon on the Mount, it is possible to structure it in a symmetrical distribution, which could well have been intended by Matthew. It can be visualized as above.[27]

Both interpretations underscore the importance of the Sermon on the Mount for Christian life as unified and integrated existence of all its aspects under the loving glance of our Father God. Relationship to God is not something added onto our lives but is the foundation of all we do. Our good and ordered relationships to others and to material goods are a consequence of our relationship with God. This implies a strong unity of life: everything we do and wish should be imbued with our filial trust in God and fraternal love for our brothers and sisters.

The Sermon on the Mount also teaches that our interior attitude

26. Dumais, *Il Discorso*, 107–12, and Lambrecht, *Sermon*, 155–64.

27. The distribution is my own, though I follow Dumais and Lambrecht.

and outer works go together. First comes the interior attitude of heart, then come the actions that are a necessary manifestation of interior life and goodness. Jesus' words in the Sermon on the Mount are certainly radical, in the sense of *radix*, root: they require a new principle of life and action in our hearts. The radicalism of the Sermon on the Mount invites us to discover the specific answer of love in all the situations in which we happen to find ourselves. The Sermon on the Mount gives the inspiration, the moral urge, the aims, and the values of action. It is our reason, however, that is called to ponder what this means in each specific situation. In the light of the principles of the Sermon on the Mount, human wisdom and science can discover the concrete action that is required of a Christian. In accordance with contemporary Catholic exegesis, we can say that Matthew adapted Jesus' words to the situation of the first Christians in order to transmit Christ's teaching that we must love people—meaning each concrete individual—in heart, word, and deed. He has taught us *that* we must love, not *what* precisely this consists in. Such a statement in no way reduces the authority of holy scripture: the whole of the Sermon on the Mount and all of its parts are inspired and canonical. It is the normative word of the risen and living Christ to the first Christians in their historical social and ecclesial surroundings.[28]

The center of Christian life according to the Sermon on the Mount is to establish a filial relationship with God and a fraternal one with our brothers and sisters. The fullness of love with which God loves us explains the radicalism and the absoluteness with which Jesus formulates the Sermon on the Mount. Christian ethics is an ethics of imitation of both the Father and the Son. Jesus is the living model of how to fulfill the Sermon on the Mount. His words "If you wish to be perfect ... come, follow me" (Mt 19:21) are an interpretation or application of the words "So be perfect, just as your heavenly Father is perfect" (Mt 5:48).

The ethics contained in the Sermon on the Mount is a profound humanism precisely because it goes beyond an immanent, atheist

28. See Dumais, *Il Discorso*, 57.

form of humanism: it develops the innermost potentialities of human nature in the most intense way because it brings the notion of man's creation in God's image to its fullest expression. Image of God and divine filiation are contiguous and overlapping concepts. We are fully human when we live our human lives in a divine way. In the Sermon on the Mount theonomy and autonomy converge: God reveals us to ourselves, thereby illumining our consciences and giving us the criteria of self-determined action.

As regards social ethics, there is a growing consensus among theologians that the Sermon on the Mount ought to influence social life. Jesus addresses the disciples (the church) but also the whole world represented by the multitudes Matthew mentions at the end of the Sermon on the Mount and in the closing lines of his gospel, when Jesus commands the disciples to "teach all nations" (Mt 28:19). Even though the Sermon on the Mount is not a political or social codebook, Jesus clearly wants us to go beyond the law of mere commutative justice that characterizes our commercial society. Without the love as taught in the Sermon on the Mount social life would wither away. The notion of gift thus underlies the Sermon on the Mount. Christians who implement the logic of gift in their behavior in business act as leaven in church and society.[29] We will reflect on the logic of gift later in this chapter.

GREATER RIGHTEOUSNESS

So far we have seen that the Sermon on the Mount connects prayer with ethics, divine filiation with universal fraternity. These aspects are all brought into focus by one central concept: righteousness. "I tell you, unless your righteousness surpasses that of the scribes and Pharisees, you will not enter into the kingdom of heaven" (Mt 5:20). The word "righteousness" (*dikaiosyne*) appears five times in the Sermon on the Mount: twice in the Beatitudes, then in 5:20, 6:1 (against vanity),

29. See ibid., 390–96.

and 6:33 (the righteousness of the Kingdom of God). Righteousness (*dikaiosyne*) is a favorite with Matthew. He stresses the need for Christians to engage actively in response to the salvation God offers us; we cannot be passive receivers.[30]

Let us turn first to the Beatitudes. They are structured in two stanzas with four verses each. In both stanzas the last verse contains the word "righteousness." The first and the eighth Beatitude, both of which promise the Kingdom of Heaven, hold the whole section together. The first stanza encourages those who suffer passively and can do nothing or little about it (poverty, sadness). The second one addresses those who can actively shape and improve society (mercy, peace building). The Beatitudes describe moral dispositions. They are not just factual statements or words of consolation but refer to morally engaged and motivated, virtuous people. The Beatitudes form a catalogue of virtues. A Christian must possess all these qualities at once, not just one of them. They are guidance for Christian life as a whole.[31]

A central element and a structuring principle of the Beatitudes, as we have seen, is righteousness. Righteousness is what a follower of Jesus should aspire to. What kind of righteousness is meant? Is it the same as social or modern justice? Why are God's justice or righteousness and that of his Kingdom "greater and surpassing"? Is there a difference between righteousness and justice? Today we associate justice with human dignity and peace, with protest against discrimination and exploitation. Is the biblical concept the same?

A glance at the Hebrew notion can help us to understand what Jesus had in mind and make it fruitful. As Lapide explains, the Hebrew concept of righteousness, "*sedaqa*," is wider than the Greek or Latin concept of *dikaiosyne* or *justitia*. *Sedaqa* combines God's justice with his grace and mercy. It is a form of justice that, out of mercy and compassion for the poor, actively takes up their cause. As a consequence of our being images of God, believers are expected to imitate God in

30. See Lambrecht, *Sermon*, 164–65.
31. See ibid., 63–64.

this particular blend of justice and mercy. *Sedaqa* unites the religious dimension with the social one: God protects the weak, the poor, the widows and the orphans. We are obliged to help them out of justice, not out of condescending generosity or beneficence. We thus imitate God who generously gives his creation to all. In the Jewish and Christian faith nobody can be just or righteous as an individual alone but only as part of a community, in relationship with God (the vertical dimension) and also with our neighbor (the horizontal dimension).[32] In the Hebrew *sedaqa* there is a dynamism that takes us from overcoming conflict (one *against* the other), to indifference (one *next* to the other), to fruitful cooperation (one *with* the other), finally to loving service (one *for* the other).[33] Lapide calls Jesus' strategy to reach this aim "theopolitics in small steps": It means reducing conflicts, appeasing tensions, renouncing rights, fulfilling the commandment of love. A striking image for this is the "miracle of the cooking pot": every day it fulfills the miracle of putting fire at the service of water, even though both are incompatible, and the bottom of the pot is very thin.[34] This is what the greater righteousness that Jesus requires of us should achieve: bringing antagonist forces into cooperation.

Jesus says that he has not come to call the just, but the sinners, and that he seeks mercy, not sacrifice (Mt 9:11–13; quoting Hos 6:6). This seems to be a contradiction to his demand of a greater justice in the Sermon on the Mount. However, the justice Jesus means includes mercy to those who offend us. The "justice" of the elder brother in the parable of the prodigal son (Lk 15:25–30), who complains about having been apparently treated unjustly by his father in comparison with the lazy runaway, is a wrong form of calculating human justice. The New Testament concept of justice is different from the juridical *suum cuique* (to each his own). It rather corresponds to the Father's answer in the same parable: "All that is mine is yours" (Lk 15:31). The

32. See Lapide, *Il discorso*, 31–33.
33. See ibid., 90.
34. See ibid., 47ff.

greater righteousness of Matthew 5:20 thus requires love and charity because God's justice is synonymous both with law, order, and retribution and with mercy, salvation, meekness, and goodness. God's own perfection is the measure of ours: Matthew 5:20 is mirrored by Matthew 5:48 ("Be perfect just as your heavenly father is perfect"). The greater justice Jesus preaches is the perfection and holiness of God the Father. Therefore, justice means the whole set of virtues that God demands of us. Being just means fulfilling God's will in all fields of life: in our relationship with God and with our fellow human beings. Everything that God asks of us—because it is God's will—is a part of justice. Greater justice involves the whole person in all her dimensions, energies, and activities; it has its center in love and its measure in God's own perfection.[35]

At this point we understand better why in the past the Sermon on the Mount has been considered impossible to fulfill. We feel overwhelmed and dizzied by its lofty aims. However, God's righteousness is his gift: he gives what he demands. We are justified by his grace and live in his justice. God's justifying grace gives us the faith that is active in love.

THE MODERN NOTION OF JUSTICE AND THE CHRISTIAN NOTION OF RIGHTEOUSNESS

Is the modern notion of the struggle for a just world a way of realizing the Christian notion of greater righteousness? As has been stated, the Sermon on the Mount and its notion of justice are not a closed code or law, but contain open concepts. Therefore, what they mean and imply must not be limited to only one manifestation or one certain form of active faith, as is the case of a political party: By necessity political parties opt for certain contingent and determinate possibilities, excluding others that on a theoretical basis can be equally valid. The struggle for a just world or social justice tends to be a political program and can

35. See Lambrecht, *Sermon*, 110–13.

thus easily become identified with a political movement or an ideology, which the Christian faith is not. The universal Christian faith is at the same time more and less—more because it transcends history, less because it requires concretization in order to become historically effective.

This is true also for the shorter version of the Sermon on the Mount in Luke and its woes concerning the rich. The categories of rich and poor in the Bible must not be taken simply in their present meaning. In antiquity, the rich were a small class of wealthy landowners who did not have to work but could dedicate their time to leisure, politics, and military command. All the rest who had to work in order to make a living (that is nearly everybody else) were considered to be poor, either as *ptochoi* (those in misery, beggars) or as *penetes* (working people, they could own a house and slaves). Luke is the gospel of God's mercy toward the poor, the sick, and the sinners. This becomes apparent also in his descriptions of the life of the church in Jerusalem with the ideal of shared common property (see Acts 2:44–45 and 4:32). Luke is skeptical about the rich and must have experienced their hardheartedness (as becomes apparent in the story of the rich man and Lazarus, Luke 16:19–25) and their foolish self-reliance on their material goods (see Luke 12:21: "You fool . . . !") Luke's Blessings and Woes are thus meant to motivate operative charity for the poor, to overcome avarice and greed, and to establish a true and lasting hierarchy of values.[36]

Individual Christians can and should participate in politics but remain aware of the fact that they cannot pretend that their political party has a monopoly on the Christian faith and all of its values. On the other hand, Christian justice and love as expressed in the Sermon on the Mount create institutions and build justice in this world. However, they remain a wild force, a beating heart, and a watchful eye that cannot be locked into structures and systems. The Sermon on the Mount always transcends history, social systems, and legal structures,

36. See ibid., 73–74.

and at the same time pushes development on toward a more just and charitable world. In this sense, the greater righteousness of the Sermon on the Mount also refers to the creation of just structures and systems, not only to individual behavior. The justice Jesus demands of his followers means struggling for a better world—for instance, for an inclusive economy. Christian spirituality is not only an individual matter as Pope Francis has repeatedly reminded us. It includes social discernment and the question of how to act adequately as a Christian concerning structural problems. In a perspective of social discernment, spirituality mediates on a practical level between, on the one hand, the vision and the principles and, on the other hand, an adequate understanding of the context as a result of a careful analysis. Spirituality thus connects the individual and the social-structural perspectives.

However, we should bear in mind that the Bible also calls St. Joseph "just" (Mt 1:19), who leads a hidden, simple life full of honest, inconspicuous work. Nobody therefore needs to feel overwhelmed but should do good to the poor he can reach. Jesus' answer to the question "Who is my neighbor?" can easily be translated as "the one next to you."[37]

Businesspeople have many occasions of acting like St. Joseph. They create opportunities for society, produce needed goods, render services that make life worth living; they organize work and give hope to young generations, they innovate and contribute to progress. In other words, they take care of the material needs and wants of life on this earth. Without these being satisfied, it would be much more difficult to attend to the spiritual and intellectual dimension of our human existence. However, must it not be the case that precisely such businesspeople feel irritated by Jesus' chastising of care for food, drink, and clothing (Mt 6:25)? Only the pagans are concerned for such things, teaches our Lord; a child of God should leave tomorrow for tomorrow, seek the Kingdom of God and its justice, and trust completely in God's providence (Mt 6:31–34). Matthew 6:25–34 certainly is a challenge for

37. See ibid., 116–17.

our mentality (and surely also for the mentality of Jesus' audience in his time). On the one hand, we feel attracted by our Lord's injunction to trust completely in God and not to busy ourselves in order to supply for our bodily needs. On the other hand, we rightly ask: how can it be a sign of trust in God not to work and not to busy oneself? Not caring for one's future is downright dangerous, and nothing we would recommend our children to do! Correctly understood, Matthew warns against the wrong, exaggerated concern of the heathens who do not believe in God's providence. Jesus' words turn against fear and anxiety that separate us from God, not against diligent foresight and caring for one's family. This is something Jesus himself did as a carpenter and worker. The positive moral value and the contrasting lifestyle Jesus recommends in Matthew 6:33 is seeking God's kingdom and its justice. This is what everything that comes before leads up to. Jesus wants us to be active promoters of the Kingdom who seek first and foremost God's justice.[38]

APPLICATIONS TO BUSINESS

After all that has been said about the Sermon on the Mount and especially its central concept of greater justice, what can we glean from it for business life? There have been convincing applications of individual Beatitudes to business, like that of meekness, or applications of the Beatitudes in their entirety.[39] In this essay I would like to reflect on the meaning of the Sermon on the Mount as a whole, of its spirit, and thus of the core of Christian ethics, for the economy.

As has been stated, the Sermon on the Mount is a continuing and never-ending challenge to the individual Christian conscience: each one of us is called to discover what poverty in spirit, meekness, loving

38. See ibid., 166–69.

39. Regarding meekness, see David Molyneaux, "'Blessed Are the Meek, for They Shall Inherit the Earth'—An Aspiration Applicable to Business?" *Journal of Business Ethics* 48, no. 4 (2003): 347–63; on the Beatitudes in their entirety, see Donald Capps, "The Beatitudes and Erikson's Life Cycle Theory," *Pastoral Psychology* 33, no. 4 (1985): 226–44.

our enemies, generosity, etc., mean in our specific circumstances. What does it mean to live out the narrative of a child of God with whose life Jesus himself would be able to identify? Finding the answer is very personal; nobody can lift it off our shoulders or our conscience. However, some general remarks can perhaps help in this personal endeavor.

STRUCTURAL CONSEQUENCES

The Biblical notion of *sedaqa* and of surpassing justice as taught by Jesus in the Sermon on the Mount has resulted in the widespread conviction of the equality of all human beings in dignity and rights and in the option for the poor. In the Sermon on the Mount and in his description of the Last Judgment (Mt 25:31–46) Jesus not only teaches us to positively treat everyone else as we ourselves wish to be treated but he identifies himself with the hungry, thirsty, homeless, and jailed—in other words, with the poor and marginalized. For a Christian the poor are really Christ, therefore God. It is the most radical inversion of the pyramid of human social values. The pyramid of honor is set on its head. This has produced typical forms of "ethical" or "social capitalism" that prohibit cutthroat market warfare, break vicious circles of negative reciprocity or of animosity, ensure fair competition, and care for workers and their rights. Concern about growing inequality has brought attention to the need of including the poor structurally into the market economy, enabling them thus to exercise their dignity by earning their own livelihood. An example for this wish for an inclusive market economy is the words of Pope Francis:

> The need to resolve the structural causes of poverty cannot be delayed, not only for the pragmatic reason of its urgency for the good order of society, but because society needs to be cured of a sickness which is weakening and frustrating it, and which can only lead to new crises. Welfare projects, which meet certain urgent needs, should be considered merely temporary responses.[40]

40. Francis, Apostolic Exhortation *Evangelii gaudium* (November 24, 2013), no. 202.

This ethical and cultural dimension elevates business to a profession with a high ethical standard. It is a vocation to holiness. Again with the words of Pope Francis:

> Business is a vocation, and a noble vocation, provided that those engaged in it see themselves challenged by a greater meaning in life; this will enable them truly to serve the common good by striving to increase the goods of this world and to make them more accessible to all.[41]

The vocation of the businessperson is to serve others with goods that are really good and services that truly serve.

By tracing dignity and equality to Jesus' words I do not imply that they are exclusively Christian values that cannot be found in other religions or cultures or that all Christians are role models in these values (unfortunately, we are not). However, the Sermon on the Mount is a crystalline formulation and a constant challenge to rethink our dealings with others. It certainly is one of the roots of Western culture, and therefore also of our globalized economy, which is a universalized form of the Western economy.

SPECIAL BUSINESS ORGANIZATIONS

The Sermon on the Mount and the Christian spirit also foster forms of economic organization and business initiatives that have been called "nonprofit" or "third-sector" business. They often pursue social objectives, like healthcare and basic needs, and are typically active on a local level or in neighborhoods. Even though these businesses make enough profit to keep going, people who work in them are attracted by the rewarding experience of cultivating human relations and the meaning they find in this work. A growing number of people seek the service and love that are put into practice in social capitalism, social entrepreneurship, impact investment, and the like. It is a sign that the values contained in the Sermon on the Mount resonate in the hearts of people who perhaps have never even read it, yet long for its realization.

41. Ibid., no. 203.

In the past, and therefore of longer tradition, the same spirit gave rise to the formation of cooperatives in which the members share certain means of production on a voluntary basis. This organization works well in agriculture and other simpler activities; however, it becomes increasingly unwieldy as the business grows, becomes international, and needs innovation and unified leadership. For these and other reasons, the special forms of business organization that the Christian spirit of the Sermon on the Mount has inspired will probably remain a program for only a portion of the business world and not its universal form. However, for any form of business organization the spirit of the Sermon on the Mount inculcates the responsibility of Christians to seek ways of inclusion of the poor into the market economy but also to defend the poor—once included—against any form of exploitation, disrespect, or indecency in work. Such abuse can be hidden to the eyes of consumers in developed countries when the poor are victims of subcontractors who pay extremely low wages or unjust salaries or do not guarantee physical, moral, or social safety.

THE CHRISTIAN CHALLENGE

All the more urgent is the question of how to put the Sermon on the Mount into effect in normal commercial dealings. Besides, in developed economies there are real practical problems to which a Christian spirituality can respond, such as: the loss of meaning in work (which is also a structural and cultural problem); burnout; neglecting the distinction in management between rational and reasonable decisions; lessening self-esteem by imposing impossible targets and negative evaluations; depersonalization; increasing surveillance systems; and erosion of trust. One attempt to show a path forward is the challenge posed by Pope Benedict XVI in his encyclical *Caritas in veritate*. Benedict XVI desires to include fraternity, the logic of gift, and gratuitousness into normal business:

> The great challenge before us ... is to demonstrate, in thinking and behavior, not only that traditional principles of social ethics like transparency, honesty and responsibility cannot be ignored or attenuated, but also that in *commercial relationships* the *principle of gratuitousness* and the logic of gift as an expression of fraternity can and must *find their place within normal economic activity.*[42]

These words are a challenge because they seem to be contrary to for-profit business. The logic of gift, for instance, does not seem to make a lot of sense in competitive economic surroundings, and yet it does. "Gift" is not to be confused with "present." The logic of gift does not require businesspeople to hand out their goods and services for free. This would be a "present" and the end of their business. The word "gift" comes from "giving," and it implies giving the commercial relationships we engage in a humane meaning. Market relationships can have many colors: they can be friendly or unfriendly, just or exploitative, respectful and humane or aggressive and inhumane. The logic of gift thus requires us to discover that market relationships are not only about money but are always also relationships between real human beings with dignity. The market is not an anonymous machine made out of inanimate bits and pieces but a living social organism that ought to fulfill a mission of service and sense.

Something very similar is true of gratuitousness. Again, it cannot mean giving things away for free, even though there is and must be a social space for free donations, like blood or organ donations, open-source software, and the like. Gratuitousness requires the awareness that the human person and social life as such are priceless, and that some elements of material life must resist commoditization. Kant already wrote that the human person has dignity but not a price. Not everything is up for sale, not everything can be quantified in a monetary way. Friendship, love, awards, honor cannot be bought, nor must votes or laws. Money has become too important. The Sermon on the Mount clearly warns us of this idolatry of mammon.

42. Benedict XVI, Encyclical Letter *Caritas in veritate* (June 29, 2009), no. 36.

Finally, the concept of fraternity strives to reintroduce the notion of the common good into the economy. Certainly, an entrepreneur who keeps his or her company afloat, pays the employees, and produces quality goods and services already serves the common good. Nevertheless, in the era of financial capitalism, bent on revenue from financial capital and not from industry, it is important to recall that the economy as a whole ought to serve human needs, material and immaterial. This is expressed in the notion of the common good, which does not only consist in the rules of peaceful social cooperation but also in the indivisible good of being together, of belonging to a community, albeit often at a great distance and without knowing one another. The common good is indivisible because it only exists in the singular: either it exists through sharing or it is destroyed. Take marriage as an example: in the case of divorce a couple can split the material common goods in the plural (one takes the house, the other the car and the money), but not the good of being a couple. This has been destroyed. On a bigger scale, something similar is true for society as a whole, the community of communities. It needs a nucleus of freely shared values that go beyond formal rules of nonbelligerent cooperation. Fraternity brings the spirit of community and friendship into business that is expressed in the notion of "greater righteousness." It requires the defense of freedom and individual rights as expressions of human dignity, but also measuring them again and again with the rule of the common good. Acting against the common good is self-destructive of the pursuit of personal happiness. Individual happiness and the common good relate to each other like color and surface: the bigger the surface the more color I can apply, the smaller the surface the less color there will be. Personal happiness, which we pursue in the creation of wealth through business, and the service to the common good to which we aspire in this very activity (and not afterward through redistribution) are not a sum but a product. In a sum one of the elements can be zero without the sum changing. In a product, if one of the factors is zero the result is also zero: who pursues personal happiness in a way that is destructive of the common good, that is against fraternity and the spirit of the Sermon on the Mount, ends up destroying his or her own happiness. And to the contrary, who pursues the common good will also find personal fulfillment: he or she will be blessed, as Jesus teaches in the Sermon on the Mount.

BIBLIOGRAPHY

Allison, Dale C. *The Sermon on the Mount: Inspiring the Moral Imagination*. New York: Crossroad, 1999.

Andrews, Charles F. *Mahatma Gandhi: His Life and Ideas*. Woodstock, Vt.: Skylight Paths, 2003.Originally published in 1930.

Augustine. *Commentary on the Lord's Sermon on the Mount with Seventeen Related Sermons*. Translated by Denis J. Kavanagh, OSA. Washington, D.C.: The Catholic University of America Press, 1951.

Benedict XVI. Encyclical Letter *Caritas in veritate*. June 29, 2009.

Bonhoeffer, Dietrich. *The Cost of Discipleship*. New York: Macmillan, 1979.

Bornkamm, Günther. "Der Aufbau der Bergpredigt." *New Testament Studies* 24, no. 4 (1978): 419–32.

Capps, Donald. "The Beatitudes and Erikson's Life Cycle Theory." *Pastoral Psychology* 33, no. 4 (1985): 226–44.

Davenport, Gene L. *Into the Darkness: Discipleship in the Sermon on the Mount*. Nashville: Abingdon, 1988.

"Didache." In *The Apostolic Fathers*, translated by Francis X. Glimm, Joseph M.-F. Marique, SJ, and Gerald G. Walsh, SJ. Washington, D.C.: The Catholic University of America Press, 1947.

Dumais, Marcel. *Il Discorso della Montagna: Stato della ricerca, Interpretazione, Bibliografia*. [The Sermon on the Mount: The State of Research, Interpretation, Bibliography]. Turin: Elledici, 1999.

Francis. Apostolic Exhortation *Evangelii gaudium*. November 24, 2013.

———. *Peace Message*. January 1, 2017.

Greenman, Jeffrey P., Timothy Larsen, and Stephen R. Spencer, eds. *The Sermon on the Mount through the Centuries: From the Early Church to John Paul II*. Grand Rapids, Mich.: Brazos, 2007.

Guelich, Robert A. *The Sermon on the Mount: A Foundation for Understanding*. Waco: Word Books, 1982.

Holtom, Jeremy. "Gandhi's Interpretation of the Sermon on the Mount." In *The Oxford Handbook of the Reception History of the Bible*, edited by Michael Lieb,

Emma Mason, and Jonathan Roberts, 542–56. Oxford: Oxford University Press, 2013.

Jeremias, Joachim. *Die Bergpredigt* [The Sermon on the Mount]. Stuttgart: Calwer, 1965.

Lambrecht, Jan. *The Sermon on the Mount: Proclamation and Exhortation*. Wilmington, Del.: Michael Glazier, 1985.

Lapide, Pinchas. *Il discorso della montagna: Utopia o programma?* [The Sermon on the Mount: Utopia or Program for Action?]. Brescia: Paideia, 2003. Originally published in 1992.

Lohfink, Gerhard. *Wem gilt die Bergpredigt? Beiträge zu einer christlichen Ethik* [To Whom Does the Sermon on the Mount Apply? Contributions to Christian Ethics]. Freiburg: Herder, 1988.

Luther, Martin. *D. Martin Luthers Werke: Kritische Gesammtausgabe* [D. Martin Luther's Works: Complete Critical Edition]. 120 vols. Weimar: Hermann Böhlaus Nachfolger, 1883–1938.

Molyneaux, David. "'Blessed Are the Meek, for They Shall Inherit the Earth'—An Aspiration Applicable to Business?" *Journal of Business Ethics* 48, no. 4 (2003): 347–63.

Pinckaers, Servais. *The Sources of Christian Ethics*. Washington, D.C.: The Catholic University of America Press, 1995.

Schnackenburg, Rudolf. *Von Jesus zur Urkirche* [From Jesus to the Early Church]. Vol. 1, *Die sittliche Botschaft des Neuen Testaments*. Freiburg: Herder, 1986.

Schockenhoff, Eberhard. *Die Bergpredigt: Aufruf zum Christsein* [The Sermon on the Mount: A Call to Being a Christian]. Freiburg: Herder, 2014.

Tolstoy, Leo. *The Kingdom of God Is within You* [1894]. Doylestown, Pa.: Wildside, 2005.

PART 2

THE LOGIC OF GIFT IN BUSINESS

5

SPIRITUAL ROOTS OF THE "LOGIC OF GIFT" AND "THE PRINCIPLE OF GRATUITOUSNESS" IN ECONOMIC ACTIVITY

DOMÈNEC MELÉ

> The great challenge before us ... is to demonstrate, in thinking and behavior ... that in *commercial relationships* the *principle of gratuitousness* and the logic of gift as an expression of fraternity can and must *find their place within normal economic activity.*
>
> —Benedict XVI, *Caritas in veritate*, 36

Benedict XVI introduced the expressions "logic of gift" and "the principle of gratuitousness" in Catholic social teaching and suggested their application within normal economic activity.[1] This is a challenge since, for more than three hundred years, economic activity has been built upon contracts, the rule of the law, and perhaps also the influence of governmental policies. Even more surprising may be that this proposal is presented "as expression of fraternity." Addressing this challenge requires, first of all, a better understanding of Benedict's proposal and how the "logic of gift" and "the principle of gratuitousness" can find their place within normal economic activity. Some work has been done on these topics, although further research is still necessary, to which I wish to contribute with this chapter.

A few scholars have undertaken the task of interpreting what Ben-

1. Benedict XVI, Encyclical Letter *Caritas in veritate* (June 29, 2009), no. 36.

edict means by the "logic of gift" and "the principle of gratuitousness," as well as the connection between these two concepts. One such is Dennis McCann, who focused on the "principle of gratuitousness" and its connection with "the logic of gift" and compared Benedict's vision of the principle with those found in anthropological studies dealing with the same phenomenon.[2] Another is Guglielmo Faldetta, who argued that the logic of gift entails not only moving beyond contractual logic in one's vision of business relationships, but also providing a new qualification of the relationships established through the gift.[3]

Other scholars have discussed the place of the logic of gift within normal economic activity. Frémeaux and Michelson propose the idea of "existential gift" in the business context—understood as giving for its own sake—and posit that the existential gift provides human actors with greater freedom in their choices and relationships and a new "ethic of generosity," whereby significant progress can be made toward developing more human models and practices in business.[4] Argandoña indirectly deals with the logic of gift by considering gift-love in the organization; he argues that love can and must be lived in firms for them to operate efficiently, be attractive to those who take part in them, and act consistently in the long term.[5] Baviera, English, and Guillén analyze three types of logic in organizations—the logic of exchange, the logic of duty, and the logic of gift—trying to explain how their balanced integration promises to enhance organizational life and outcomes.[6]

2. Dennis McCann, "The Principle of Gratuitousness: Opportunities and Challenges for Business in *Caritas in Veritate*," *Journal of Business Ethics* 100, supp 1 (2011): 55–66.

3. Guglielmo Faldetta, "The Logic of Gift and Gratuitousness in Business Relationships," *Journal of Business Ethics* 100, supp 1 (2011): 67–77.

4. Sandrine Frémeaux and Grant Michelson, "'No Strings Attached': Welcoming the Existential Gift in Business," *Journal of Business Ethics* 99, no. 1 (2011): 63–75.

5. Antonio Argandoña, "The 'Logic of Gift' in the Business Entreprise," in *Human Development in Business: Values and Humanistic Management in the Encyclical "Caritas in Veritate,"* ed. Domènec Melé and Claus Dierksmeier (New York: Palgrave-Macmillan, 2012), 198–216; Argandoña, "Beyond Contracts: Love in Firms," *Journal of Business Ethics* 99, no. 1 (2011): 77–85.

6. Tomás Baviera, William English, and Manuel Guillén, "The 'Logic of Gift' Inspiring Behavior in Organizations beyond the Limits of Duty and Exchange," *Business Ethics Quarterly* 26, no. 2 (2016): 159–80.

In this chapter, we will try to contribute to a better understating of Benedict's "logic of gift" and "principle of gratuitousness." First, we will contrast this "logic of gift" with other meanings of "gift" in economics and sociological thought, stressing that Benedict presents this logic as distinct from but not in opposition to the logics of the market and the state. Then, we will argue that the deep roots of these concepts are in Christian spirituality, and it is precisely this spirituality that provides the deep meaning of these concepts and a spiritual motivation for their application.

MEANINGS OF THE "LOGIC OF GIFT" IN ECONOMICS

The first academic approach to gift in economic activity was probably that of the French sociologist and anthropologist Marcel Mauss in the early twentieth century. In his work *Essai sur le don: Forme et raison de l'échange dans les societies archaïques,* Mauss analyzed archaic societies, finding that gift had a central role not as a matter of gratuitousness but as reciprocal exchange.[7] Gift-giving was performed between groups rather than individuals, and this produced social cohesion. This practice took place in three stages understood as obligations: giving, receiving, and, most importantly, reciprocating. Gift-giving was significant and pervaded all aspects of the societies studied. In contrast, for Benedict, the logic of gift is associated with gratuitousness and not a form of reciprocal exchange.

The current economic system, obviously, is not based on gift but on market exchange, although gifts can also be used as a part of the logic of exchange. This is the case of certain gifts given by companies for promotional purposes. However, in some economic activities, one can acquire goods and services for free, like a gift. This is the so-called gift-economy. Examples of participants in the gift economy include

7. Marcel Mauss, *The Gift: Forms and Functions of Exchange in Archaic Societies* [1925] (London: Cohen and West, 1966).

organ donors, who do not receive any compensation for the donation, and blood donors, who in many countries do not obtain an explicit reward for donations. Free software communities are another example of the gift economy. Programmers put the source code of their programs on the Internet so that anyone can copy it or, more importantly, modify and improve it. Scientific research with findings freely published or shared with the scientific community, along with other forms of information sharing such as Wikipedia, online dictionaries, encyclopedias, and the like, are also expressions of the gift economy. Although these examples do not require exchange, they often bring about admiration and recognition. In addition, this can stimulate others to do the same without expecting economic contribution. Lewis Hyde has theorized on the modern gift economy and how it differs from the market economy.[8] In the modern gift economy the gift is not made through obligation as Mauss suggested, but voluntarily, and probably with a sense of gratitude. According to Hyde, the spirit of the gift economy is that gift must be reciprocated, and it does not matter whether that is to the original giver or to someone else, a "pay it forward." He offers the example of Alcoholics Anonymous, in which some of those who have stopped drinking alcohol with the aid of former addicts try to help others do the same.

Influenced by Hyde is the American semiotician, peace activist, and feminist Genevieve Vaughan, though she is critical of locating gratitude in the gift economy.[9] The starting point for Vaughan is the maternal gift economy in the relationship between mother and child for at least the first four or five years, in which the latter receives based not on exchange but gift. Vaughan criticizes the position of Mauss and his followers, saying, "The insistence upon reciprocity hides the communicative character of simple giving and receiving without reciprocity and does not allow [Mauss's followers] to make a clear distinction

8. Lewis Hyde, *The Gift: Imagination and the Erotic Life of Property* (New York: Vintage, 1981).

9. Genevieve Vaughan, *For-Giving: A Feminist Criticism of Exchange* (Austin, Tex.: Anomaly Press and Plain View Press, 2002).

between giftgiving and exchange as two opposing paradigms."[10] According to Vaughan, gift-giving is not a matter of reciprocity, obligation, or gratitude, but simply the recognition of other people's needs. She affirms, "The logic of gift giving is a maternal economic logic, the logic of the distribution of goods and services directly to needs."[11] In a collective work edited by her, several current indigenous economies based on gift-giving and an active role of women are presented.[12] However, these cases refer to small and closed societies, quite different in many aspects from most societies, and this may lead us to question whether maternal gift logic can work in most societies.

A gift economy can function in small communities with a great degree of trust, such as a family or a small group of close friends, as well as in the indigenous communities in certain social conditions, like those described in Vaughan's volume. However, it is not realistic to propose maternal gift logic as an exclusive economic structure. Any economic system requires sufficient trust among participants, and among strangers this can only be supported by institutions that guarantee and protect trade or commerce.

In modern organizations, the logic of exchange can be related to extrinsic motivation and the logic of gift to intrinsic motivation. The latter is relevant and, in some cases, like blood donation, it has been reported that offering payment to blood donors reduced both the number of donations and the quality of the blood.[13] Similarly, other studies show that introducing financial incentives to agents to contribute to a socially desirable outcome may actually decrease the number of contributions.[14] In other words, with a monetary incentive

10. Ibid., 54.

11. Vaughan, ed., *Women and the Gift Economy: A Radically Different Worldview Is Possible* (Toronto: Innana, 2007), 7.

12. Ibid.

13. Richard Titmuss, *The Gift Relationship* (London: Allen and Unwin, 1970). See also Bruno S. Frey, *Not Just for the Money* (Cheltenham: E. Elgar, 1997); Edward L. Deci, Richard Koestner, and Richard M. Ryan, "Meta-Analytical Review of Experiments Examining the Effects of Extrinsic Rewards on Intrinsic Motivation," *Psychological Bulletin* 125, no. 6 (1999): 627–68.

14. Kristen Underhill, "When Extrinsic Incentives Displace Intrinsic Motivation: Designing Legal Carrots and Sticks to Confront the Challenge of Motivational Crowding-Out," *Yale Journal*

the intrinsically motivated person finds the opportunities for conduct consistent with his or her value system reduced. Economic incentives thus not only diminish self-determination and the range of possibilities for personal self-expression, but undermine the very basis of what Adam Smith called "self-esteem."[15]

THE LOGIC OF GIFT ADDED TO THE "LOGIC OF THE MARKET" AND THE "LOGIC OF THE STATE"

The logic of gift of which Benedict writes is not based on reciprocal exchange, nor is it a matter of gratitude—although these could be other relevant motives for gift-giving in some cases, as noted. In fact, Benedict XVI distinguishes between the "logic of exchange" and the "logic of gift."[16] The former is associated with the market, while the latter is related to the freely given gifts of people within society, not a mere exchange, although the action can motivate certain reciprocity. Both logics are different from that of the state, which is a "logic of duty."[17]

Benedict XVI associates the "logic of gift" not to gratitude but to gratuitousness. *Gratuitous*—the adjective that gives us gratuitousness—derives from the Latin *gratuitus,* "done without pay, spontaneous, voluntary," from *gratus*, "pleasing, agreeable," or from *gratia*, "favor." Etymologically it means "freely bestowed."[18] As McCann points out, in Benedict's analysis, the principle of gratuitousness is embodied in the logic of gift.[19]

on Regulation 33, no. 1 (2016): 213–79; Maarten C. W. Janssen and Ewa Mendys-Kamphorst, "The Price of a Price: On the Crowding out and in of Social Norms," *Journal of Economic Behavior and Organization* 55, no. 3 (2004): 377–95.

15. See Stefano Zamagni, "Reciprocity, Civil Economy, Common Good," in *Pursuing the Common Good*, ed. Margaret S. Archer and Pierpaolo Donati (Vatican City: Pontifical Academy of Social Sciences, 2008), 467–502.

16. See ibid.

17. See ibid.

18. *Online Etymology Dictionary*, s.v. "gratuitous," http://www.etymonline.com/index.php?term=gratuitous&allowed_in_frame=0, accessed on April 14, 2017.

19. McCann, "Principle."

The Holy Father points out the insufficiency of the "logic of the market" and the "logic of the State," even acting together, to maintain solidarity—and therefore social cohesion—between citizens:

> When both the logic of the market and the logic of the State come to an agreement that each will continue to exercise a monopoly over its respective area of influence, in the long term much is lost: solidarity in relations between citizens, participation and adherence, actions of gratuitousness, all of which stand in contrast with *giving in order to acquire* (the logic of exchange) and *giving through duty* (the logic of public obligation, imposed by State law).[20]

We may remember that conventional logics of business and the whole of economic activity are based, on one hand, on commutative contracts whereby something is given so that something may be received in return and, on the other hand, on the role of the state.

The market is based on a logic of exchange or reciprocity, following the classic Latin aphorism *do ut des* (I give that you may give), which expresses the logic of exchange. This logic is explicit in one of the most famous quotes by Adam Smith in the *Wealth of Nations*, in which he also excludes benevolence and adds the motivation of self-love. He wrote, "It is not from the benevolence of the butcher, the brewer, or the baker that we expect our dinner, but from their regard to their own interest. We address ourselves not to their humanity but to their self-love."[21] This Smithian remark has been understood in modern economics as a tribute to self-interest, which is considered the sole motivation for conducting business.

Furthermore, the business firm is often seen as a mere set of contracts and its external relations exclusively as economic transactions based on commutative contracts. Exchange is therefore central, whether it be the exchange of products and services or exchange of work for a certain remuneration or other rewards. This is particularly true in the case of the current neoclassic economic-based manage-

20. Benedict XVI, *Caritas in veritate*, no. 39.

21. Adam Smith, *An Inquiry into the Nature and Causes of the Wealth of Nations* [1776] (London: Dent, 1910), 1:13.

ment theories like Agency Theory and Transactional Cost Theory, which understand the firm as a set of contracts for which the ultimate cause is self-interest.[22]

In recent decades many authors have considered the existence of "psychological contracts" in addition to formal contracts between an employer and an employee.[23] These are unwritten mutual expectations for each side. They include how the employee is treated by the employer and what the employee puts into the job. Using practical terms, the psychological contract can be explained as follows: "Now employees are expected to give more in terms of time, effort, skills, and flexibility, whereas they receive less in terms of career opportunities, lifetime employment, job security, and so on. Violation of the psychological contract is likely to produce burnout because it erodes the notion of reciprocity, which is crucial in maintaining well-being."[24]

Another widely used theory in business and other social relations is Social Exchange, which assumes that social change and stability occur through a process of negotiated exchanges between parties.[25] Social relations should be the result of a subjective cost-benefit analysis and the comparison of alternatives. In a certain sense, the psychological contract is a particular case of social exchange.

The existence of interdependence and exchanges through self-interest are fundamental in social exchange theory as well as in the assumption of a psychological contract.[26] The anthropological assumption of the self-interest of both parties is also inherent to business contracts.

22. Sumantra Ghoshal, "Bad Management Theories Are Destroying Good Management Practices," *Academy of Management Learning and Education* 4, no. 1 (2005): 75–91.

23. This concept was first introduced by Chris Argyris, *Understanding Organizational Behavior* (Homewood, Ill.: Dorsey, 1960), and then developed by Denise M. Rousseau, "Psychological and Implied Contracts in Organizations," *Employee Responsibilities and Rights Journal* 2, no. 2 (1989): 121–39.

24. Christina Maslach, Wilmar B. Schaufeli, and Michael P. Leiter, "Job Burnout," *Annual Review of Psychology* 52, no. 1 (2001): 409.

25. Anthony Heath, *Rational Choice and Social Exchange: A Critique of Exchange Theory* (Cambridge: Cambridge University Press, 1976).

26. See Edward J. Lawler and Shane R. Thye, "Bringing Emotions into Social Exchange Theory," *Annual Review of Sociology* 25 (1999): 217–44.

The logic of exchange entails both normative and descriptive senses. Commutative justice, which entails equitable exchange of goods as a moral duty, provides the normative sense to the logic of exchange. Another nonmoral normative approach is that contracts motivated by self-interest and the maximization of shareholder value are best for wealth creation.[27] The descriptive sense comes from the empirical verification of reciprocity in the business relationship.

The state has traditionally been seen as the counterweight of the market through laws, regulations, and governmental actions, including social policies. The contracts themselves are regulated by law, and the courts guarantee compliance with them. In addition, the state can try to assist those least favored by the market or fully excluded without income. Thus, two mechanisms, one based on the "logic of exchange" and the other on the "logic of the state," assure the effectiveness of the socioeconomic system, possibly complemented by individual charity or occasionally by actions of corporate philanthropy. Underlying these two "logics" there can often be an extreme individualism and an atomistic view of society, which is seen as a "social contract" among people endowed with interests. There is no space for the logic of gift, except for individual donations that are often tinted by self-interest—for the giver's reputation, self-satisfaction, and certain rewards.

In this bipolar scheme individual persons and civil society have only a minor role and, in some cases, no role at all. As citizens, people can vote for political representatives in elections, and as buyers, they have "monetary votes" to buy one product as opposed to another. Today, however, such bipolarity must be questioned. Civil society, which includes a variety of associations, mass media, social networks, nongovernmental organizations, religious groups, and so on, is a genuine third pole, and one that is often very powerful.

The market-state scheme is not only unrealistic, but also ethically questionable. It is a well-known fact that the market is effective in

27. Michael C. Jensen, "Value Maximization, Stakeholder Theory, and the Corporate Objective Function," *European Financial Management* 7, no. 2 (2001): 297–317.

assignment of resources, but it is not necessarily equitable in terms of wealth distribution. The state can contribute to a redistribution of wealth. In addition, it can promote welfare actions and certain minimum standards for living together, but market and state alone are insufficient for promoting a good society, which is much more than wealth, welfare, and standards to dissuade from the commission of offenses.

A good society requires economic, social, and cultural elements for human development in an integral sense. Even state action effective in developing policies of social justice requires a culture of solidarity. Actions of gratuitousness foster solidarity and social cohesion within society and therefore have a role that is both different from and complementary to those of the market and the state.

Another important problem with both the logic of the market and the logic of the state is their underlying anthropological reductionism. The human being is exclusively seen as a self-interested individual, which is to ignore the fact that the person also has the capacity of gift-giving with gratuitousness. Zamagni pointed out that Benedict offers us a view of the human being alternative to the *homo economicus* and the conceptions of self-interest on which it is based, including marginal utility theory, and in doing so the pope suggests a new way for explaining economic behavior.[28] Drawing from Zamagni, McCann adds that recovering the economic significance of the logic of gift allows us to dissolve another binary model, "namely, the modernist dichotomy of self-interest and altruism, in favor of an anthropology that is both social and pluralistic in its interpretation of human motivation and choice."[29]

Benedict XVI summarizes the importance of overcoming the binary model of market-plus-state by saying:

28. Zamagni, "Caritas in Veritate," observations presented at the conference "Civilizing the Economy: A New Way of Understanding Business Enterprise?," Faith and Work Initiative of Princeton University, Princeton, N.J., April 8–9, 2010; referenced in McCann, "Principle," 58.

29. Zamagni, "Reciprocity," 58.

> The exclusively binary model of market-plus-State is corrosive of society, while economic forms based on solidarity, which find their natural home in civil society without being restricted to it, build up society. The market of gratuitousness does not exist, and attitudes of gratuitousness cannot be established by law. Yet both the market and politics need individuals who are open to reciprocal gift.[30]

Benedict does not propose an economy based exclusively on the "logic of gift" but challenges us to develop new forms of economic activity in which the logic of gift and the principle of gratuitousness are fully present.

> Economic life undoubtedly requires contracts, in order to regulate relations of exchange between goods of equivalent value. But it also needs just laws and forms of redistribution governed by politics, and what is more, it needs works redolent of the spirit of gift. The economy in the global era seems to privilege the former logic, that of contractual exchange, but directly or indirectly it also demonstrates its need for the other two: political logic, and the logic of the unconditional gift.[31]

As a practical orientation, Benedict suggests hybrid forms of enterprises—in fact, they already exist in many countries—that, without rejecting profit, aim at a higher goal than the mere logic of the exchange of equivalents, with profit as an end in itself. However, if my interpretation is correct, the principle of gratuitousness and the logic of gift go beyond these types of organizations. Otherwise, he would not say that "in *commercial relationships* the *principle of gratuitousness* and the logic of gift as an expression of fraternity can and must *find their place within normal economic activity*."[32]

What is clear is that Benedict does not assume a naïve model of *homo donor*—purely a gift giver—instead of the *homo economicus*—purely self-interested—but of a certain "*homo integralis*" who acts at once with a sense of reciprocity and gratuitousness in ordinary economic activity, without understanding this gratuitousness as being

30. Benedict XVI, *Caritas in veritate*, no. 39.
31. Ibid., no. 37.
32. Ibid., no. 36.

exclusively for altruistic actions that go beyond or are the aim of ordinary economic activity.

Therefore, the "logic of gift" embodied in the principle of gratuitousness does not exclude logic of exchange—the logic of the market—based on commutative justice, nor the logic of the state that responds to criteria of distributive justice. In fact, in *Caritas in veritate*, Benedict XVI explicitly affirms that "the logic of gift does not exclude justice, nor does it merely sit alongside it as a second element added from without";[33] but adds, "Economic, social and political development, if it is to be authentically human, needs to make room for the *principle of gratuitousness* as an expression of fraternity."[34]

Because the logic of exchange is necessary, the corresponding ethical elements such as transparency, honesty, and responsibility are also required. These values "cannot be ignored or attenuated," but they are not enough; the principle of gratuitousness and the logic of gift in business activity are also necessary.[35]

The action of the state and welfare structures are also essential, but "in order to defeat underdevelopment, action is required not only on improving exchange-based transactions and implanting public welfare structures, but above all on gradually *increasing openness, in a world context, to forms of economic activity marked by quotas of gratuitousness and communion.*"[36]

Within business organizations and in the market, there can be a place for these quotas of gratuitousness and communion.[37] This can be by the recognition of the dignity of each person and an attitude of benevolence instead of a view of the other as a mere instrument for gain and by imbuing business with a sense of true human relation and not seeing it as a mere economic transaction.

33. Ibid., no. 34.

34. Ibid.

35. See ibid., no. 36.

36. Ibid., no. 39.

37. See Argandoña, "Beyond Contracts"; Frémeaux and Michelson, "No Strings"; and Baviera, English, and Guillén, "The 'Logic of Gift.'"

ROOTED IN CHRISTIAN SPIRITUALITY

Spirituality is a part of human life. Benedict notes that "the supremacy of technology tends to prevent people from recognizing anything that cannot be explained in terms of matter alone. Yet everyone experiences the many immaterial and spiritual dimensions of life.... In all knowledge and in every act of love the human soul experiences something 'over and above' that seems very much like a gift that we receive or a height to which we are raised. The development of individuals and peoples is likewise located on a height, if we consider *the spiritual dimension* that must be present if such development is to be authentic."[38]

Religious and nonreligious spirituality is connected to ethics and can provide normative elements for economic activity.[39] In addition, spirituality is a source of motivation, which is particularly important in regard to gratuitousness since—as noted—attitudes of gratuitousness cannot be established by law.[40]

This is the case of the principle of gratuitousness and the logic of gift proposed by Benedict XVI, which, as we will try to show, are rooted in Christian spirituality. This can be deduced from several passages of *Caritas in veritate*.

First, as has been mentioned, the principle of gratuitousness and the logic of gift are presented "as an expression of fraternity."[41] Christian spirituality fully supports dealing with people with a sense of fraternity and the *recognition that the human race is a single family*. This is founded on the understanding of God as the common Father of all of humanity—there is no fraternity without a common father, and God is the Father of all. As the Bible says, God "from one man has created the whole human race and made them live all over the face of the earth."[42] To this regard, the church reminds us that "God, Who has

38. Benedict XVI, *Caritas in veritate*, 77.

39. William C. Spohn, "Spirituality and Ethics: Exploring the Connections," *Theological Studies* 58, no. 1 (1997): 109–23.

40. Benedict XVI, *Caritas in veritate*, no. 39.

41. Ibid., nos. 34, 36.

42. Acts 17:26.

fatherly concern for everyone, has willed that all men should constitute one family and treat one another in a spirit of brotherhood."[43] The recognition of God as common Father entails openness to God, and "openness to God makes us open towards our brothers and sisters and towards an understanding of life as a joyful task to be accomplished in a spirit of solidarity."[44]

A second connection with Christian spirituality is that treating one another in a spirit of brotherhood requires *agape* (*caritas* in Latin)—that is, love in the sense of gift-giving, and *agápe* is a central value in Christian spirituality, as is *logos* or "truth." Love the Lord and love your neighbor as yourself summarizes the whole moral law and the prophets of the Old Testament.[45] Jesus adds as a new commandment, "Love one another. As I have loved you, so you also should love one another."[46] Love of God cannot be separated from love of neighbor: "Whatever other commandment there may be, [is] summed up in this saying, namely, 'You shall love your neighbor as yourself.... Hence, love is the fulfillment of the law."[47] Love (charity) is so central in Christian spirituality that love is the distinguishing mark of Christ's disciples and fraternity is a genuine fruit of Christian love (*agápe*).[48] *Logos*—"truth"—is also significant in Christian spirituality, the truth known both by reason and by faith.[49] Agápe adds the idea of *communion* to fraternity, a spiritual concept mentioned in *Caritas in veritate*—often in connection with fraternity or the unity of the human family.[50]

43. Vatican Council II, Pastoral Constitution *Gaudium et spes* (December 7, 1965), no. 22.

44. Benedict XVI, *Caritas in veritate*, no. 77.

45. Mt 22:37–40.

46. Jn 13:34.

47. Rom 13:9–10; see Gal 5:14; 1 Jn 4:20.

48. See Jn 13:35 and Domènec Melé, "The Christian Notion of Αγάπη (Agápē): Towards a More Complete View of Business Ethics," in *Leadership through the Classics: Learning Management and Leadership from Ancient East and West Philosophy*, ed. Gregory P. Prastacos, Fuming Wang, and Klas Eric Soderquist (Heidelberg: Springer, 2012), 79–91.

49. Jesus, who presents himself as the truth (Jn 14:6) and was sent to testify to the truth (Jn 18:37), affirms, "If you remain in my word, you will truly be my disciples, and you will know the truth, and the truth will set you free" (Jn 8:31–32).

50. Benedict XVI, *Caritas in veritate*, nos. 34, 42, 51, 53, 73.

According to Benedict XVI, love and truth go together: "*Only in truth does charity shine forth*, only in truth can charity be authentically lived. Truth is the light that gives meaning and value to charity."[51] That light—the light of reason and the light of faith—grasps the meaning of charity "*as gift, acceptance, and communion.*"[52]

A third aspect of Christian spirituality related to the logic of gift is the recognition that God has given us the gift of his love, and this calls us to give our gift to others. In this sense, Benedict affirms, "Love is God's greatest gift to humanity"[53] and the "primordial truth of God's love, grace bestowed upon us, that opens our lives to gift."[54] He adds:

> Charity in truth feeds on hope and, at the same time, manifests it. As the absolutely gratuitous gift of God, hope bursts into our lives as something not due to us, something that transcends every law of justice. Gift by its nature goes beyond merit, its rule is that of superabundance. It takes first place in our souls as a sign of God's presence in us, *a sign of what he expects from us.*[55]

In Benedict's words, "*Charity in truth* places man before the astonishing experience of gift. Gratuitousness is present in our lives in many different forms, which often go unrecognized because of a purely consumerist and utilitarian view of life. The human being is made for gift, which expresses and makes present his transcendent dimension."[56]

A fourth connection between the logic of gift and Christian spirituality comes from the recognition of God as the ultimate source of love, and God himself infuses his love into our hearts. Thus, according to the Bible, "The love of God has been poured out into our hearts through the holy Spirit that has been given to us."[57] Benedict XVI adds, "Truth, and the love which it reveals, cannot be produced: they can only be received as a gift. Their ultimate source is not, and can-

51. Ibid., no. 3.
52. Ibid., emphasis added.
53. Ibid., no. 2.
54. Ibid., no. 8.
55. Ibid., no. 34.
56. Ibid., no. 34.
57. Rom 5:5.

not be, mankind, but only God, who is himself Truth and Love."[58] In other words, the presence of the Spirit of God in the faithful pushes them to act with love and therefore with gratuitousness and with a logic of gift. This reinforces the sense of fraternity and the practice of love—*agápe*. "The unity of the human race, a fraternal communion transcending every barrier, is called into being by the word of God-who-is-Love."

FRATERNITY IN ECONOMIC ACTIVITY

Benedict XVI insists that the establishment of authentic fraternity is an urgent necessity in economic activities.[59] Globalization and human development particularly require fraternity. Benedict affirms that "as society becomes ever more globalized, it makes us neighbours but does not make us brothers,"[60] and he recalls Paul VI's view that underdevelopment has an important cause in "the lack of brotherhood among individuals and peoples."[61]

He also reminds us that "today humanity appears much more interactive than in the past: this shared sense of being close to one another must be transformed into true communion. *The development of peoples depends, above all, on a recognition that the human race is a single family* working together in true communion, not simply a group of subjects who happen to live side by side."[62]

Fraternity, although it is used in a secular sense, falls short of its profound meaning if it does not accept a superior being as the common father. Benedict notes the difference between recognizing a certain equality among all human beings and fraternity: "Reason, by itself, is capable of grasping the equality between men and of giving stability to their civic coexistence, but it cannot establish fraternity.

58. Benedict XVI, *Caritas in veritate*, no. 52.

59. See ibid., no. 20.

60. Ibid., no. 19.

61. Paul VI, Encyclical Letter *Populorum progressio* (March 26, 1967), no. 66.

62. Benedict XVI, *Caritas in veritate*, no. 53.

This originates in a transcendent vocation from God the Father, who loved us first, teaching us through the Son what fraternal charity is."[63]

However, fraternity entails a rationale—equality as members of the same species—that can be adopted by those who do not share the Christian faith. In addition, many can assume "the Christian ideal of a single family of peoples in solidarity and fraternity"[64] and join with the Catholic Church in working to bring about "the advancement of humanity and of universal fraternity."[65]

This rationale provides a wider vision than that of a contractual view based on individual interests. Contracts are essential in business relations and are effectively the skeleton of economic activity. The church itself recognizes that a significant part of economic and social life depends on the honoring of contracts between physical or moral persons and encourages the strict observation of contracts, as long as the commitments made in them are morally just and they are made and executed in good faith.[66]

It is not necessary to be a Christian to see honoring contracts as necessary for a proper development of commerce and organizational life, long-term wealth creation, and for the advancement of a humanistic culture. All of these require concern for the other and a culture of trust and solidarity.

A common observation is that organizations are much more than a set of contracts, since people are linked by a variety of relationships and motives.[67] Commerce is not a mere set of contracts. Previous to any commercial exchange there is a human meeting and the development of trust. In addition, business dynamism requires loyal clients and committed employees, which are not possible without trust. Trust

63. Ibid., no. 19.

64. Ibid., no. 13.

65. Ibid., no. 11.

66. See *Catechism of the Catholic Church* (Vatican City: Libreria Editrice Vaticana, 1993), no. 2410.

67. Robert C. Solomon, *Ethics and Excellence: Cooperation and Integrity in Business* (New York: Oxford University Press, 1992), 145–52; Domènec Melé, "The Firm as a 'Community of Persons': A Pillar of Humanistic Business Ethos," *Journal of Business Ethics* 106, no. 1 (2012): 89–101.

brings about confidence, predictability, and willingness to cooperate,[68] which are all crucial for business.

Trust entails—in addition to the recognition of his or her technical competences—the trustee's adherence to a set of principles that the trustor finds acceptable and the belief that the trustee wants to do good to the trustor, not simply act through egocentric motives of profit.[69]

It seems that the mere logic of exchange and reciprocity is necessary but not sufficient. This is even clearer when considering the organization of production and the problem of distribution of goods.[70] An objection here might be that the logic of exchange is sufficient to describe business activity. No doubt many behaviors in the business context can be explained by formal contracts alone, but the proof that they are insufficient is the necessity of extending the idea of contract to "psychological contracts," which include anthropological aspects related to gift-giving such as respect, compassion, trust, empathy, fairness, and objectivity. According to Chapman, "Qualities like these characterize the Psychological Contract, just as they characterize a civilized outlook to life as a whole."[71] It is hard to accept that all these elements are only a matter of exchange. However, proponents of "psychological contracts" are reluctant to accept gratuitousness and instead adopt the perspective of Social Exchange Theory. In this sense, they assume that the human being has only self-interest and acts exclusively through the motivation of reciprocity by applying the "logic of exchange," whereas the human being in fact also has the capacity for giving without expecting anything in return—something generally excluded in the perspectives of ordinary economic activity.

Benedict XVI's teaching on the "logic of gift" in the principle of

68. F. David Schoorman, Roger C. Mayer, and James H. Davis, "An Integrative Model of Organizational Trust," *Academy of Management Review* 20, no. 3 (1995): 709–34.

69. These elements have received support from empirical research; see ibid., 344–54.

70. Amartya Sen, "Does Business Ethics Make Economic Sense?" *Business Ethics Quarterly* 3 (1993): 45–54.

71. Alan Chapman, "The Psychological Contract," *businessballs.com*, http://www.businessballs.com/psychological-contracts-theory.htm, accessed April 12, 2017.

gratuitousness in economic activity is aligned with Catholic tradition and more specifically with Catholic Social Teaching (CST). Although CST has emphasized duties of justice, it has never denied the centrality of charity (love) in the Christian approach to socioeconomic issues (justice is the first requirement or minimum measure of charity, but charity goes beyond justice).[72] Charity is a virtue and a principle for interpersonal relationships as well as for macro-relationships (social, economic, and political), as Benedict XVI points out.[73] This is an idea often repeated in CST. Leo XII referred to bonds based not only on friendship, but also "those of brotherly love";[74] Pius XI talked explicitly of "social charity,"[75] and Paul VI encouraged promoting what he called "the civilization of love."[76] The Second Vatican Council reminds us that Jesus taught that "the new command of love was the basic law of human perfection and hence of the world's transformation"[77] and mentions both "obligations of justice and love" in the contribution of a good society beyond an "individualistic ethics."[78] The *Catechism of the Catholic Church* recalls that "charity is the greatest social commandment,"[79] and the *Compendium of the Social Doctrine of the Church* concluded by advocating "a civilization of love"[80] and stating that "*love must be present in and permeate every social relationship.*"[81]

The novelty introduced by Benedict XVI is in expressing "social charity" and its inherent fraternity as a guiding principle—gratuitousness—for economic activity and presenting this as a consequence of the logic of gift, which must find its place within normal economic activity.

72. See Benedict XVI, *Caritas in veritate*, no. 6.
73. Ibid., no. 2.
74. Leo XIII, Encyclical Letter *Rerum novarum* (May 15, 1891), no. 25.
75. Pius XI, Encyclical Letter *Quadragesimo anno* (May 15, 1931), nos. 88, 126.
76. Paul VI, *Message for the World Day of Peace*, January 1, 1977.
77. Vatican Council II, *Gaudium et spes*, no. 38.
78. Ibid., no. 30.
79. *Catechism of the Catholic Church*, no. 1889.
80. Pontifical Council for Justice and Peace, *Compendium of the Social Doctrine of the Church* (Vatican City: Libreria Editrice Vaticana, 2004), nos. 575–83.
81. Ibid., no. 251.

CONCLUSION

In Pope Benedict XVI's teaching, the logic of gift and the principle of gratuitousness, which embodies the former, have deep roots in Christian spirituality. They are an expression of fraternity and ultimately of love in truth. Benedict holds that "charity can be recognized as an authentic expression of humanity and as an element of fundamental importance in human relations, including those of a public nature."[82] The same can be said of logic of gift and the principle of gratuitousness, since they are anchored in charity. In addition, "charity in truth is a force that builds community, it brings all people together without imposing barriers or limits," and the human community has to become "a fully fraternal community."[83]

Christian humanism, inasmuch as this "enkindles charity and takes its lead from truth, accepting both as a lasting gift from God,"[84] should include the logic of gift and the principle of gratuitousness as crucial elements. These provide a humanistic approach and foster a sense of community.

BIBLIOGRAPHY

Argandoña, Antonio. "Beyond Contracts: Love in Firms." *Journal of Business Ethics* 99, no. 1 (2011): 77–85.

———. "The 'Logic of Gift' in the Business Enterprise." In *Human Development in Business: Values and Humanistic Management in the Encyclical "Caritas in Veritate,"* ed. Domènec Melé and Claus Dierksmeier, 198–216. New York: Palgrave-Macmillan, 2012.

Argyris, Chris. *Understanding Organizational Behavior*. Homewood, Ill.: Dorsey, 1960.

Baviera, Tomás, William English, and Manuel Guillén. "The 'Logic of Gift': Inspiring Behavior in Organizations Beyond the Limits of Duty and Exchange." *Business Ethics Quarterly* 26, no. 2 (2016): 159–80.

82. Benedict XVI, *Caritas in veritate*, no. 3.
83. Ibid., no. 34.
84. Ibid., no. 77.

Benedict XVI. Encyclical Letter *Caritas in veritate*. June 29, 2009.

Frey, Bruno S. *Not Just for the Money*. Cheltemham: E. Elgar, 1997.

Catechism of the Catholic Church. Vatican City: Libreria Editrice Vaticana, 1993.

Chapman, Alan. "The Psychological Contract." *Businessballs.com*. http://www.businessballs.com/psychological-contracts-theory.htm. Accessed April 12, 2017.

Deci, Edward L., Richard Koestner, and Richard M. Ryan. "Meta-Analytical Review of Experiments Examining the Effects of Extrinsic Rewards on Intrinsic Motivation." *Psychological Bulletin* 125, no. 6 (1999): 627–68.

Faldetta, Guglielmo. "The Logic of Gift and Gratuitousness in Business Relationships." *Journal of Business Ethics* 100, supplement 1 (2011): 67–77.

Frémeaux, Sandrine, and Grant Michelson. "'No Strings Attached': Welcoming the Existential Gift in Business." *Journal of Business Ethics* 99, no. 1 (2011): 63–75.

Ghoshal, Sumantra. "Bad Management Theories Are Destroying Good Management Practices." *Academy of Management Learning and Education* 4, no. 1 (2005): 75–91.

Heath, Anthony. *Rational Choice and Social Exchange: A Critique of Exchange Theory*. Cambridge: Cambridge University Press, 1976.

Hyde, Lewis. *The Gift: Imagination and the Erotic Life of Property*. New York: Vintage, 1981.

Janssen, Maarten C. W, and Ewa Mendys-Kamphorst. "The Price of a Price: On the Crowding out and in of Social Norms." *Journal of Economic Behavior and Organization* 55, no. 3 (2004): 377–95.

Jensen, Michael C. "Value Maximization, Stakeholder Theory, and the Corporate Objective Function," *European Financial Management* 7, no. 2 (2001): 297–317.

Lawler, Edward J., and Shane R. Thye. "Bringing Emotions into Social Exchange Theory." *Annual Review of Sociology* 25 (1999): 217–44.

Leo XIII. Encyclical Letter *Rerum novarum*. May 15, 1891.

Maslach, Christina, Wilmar B. Schaufeli, and Michael P. Leiter. "Job Burnout." *Annual Review of Psychology* 52, no. 1 (2001): 397–422.

Mauss, Marcel. *The Gift: Forms and Functions of Exchange in Archaic Societies* [1925]. London: Cohen and West, 1966.

Mayer, Roger C., James H. Davis, and F. David Schoorman. "An Integrative Model of Organizational Trust." *Academy of Management Review* 20, no. 3 (1995): 709–34.

McCann, Dennis. "The Principle of Gratuitousness: Opportunities and Challenges for Business in *Caritas in Veritate*," *Journal of Business Ethics* 100, supplement 1 (2011): 55–66.

Melé, Domènec. "The Christian Notion of Αγάπη (Agápē): Towards a More Complete View of Business Ethics." In *Leadership through the Classics: Learning Management and Leadership from Ancient East and West Philosophy*, edited by

Gregory P. Prastacos, Fuming Wang, and Klas Eric Soderquist, 79–91. Heidelberg: Springer, 2012.

———. "The Firm as a 'Community of Persons': A Pillar of Humanistic Business Ethos." *Journal of Business Ethics* 106, no. 1 (2012): 89–101.

Online Etymology Dictionary. "Gratuitous." http://www.etymonline.com/index.php?term=gratuitous&allowed_in_frame=0. Accessed on April 14, 2017.

Paul VI. Encyclical Letter *Populorum progressio*. March 26, 1967.

———. *Message for the World Day of Peace*. January 1, 1977.

Pius XI. Encyclical Letter *Quadragesimo anno*. May 15, 1931.

Pontifical Council for Justice and Peace. *Compendium of the Social Doctrine of the Church*. Vatican City: Libreria Editrice Vaticana, 2004.

Solomon, Robert C. *Ethics and Excellence: Cooperation and Integrity in Business*. New York: Oxford University Press, 1992.

Rousseau, Denise M. "Psychological and Implied Contracts in Organizations." *Employee Responsibilities and Rights Journal* 2, no. 2 (1989): 121–39.

Schoorman, F. David, Roger C. Mayer, and James H. Davis. "An Integrative Model of Organizational Trust: Past, Present, and Future." *Academy of Management Review* 32, no. 2 (2007): 344–54.

Sen, Amartya. "Does Business Ethics Make Economic Sense?" *Business Ethics Quarterly* 3 (1993): 45–54.

Smith, Adam. *An Inquiry into the Nature and Causes of the Wealth of Nations* [1776]. London: Dent, 1910.

Spohn, William C. "Spirituality and Ethics: Exploring the Connections." *Theological Studies* 58, no. 1 (1997): 109–23.

Titmuss, Richard. *The Gift Relationship*. London: Allen and Unwin, 1970.

Underhill, Kristen. "When Extrinsic Incentives Displace Intrinsic Motivation: Designing Legal Carrots and Sticks to Confront the Challenge of Motivational Crowding-Out." *Yale Journal on Regulation* 33, no. 1 (2016): 213–79.

Vatican Council II. Pastoral Constitution *Gaudium et spes*. December 7, 1965.

Vaughan, Genevieve. *For-Giving: A Feminist Criticism of Exchange*. Austin, Tex.: Anomaly Press and Plain View Press, 2002. Originally published in 1997.

———, ed. *Women and the Gift Economy: A Radically Different Worldview Is Possible*. Toronto: Innana, 2007.

Zamagni, Stefano. "Reciprocity, Civil Economy, Common Good." In *Pursuing the Common Good*, edited by Margaret S. Archer and Pierpaolo Donati, 467–502. Vatican City: Pontifical Academy of Social Sciences, 2008.

———. "Caritas in Veritate." Observations presented at the conference "Civilizing the Economy: A New Way of Understanding Business Enterprise?" Faith and Work Initiative of Princeton University. Princeton, N.J., April 8–9, 2010.

6

THE SOCIAL PERSPECTIVE OF CHRISTIAN ETHICS

Challenges for Business Management

CLEMENS SEDMAK

INTEGRITY AND BUSINESS LIFE

What are the specific challenges in business life from the perspective of Christian ethics? Or, to put the question differently: what does it mean to be a Christian *and* a businessperson? In order to gain a realistic view of this issue I would suggest looking at an example, the story of Tom Monaghan, the founder of Domino's Pizza. He was raised a Catholic and was dedicated to being faithful to his religious commitments. James Leonard begins his account of Monaghan's life with the words "Monaghan dreamed big dreams, set impossible goals, and achieved great things, all while trying to live so his soul would go to heaven when he died."[1] Monaghan himself credits his success mainly to his values. In his 1986 autobiography *Pizza Tiger* he is very clear about his moral positions and commitments.

He grounds his life in his faith ("My religious faith is strong. I know I can never be a success on this earth unless I am on good terms with God")[2] and sets his priorities in the light of a religious insight he had as a young man serving in the marines when he traveled from the

1. James Leonard, *Living the Faith: A Life of Tom Monaghan* (Ann Arbor: University of Michigan Press, 2012), xi; see also Joseph L. Badaracco Jr., *Tom Monaghan: In Business for God; Teaching Note*, Harvard Business School Teaching Note 392-140, May 1992.

2. Tom Monaghan, with Robert Anderson, *Pizza Tiger* (New York: Random House, 1986), 8.

Philippines to Japan: "I would never get to the point where I would violate my Catholic upbringing. I couldn't knowingly do things that were wrong. From these kinds of thoughts I developed my priorities."[3] He bases the more secular aspects of his life, as he describes his business activities, on the "Golden Rule."[4] He describes himself as a "hands-on" person whose habits were translated into his working style at the company ("there isn't an executive in Domino's, including me, who will stand by and look on if a crew is working short-handed").[5] He has been conscientious from the beginning of his work life; when he landed a job delivering newspapers, for instance, he "tried to be the hardest worker in the place, the fastest stripper, the fastest bundler."[6] He was willing to humbly face the truth when he had to meet the president of a bank in the middle of his first near-bankruptcy, and it was his honesty that kept the trust of creditors.[7] His business life was based on clear values.

There were a number of success factors in his story worth mentioning—first, the fact that he enjoyed what he was doing and that he cared about his product and its quality. "By the time we opened DomiNick's, I had come to *love* pizza and could eat a ton of it."[8] The manual work of rolling out the dough appealed to him; he was committed to using high-quality ingredients, and he was determined to succeed; he had high hopes, daring dreams, and big plans—he learned from DiVarti that the secret of a good pizza is the pizza sauce. Second, there was his "hunger for expansion and growth" and his desire to identify opportunities. An experience that illustrates this desire as well as this skill is an early expansion undertaken soon after the acquisition of a newsstand: "I discovered that because there were so many college professors in town, there was a great demand for the *New York Times*. This looked like opportunity to me, so in every spare moment, I would put

3. Ibid., 48.
4. Ibid., 9.
5. Ibid., 19.
6. Ibid., 40.
7. Leonard, *Living the Faith*, 71.
8. Monaghan, *Pizza*, 59.

on my one suit and tie and go knocking on doors in finer residential sections of town. I'd ask the homeowners if they would like to have the Sunday *New York Times* delivered, and enough of them did to make up the first home-delivery route the paper had west of the Allegheny Mountains."[9] Clearly Tom Monaghan had the skill—and used it well—to identify possibilities and translate them into opportunities. He was constantly thinking about improvements and growth ("any extra time I had went into making improvements in the store").[10]

A third success factor in Tom Monaghan's life is relationships—his stable marriage and his friends: "Nobody can succeed in business without the help of friends."[11] His social capital was the source of support, ideas, and insights: his brother brought him into the pizza business. The owner "[Dominick] DiVarti let the Monaghan brothers keep using his name and sauce recipe and also showed them how to make pizza."[12] Two unemployed factory workers were willing to do deliveries with their own cars. A customer suggested to Monaghan he open a place near Central Michigan University campus.[13] An Italian restaurant in Lansing shared its recipe for an excellent pizza sauce ("To my surprise, the owner didn't hesitate to give me the recipe, and it was a big hit with our customers").[14] Another employee, Jim Kennedy, came up with the new name of the company.[15] A pizza place in Detroit gave him a tour of the company and showed him the system of sliding pizzas into the oven. He was also lucky in meeting a good attorney, Larry Sperling. And these are just a few examples. Clearly, Tom Monaghan was not a "self-made" man, but owed his success to a network of players. It has to be mentioned that some of his relationships and partnerships were also responsible for failures, sometimes expen-

9. Ibid., 55–56.

10. Ibid., 63.

11. Ibid., 12.

12. Leonard, *Living the Faith*, 42. "DiVarti allowed us to continue to use his name on the place, which was good since we didn't think that Monaghan's Italian Pizza had the right sound"; Monaghan, *Pizza*, 57.

13. Monaghan, *Pizza*, 65.

14. Ibid., 59.

15. Ibid., 85.

sive ones. One of his bleakest experiences was when he was sued by his own franchisees. Relationships and their quality mattered to him.

Fourth, Monaghan's achievements were based on his willingness to embrace innovations, to work on new developments, to make changes. He dropped sandwiches and six-inch pizzas from the menu ("I realized then that it took just as much time to make a small pizza as a large one, and it took just as long to deliver a small pizza"),[16] he utilized a German machine originally designed for making bratwurst for cheese and dough processing, he used fiberglass boxes for storing and proofing dough, installed a huge mechanical pizza oven, experimented with the delivery boxes, went on literally hundreds of research trips ("Over three years, Margie and I must have visited three hundred pizzerias"),[17] and was intent on getting feedback from people who were *not* his customers. He was constantly on the move, engaged in growth-generating activities.

A clear value-basis, faith in his product, the ability to identify and use opportunities, relationships and social capital, and a commitment to innovation were clearly factors contributing to Monaghan's success. In the midst of this undeniable success, based, without doubt, on a strong sense of values, we can also identify specific moral challenges from the point of view of Christian ethics, which are worth examining very briefly: (1) greed, (2) a toxic competitive attitude, and (3) ruthlessness.

1. Early Christian writers are clear about the dangers of greed. John Cassian characterizes covetousness as a principal fault of the soul.[18] Early Christian communities pondered the question as to whether business was the intense occupation with worldly affairs based on a mindset characterized by a "desire for gain."[19] There is a fine line between a commitment to growth and avarice. Success in business cannot be

16. Ibid., 64.

17. Ibid., 100.

18. John Cassian, "Institutes," book 7, in *A Select Library of Nicene and Post-Nicene Fathers of the Christian Church*, vol. 11, ed. Philip Schaff (Buffalo, N.Y.: Christian Literature, 1894).

19. Helen Rhee, *Loving the Poor, Saving the Rich: Wealth, Poverty, and Early Christian Formation* (Grand Rapids, Mich.: Baker Academic, 2012), 160.

sustained easily without a concept of growth. Monaghan was nearing bankruptcy caused by his ambition to grow: "He wanted rapid growth because he believed it would impress the financial community, something he thought would be crucial when he started selling stock in the company."[20] He wanted rapid growth, was in a hurry to expand as fast as possible, accepting recommendations to build stores in residential neighborhoods, even though deep down, he had his doubts. He would later admit, "I'd heard Ray Kroc tell banquet audiences the story of how he and his secretary and his right-hand man had celebrated when they realized that they'd become multimillionaires the instant McDonald's stock went onto the Big Board." James Leonard comments, "and Monaghan wanted some of that so badly he could taste it."[21] This is, one could say, an expression of greed, greed based on an attitude of comparing oneself to and aspiring to be even better than others. In his frenzy to get to the top quickly he took risky decisions, such as streamlining the fleet of delivery cars (with eighty-five brand-new Javelins) and impetuously changing his accounting system in an operation that caused him to lose huge amounts of data. Such rash decision-making meant the company almost collapsed, and he partly lost control over it. He realized—almost too late—that "he'd rushed expansion."[22] After rebuilding the company in 1971 he regained a degree of former success and engaged in buying luxury and status goods. One does not come across many Christian authors supporting this type of attitude and behavior.

2. A second moral challenge was his overly (almost toxic) competitive attitude in business, which may have been born of his own greed and pride. "Toxic competitiveness" could be understood to be stressful competition that erodes the possibility for peace of mind and reduces certain human beings to competitors. Competitiveness is the desire to have more "x" or to be more "x" than others, which implies comparison and the recognition of the positions of others as identity-

20. Leonard, *Living the Faith*, 67. "Monaghan wanted to do more than merely survive. He wanted to thrive, and he believed the way to do it was through franchising"; ibid., 59.

21. Ibid., 67.

22. Ibid., 79.

conferring points of reference. Greed and competition are closely related to pride in many ways: the fact that "drivenness" can make people succeed and that this success can lead to a strong feeling of pride. It is well known that Tom Monaghan read *Mere Christianity* and was deeply moved by C. S. Lewis's insights into pride as "the great sin." C. S. Lewis describes the competitive nature of pride;[23] pride has been characterized as a root sin by many authors, but C. S. Lewis sees it as particularly dangerous, since it can arrive in many disguises and is perfectly compatible with a surface life of values. Lewis stands in the tradition that considers pride to be a sin that breeds further sins; it is obsessed with making comparisons and is linked to greed that allows a person neither to move toward contentment nor to settle there once it is reached. Monaghan identified pride as a major moral challenge in his life and conceded that he was committed to competitiveness from the very beginning: "To me, the real substance of life and work is in a constant battle to excel. I am determined to win, to outstrip our company's best performance and beat the competition."[24] His ambition was defined by a manic desire to outdo others: "I would have the best pizza sauce in the world. I spent more than a dozen years seeking it in all kinds of kitchens across the country."[25] The ambition to succeed can be laudable, and ambition-based comparisons are helpful antidotes to a morally suspicious monopolization, but there is the systemic issue of competitiveness as a mindset that makes a person see the world in a particular way, a spirituality not encouraged by gospel texts such as Mark 9:33–37 (the discussion about the greatest disciple) or John 21:21–22 (Jesus rebukes Peter for comparing himself with another disciple). Competitiveness can become toxic if it threatens a person's inner balance and quality of relationships—if we take the gospel challenges seriously.[26]

23. C. S. Lewis, *Mere Christianity* (New York: HarperCollins 1980), book 3, chapter 8, "The Great Sin."

24. Monaghan, *Pizza*, 3.

25. Ibid., 58.

26. See Clive Beed, "Jesus and Competition," *Faith and Economics* 45 (2005): 41–57.

3. Business life demands full commitment. There is the question of being divided in a commitment to respond to the person's needs and the commitment to respond to the business's need. Business calls for commitment; success in business asks for dedication. Monaghan was forced to learn this the hard way when his company went downhill and he had neglected the focus on his business ("I really lost focus there for a while, in the stores and in my whole world. I figured Domino's was doing alright. I got good people in place. We're a well-oiled machine").[27] If a company demands something like "undivided attention," how can this demand be reconciled with Matthew 6:24 or personal growth and character-formation? Monaghan honestly reports about moral failures because of long work hours: he was involved in a fist fight with an employee, he was neglecting the culture of his own domestic life ("I was getting too tense; I was feeling the pressure of working so furiously seven nights a week").[28] The pressure was enormous; Monaghan felt a tremendous sense of freedom when he sold the company.[29] A business mentality looking for "efficacy" and "efficiency" may not be compatible with other (especially spiritual) values.[30] To name one example: Jesus' approach to "accompaniment" (maybe best exemplified on the road to Emmaus) was not efficient. He spent an entire day with two individuals, patiently listening to them, rather than convincing the masses by providing a spectacular miracle. "Ruthlessness" in the sense of "being committed to business as the priority" leads to a further issue—namely, morally challenging situations that

27. Leonard, *Living the Faith*, 151.

28. Monaghan, *Pizza*, 98.

29. Julie Sloane and Tom Monaghan, "Tom Monaghan Domino's Pizza: The Pioneering Pizza-Delivery Chain I Started Almost Didn't Make It Out of the Oven," *Fortune Small Business*, September 1, 2003.

30. In his famous "Education after Auschwitz," Theodor Adorno warned that embracing efficiency as a key value may well be a road to a new Auschwitz: "The manipulative character—as anyone can confirm in the sources available about those Nazi leaders—is distinguished by a rage for organization . . . he is obsessed by the desire of *doing things* [*Dinge zu tun*], indifferent to the content of such action. He makes a cult of action, activity, of so-called *efficiency* as such which reappears in the advertising image of the active person. If my observations do not deceive me and if several sociological investigations permit generalization, then this type has become much more prevalent today than one would think"; Adorno, "Education After Auschwitz," in *Critical Models: Interventions and Catchwords* (New York: Columbia University Press, 2005), 198.

might damage people. In business life people have to be fired (bad apples have to be tossed out),[31] a disposition and necessity that may be connected to a certain level of "ruthlessness" in the pressure of putting business interests before the person (both the person of the employee and the person of the employer). Tom Monaghan had a habit of firing people, sometimes disturbingly quickly.[32] There is here the need to negotiate boundaries between business interests and a wider common-good orientation and concern with a person's well-being.

These three moral challenges cannot be reduced to biography-bound particulars of Tom Monaghan's life; they are systemic and typical in the sphere of business. They can best be framed within Christian ethics. Let us take a closer look.

CHRISTIAN ETHICS AND BUSINESS

Fundamentally, Christian ethics is based on a *commitment to follow (the example of) Jesus*, the Christ: "Being Christian is not the result of an ethical choice or a lofty idea, but the encounter with an event, a person, which gives life a new horizon and a decisive direction."[33] The distinguishing feature of the Christian ethos is living faith in Christ—that is, a faith that constitutes a form of life characterized by accepting Jesus as Savior. It is not a principle, but a person that constitutes the beginning and the basis, the point of reference and orientation, and the goal and vision of Christian ethics. Due to this commitment to Jesus and a firm belief in the presence and omnipresence of God, Christian ethics is characterized by *the appropriation of a "second-person perspective"* and leading a life in the face of God whose will is to be done. This involves a commitment to place one's own will under God's will. A second-person perspective is a way of life, of living in the presence of God. Augustine's *Confessions* is a milestone in the tradi-

31. See Monaghan, *Pizza*, 10.
32. Leonard, *Living the Faith*, 147.
33. Benedict XVI, Encyclical Letter *Deus caritas est* (December 25, 2005), no. 1.

tion of studying theology from a second-person perspective. Martin Buber, Stephen Darwall, and Eleonore Stump have in their respective styles clarified the ethical and theological implications of a perspective vis-à-vis a "Thou."[34]

The second-person perspective and discipleship make us look at Jesus, at Christ, in the context of the Christian tradition even—or perhaps particularly—for the purposes of doing business ethics. There is a temptation, though, to reconstruct the gospels as business narratives. There is the temptation to say that Jesus of Nazareth provided healing and teaching services and asked for discipleship in return, thus establishing a transparent pattern of transaction and exchange. There is also the temptation to say that because Jesus is described primarily as teacher (Mk 1:21) and healer (Mk 1:34) at the beginning of Mark's Gospel, he must have had a good head for business, a master of his art born with business acumen. One might go so far as to suppose that Jesus created a demand (to use a key marketing term), a need; his fame spread—Mark describes how many gathered around because "it became known that he was at home" (Mk 2:1–2). Jesus teaches with authority (Mt 7:29). This is innovative; it fulfills the demands of a niche market. Mark goes on to tell us that Jesus expects a certain reaction to the services he offers; in Mark 5:19 we read that after curing a man from demonic possession Jesus wanted him to tell his friends what the Lord had done for him. Jesus also expected gratitude: the Gospel of Luke (Lk 17:11–19) tells the story of ten lepers who have been healed by Jesus; Jesus is disappointed that only one of them shows his gratitude and thinks to thank Jesus for his efforts (Lk 17:17–18). Here we might be tempted to say that we see a business model emerging: healing and teaching services are offered in exchange for a transformation, for a conversion.

Of course, I must hasten to add, neither this language nor alleged

34. Stephen Darwall, *The Second-Person Standpoint: Morality, Respect and Accountability* (Cambridge, Mass.: Harvard University Press, 2006), esp. chapters 1 and 2; Eleonore Stump, "Second-Person Accounts and the Problem of Evil," in *Faith and Narrative*, ed. Keith E. Yandell (New York: Oxford University Press, 2001), 86–103; Stump, *Wandering in Darkness: Narrative and the Problem of Suffering* (Oxford: Oxford University Press, 2010).

reasoning does justice to Jesus, the Christ. It might be more promising, more worthwhile (if one were to explore links between business ethics and the gospel) to look at this issue of transformation from a leadership ethics perspective. Obviously, Jesus is described as actively recruiting. From a business ethics perspective we could ask the question "Was Jesus a good employer?" Jesus seems to be recruiting and leading people by offering transformation and in doing so is making a promise by telling the fishermen, "Come after me, and I will make you fishers of men" (Mk 1:17). If we consider the picture we are given, we can see transformation on different levels: (1) Jesus transforms the social capital of the disciples, making them move in different circles and get to know people they otherwise would not have met. They are also being called upon to build community that relies on strong internal ties for its existence and well-being (which is why the betrayal of Judas was so hurtful). (2) Jesus transforms the experiential horizons of his disciples, making them witness events and experience things they would not have experienced as fishermen. (3) Jesus transforms capabilities by empowerment as described in Luke 10, where the disciples are empowered to heal people and cast out demons, which brings them great joy (Lk 10:17). (4) Jesus transforms the imagination and the sense of possibilities in his disciples. What he says has a great effect on their thinking and perception. He is inviting them to listen; he is offering them an invitation to what could be called "metanoia": a thinking beyond the familiar categories, beyond the established ways of thinking (thinking beyond [*meta*], the thinking [*nous*]). This becomes apparent in the encounter between Jesus and Nicodemus in John 3, but also in the learning curve for Peter, described in Matthew 16:21–23, where Peter has to accept that Jesus will face suffering. The transfiguration account in Matthew 17:1–9 is sometimes interpreted as a preparation for the theology of the cross that leads to the theology of the resurrection.[35] Jesus' disciples have to think in new categories.

35. This reading was important, for example, for Archbishop Oscar Romero; see Margaret Pfeil, "Oscar Romero's Theology of Transfiguration," *Theological Studies* 72, no. 1 (2011): 87–115.

(5) Jesus transforms, we could say, the "depth of life" of his disciples: they discover a sense of mission and a sense of meaning; they also find their place as citizens of the Kingdom with a mandate to transform the face of the earth. They have embraced a sacramental view, thinking in parables, accepting a religious interpretation of the universe, a "symbolic interpretation" of experiences. An event then is not only "an event," but lends a deeper dimension to any historical event or experience, telling us something about the non-observable and deep structure of the universe. In his encounter with the rich young man, Jesus sees not only a man of wealth, but a man with a soul to be saved (Mk 10:17–25). The disciples are invited to share in this transformation.

Jesus offers deep transformations; it could be argued that a dedicated employer can be expected to offer some kind of transformation (personal growth) to his or her employees or even, *cum grano salis*, transformations enabled by the product developed and sold by a businessperson. These transformations are expressions of love; Jesus transformed his disciples' lives because he loved them (Jn 13:34, 15:12–14). Love is essentially about entering an attitude of care, about "the willingness to enter into the chaos of another."[36] Loving relationships from a Christian perspective express deep concern, salvific interest, a personal perspective, and a readiness to see a unique value in a person, the readiness to enter costly relationships. Jesus offered deep transformations of relationships, but he clearly did not turn the fishermen into business brokers: he paid the temple tax with a random coin (Mt 17:27), and Judas, the cashier, was not fully part of the innermost circle (see his questioning of the anointing in Bethany in John 12:4–8; Judas was also not part of deep transformative experiences such as the final discourses at the last supper in John 13:31–17:26).

Jesus offered a transformation of thinking and judging, as we have seen: following Jesus makes people embrace a sacramental view of the world (connecting the visible to the invisible) and the commitment

36. James F. Keenan, *The Works of Mercy: The Heart of Catholicism* (Lanham, Md.: Rowman and Littlefield, 2008), 4.

to the new commandment of love (Jn 13:34). Now, perhaps we can see how moral challenges such as those previously described can be countered: greed can be curbed with a dose of the parable of the rich fool (Lk 12:16–21); an unhealthy competitive attitude can be alleviated by inviting the sufferer *not* to think in terms of traditional hierarchical thinking (Jn 13:14 or the admonishment "unless you turn and become like children" in Mt 18:3b); ruthlessness can be healed with Christlike gentleness (Mt 11:28), the command to turn the other cheek (Mt 5:39), and a clear sense of priorities as we find in the command to "seek first the kingdom" (Mt 6:33). Christian ethics, so it seems, can provide some relevant answers. But how can one do business if one is committed to following Jesus and accepting love as the defining factor in life? How can one be a businessperson *and* a Christian?

Looking at the way Monaghan tried to integrate faith, there is the challenge of a reductionist account of faith, especially the instrumentalization of religious practices for business activities, succumbing to a "spirit of worldliness." When Monaghan says in his autobiography, "No matter how tense or tired I get, I can take time out to pray or say a rosary and feel refreshed. That's a tremendous asset,"[37] we may feel tempted to read this as a statement about faith as a performance enhancer, as an asset, a kind of capital. Christian faith is not "yet another tool in the tool-box"; it is not a business principle that helps us to make "spiritual capital." "Success" is not one of the names of God; religion is not yet another success factor in the business game.

In his 1524 treatise *On Trading and Usury* Martin Luther mentioned some of those fundamental challenges: a Christian way of doing business is a rare thing; a Christian would, according to Luther,[38] consider Matthew 5:39b–40 and 5:42 ("Give to the one who asks of you") and would be open to lending without expecting return. It is a non-Christian way of doing business if one forgets the needy and refuses to

37. Monaghan, *Pizza*, 8.

38. See John D. Singleton, "'Money Is a Sterile Thing': Martin Luther on the Immorality of Usury Reconsidered," *History of Political Economy* 43, no. 4 (2011): 683–98.

give to enemies and opponents. So, again we come back to the questions, "What does it mean to be a (real) Christian *and* a businessperson? How can one be a (successful) businessperson *and* a Christian?"

THE IDEA OF BUSINESS ACCORDING TO CATHOLIC SOCIAL TEACHING

One way of approaching this question is to employ a reference system based on gospel value principles that values business as well. Such a normative framework has been developed in the Catholic Social Tradition in documents of Catholic Social Teaching.

In light of Catholic Social Teaching I suggest we could define "a business" as *a community of persons serving the common good by responding to well-justified needs and concerns*. This definition has four main elements: community, personhood, common good orientation, and responsiveness. A business as a community means that it requires a shared system of values as basis and a quality standard of relationships; business as community needs and indeed depends on social cohesion. It can be argued that this ideal can at best be realized in smaller-scale businesses. Businesses are communities of persons—that is, of individual beings with dignity and a soul, living in and through relationships. Third, a business serves the common good; it is part of a larger context and has—as any other agent in the understanding of Catholic Social Teaching—a duty to contribute to the common good, to the good of all. This clearly indicates a shift from a profit-based shareholder orientation. Fourth, a business is responsive: it responds to needs and desires; it follows a model of "conversation" between producer and customer. From an ethical perspective, a business is encouraged to respond to well-justified needs and desires—that is, to desires that are compatible with the *summum bonum*, that contribute to (or at least do not harm) the integrity of a person. Business is responsive in the sense that it provides answers to questions and concerns of persons.

Let us look at these points in more detail in conversation with Catholic Social Teaching documents.

The social encyclical *Centesimus annus* characterizes a business "as a *community of persons* who in various ways are endeavoring to satisfy their basic needs."[39] As a community of persons a business is engaged in activities that are first and foremost personal actions, actions of human significance (before professional significance).[40] This would imply that workers be regarded as cocreators and as such should be involved in the decision-making process in concerns that are of importance to them.[41] Businesses must invest in people.[42] Employees must be treated with dignity. One way to implement this is to ensure that workers are not humiliated.[43] In the same document we find a business characterized as a "society of persons."[44] Business—or society—is meant "to serve the common good by striving to increase the goods of this world and to make them more accessible to all."[45] The common good, however, is not a value in itself, but serves the purpose of serving the person.[46] A business as a community of service is part of something bigger: it is in this context that a business can be characterized as a "vocation";[47] business interests have to be embedded in a larger context, otherwise both humans and the planet they inhabit will suffer.[48]

Business is "a means for achieving human and social ends."[49] Because of its service function the profit of a business cannot be the highest good. It may be an important indicator of how well the business is

39. John Paul II, Encyclical Letter *Centesimus annus* (May 1, 1991), no. 35.

40. Benedict XVI, Encyclical Letter *Caritas in veritate* (June 29, 2009), no. 41.

41. Vatican Council II, Pastoral Constitution *Gaudium et spes* (December 7, 1965), no. 68.

42. Francis, Encyclical Letter *Laudato si'* (May 24, 2015), no. 128.

43. John Paul II, *Centesimus annus*, no. 35.

44. Ibid., no. 43.

45. Francis, Apostolic Exhortation *Evangelii gaudium* (November 24, 2013), no. 203.

46. *"The common good of society is not an end in itself; it has value only in reference to attaining the ultimate ends of the person"*; Pontifical Council for Justice and Peace, *Compendium of the Social Doctrine of the Church* (Vatican City: Libreria Editrice Vaticana, 2004), no. 170.

47. Francis, *Evangelii gaudium*, no. 203.

48. Francis, *Laudato si'*, no. 34.

49. Benedict XVI, *Caritas in veritate*, no. 46.

doing, but clearly not the only one and certainly not its primary purpose. A business is responsive in that it responds to needs and desires of communities and members of that community; seen thus, business ethics cannot be practiced without regard for the addressees of business: there is "great need for a sense of social responsibility on the part of consumers."[50] A business is responsive in that it responds to the needs of its customers, but also to the needs of its employees who are entitled to a proper wage. At the same time, however, neither are excessive wages—that is, wages undermining the common good, compatible with Catholic Social Teaching.[51] This kind of responsiveness is a special vocation: "Business is a vocation, and a noble vocation, provided those engaged in it see themselves challenged by a greater meaning in life."[52] Likewise, "business is a noble vocation, directed to producing wealth and improving our world."[53] The responsiveness of business is linked to a particular sense of responsibility—managers have to accept long-term responsibilities, and anonymous responsibilities have to be avoided; the "community of reference" cannot be reduced to shareholders.[54]

Businesses are responsive—but how? Lord Sugar of Clapton, a successful entrepreneur, may provide a clue. In his autobiography *What You See Is What You Get*,[55] he describes his business success in terms of being able to respond to people's desires: Sugar made his first million by manufacturing stereo hi-fi systems, particularly by producing the lids of such stereo players cheaply, selling them as a luxury article with 400 percent profit margin. He got the idea over a cup of tea with his wife and his parents: "Ann and I visited my mum and dad's for tea and I noticed they had a plastic butter dish—a red-tinted one. As I lifted the lid up, I saw a moulding mark, known to me now as a sprue mark—the place where the plastic is injected—and in that moment,

50. Francis, *Laudato si'*, no. 206.

51. Pius XI, Encyclical Letter *Quadragesimo anno* (May 15, 1931), no. 72.

52. Francis, *Evangelii gaudium*, no. 203.

53. Francis, *Laudato si'*, no. 129.

54. Benedict XVI, *Caritas in veritate*, no. 40.

55. Alan Sugar, *What You See Is What You Get: My Autobiography* (London: Pan Macmillan, 2011).

something clicked in my brain. Here we had a coloured, see-through plastic butter lid, and all I needed to do was to make a similar item but much bigger, also see-through, with a nice grey tint to it."[56] Alan Sugar intuitively seemed to know what his "pet" consumer—"the lorry driver and his wife"—would buy next.[57] If they wanted a stereo, we would supply a posh one at an affordable price; the sound might not be perfect, but that was not what they were buying, after all; they wanted something that looked nice in their living room, and that is what they got. Sugar responded to the needs of a particular group, thus catering to a particular concern. Of course, one might now ask just what makes a need a need, and when does a need become a desire, and then perhaps considering the ethical perspective of such needs and their status even more in responding to them.

In light of this example, business ethics may indeed ask the following: (1) Are the questions to which a business responds ethically acceptable? (2) Are business responses (products, services) to these particular questions ethically justifiable? German entrepreneur Manfred Sauer, to give an example, has founded a company that produces fashion for wheelchair users. He offers products that answer the question, "How can I dress well as a wheelchair user?" The ethical status of the question can be taken to be the basis for an ethical evaluation of the business idea. This could give us a way of assessing the ethical foundations of doing business.

In order to be responsive you have to be close to people, have a sense of their needs and desires; a Christian, however, lives in a certain tension with the world (Jn 15:19; Rom 12:2). Christian businesspersons face a major challenge in negotiating the relationship between world and religion. According to Ernst Troeltsch (with his distinction between "church"

56. Ibid., 107.

57. "It was the buying public I was concerned about. I would bring perceived value to the average guy who could not afford the expensive kit, but wanted something that looked the part. And, let's face it, half of the people who bought the expensive stuff, did so out of snobbery, simply because they were told it was the best"; ibid., 133. Alan Sugar based his decision on the needs of the mass market in contrast to niche markets—for instance, Bang and Olufsen.

and "sect" as the form of religious communities) and Reinhold Niebuhr (with his characterization of different relationships between "Christ and culture") there are different ways of positioning religion in the world. There can be countercultural as well as adaptive models. Accordingly, business can be placed on a spectrum of being more or less adaptive or opposed to culture.[58] As responsive agents, businesses cannot afford to be too countercultural, otherwise they will not be able to respond to customers in a profitable way. So, it seems that a businessperson has to have some commitment to "being in the world" while at the same time retaining an eschatological perspective, a tension beautifully expressed in *Gaudium et spes*, no. 39. However, a business mentality has its place and its limits; Catholic Social Teaching documents are critical of "a business mentality" with regard to the church, "caught up with management, statistics, plans and evaluations."[59] This is a clear reminder that business has to be seen as part of something bigger; there is a need for a sense of proportions. It is, for ethical reasons, not profit that should drive a business, but proper responsiveness.

In the light of these points, let us revisit the question: Can you be a Christian *and* a businessperson?

THREE MORAL CHALLENGES AND RESPONSES OF BUSINESS AND CATHOLIC SOCIAL TEACHING

We have thus far identified three major moral challenges in business life from the perspective of Christian ethics: greed, a toxic competitive attitude, and ruthlessness. We have also seen that the gospel response to these challenges could consist in the message of the parable of the rich fool, the invitation to follow the example of children, and a clear sense of priorities, respectively. A business characterized as a community of persons serving the common good by responding to well-justified con-

58. Louke van Wensveen Siker, "Christ and Business: A Typology for Christian Business Ethics," *Journal of Business Ethics* 8, no. 11 (1989): 883–88.

59. Francis, *Evangelii gaudium*, no. 95.

cerns and desires is committed to a deep understanding of the human person with her inner life, her ability to love, and her ability to embrace a sacramental view of the universe.

These are three major ideas in Christian ethics that would respond to the three moral challenges of business: the idea of a well-ordered inner life as a remedy to greed, a commitment to love as a remedy to a toxic competitive attitude, and a sacramental reading of the world as a response to the challenge of ruthlessness. Accepting the idea of the soul, understanding love as the center of life leading to an idea of permeability between micro structures and macro structures, and a sacramental view of the universe leading to an understanding of ultimate questions are epistemic commitments that shape the practice of Christian ethics.[60] Let us explore what these three ideas—interiority, love, and sacramentality—could mean for economics in general and business ethics in particular.

1. In his recent analysis of economics set out in *The Economics of Good and Evil*, Czech economist Tomas Sedláček has rediscovered the concept of interiority and thereby stimulated discourse on the foundations of economics.[61] Sedláček sees economics as driven by wild desires, by greed. In this claim, Sedláček draws our attention to Bernard Mandeville: "Mandeville was the key proponent of the *need for greed* philosophy. In this sense, greed is the necessary condition for progress of a society; without greed there would be no or little progress."[62]

60. J. Philip Wogaman, in *A Christian Method of Moral Judgment* (London: SCM, 1976), chapters 3–4, distinguishes positive moral presumptions of the Christian faith (such as goodness of created existence; value of individual life; unity of human family in God; equality of persons in God) and negative moral presumptions (such as an understanding of human finitude, human sinfulness) as Christian epistemic commitments. For a systematic reflection on epistemic commitments of Christians, see Clemens Sedmak, *Lokale Theologien und globale Kirche: Eine erkenntnistheoretische Grundlegung in praktischer Absicht* [Local Theologies and Global Church: An Epistemological Foundation with Practical Aims] (Freiburg im Breisgau: Herder, 2000), 144–56.

61. Tomas Sedláček, *Economics of Good and Evil: The Quest for Economic Meaning from Gilgamesh to Wall Street* (Oxford: Oxford University Press, 2011). See Roger D. Johnson, "Economics of Good and Evil: The Quest for Economic Meaning from Gilgamesh to Wall Street" (Review), in *Faith and Economics* 59 (2012): 86–90; see also Clemens Sedmak, "Utility and Identity: A Catholic Social Teaching Perspective on the *Economics of Good and Evil*," *Studies in Christian Ethics* 28, no. 4 (2015): 461–77.

62. Sedláček, *Economics*, 189.

Sedláček draws on the motif of insaturability from myths: "We are naturally discontented."[63] Human beings are constantly "driven"; "the more we have, the more we want.... The more we have, the more additional things we need."[64] We are driven by desires and wants: "The reason why we have grown so much (in GDP) in the recent past is that we *wanted it very, very much*."[65] Strong desires, embedded in a framework of comparison-driven greed, are the engines of economic dynamics as Sedláček describes them. It is because of human greed that growth has been set as an intrinsic value pursuing "paradise on earth." Sedláček makes the bold claim that the account of the Fall in the book of Genesis is a story about excessive consumption, thus a story about greed. Original sin then, according to Sedláček, is a result of consumption. Wild things are within us, since our inner lives are untamed: "Wild things are not in the past, in heroic stories and movies, or in distant jungles. They are within us."[66] That is why any solution to the contemporary economic crisis must be found in and founded on human interiority—that is, in controlling desires:

> There seem to be two ways to minimize the discrepancy between demand and supply. One is to increase the supply of goods (in personal lives as well as in permanent GDP increases) until it satisfies our demands—to have, so to speak, all that we want to have.... The other reply to the problem of demand versus supply is an opposite one, and it can be found in the ideas of the Stoics: If there is a mismatch, a gap between demand and supply, then *decrease demand* to meet your existing *supply*.... In this view, a truly "rich" man is someone who wants nothing (more) while the needs of the poor man are many.[67]

This challenge of well-ordered interiority is taken up by Christian ethics in a particular way. The taming of desires requires the cultivation of second-order desires—that is, desires about desires (in the sense that one desires to desire the good; and in the light of this meta-

63. Ibid., 223.
64. Ibid., 227.
65. Ibid., 239.
66. Ibid., 324.
67. Ibid., 221–22.

desire organizes her desires accordingly and works on a discipline of desiring).[68] Reducing demands is about controlling desires; controlling desires is about structuring interiority. Christian ethics shares the claim that it is the inner human life that is the engine of economic dynamics and that the solution of our present economic crisis cannot be found except in our inner lives. Christian ethics offers an understanding of interiority that sees it as not hopelessly the prey to chaos, but as an intangible inner realm that can be structured. Early Christian writers have given us deep insight into and understanding of the structure and ways of structuring a person's inner life. A deep understanding of the human person will have implications concerning the choice of goods produced and services offered. (Are these goods and services conducive to the proper cultivation of interiority, or do they, as early Christian writers have described it, appeal to the dangerous leanings of the inner person such as "greed" or "pride" [and tendency bias in matters concerning leadership]?) Business leaders respecting the concept of interiority will develop a culture of self-reflection that enables and equips them to avoid the trap of "self deception."[69] A well-ordered inner life can curb the dynamics of greed. As a community of persons a business must be committed to the idea of interiority, to taking the inner lives of its stakeholders seriously. This changes the way we look at the person.[70] The person is part of a wider context of a hierarchy of goods and desires. Christian ethics would oblige the businessperson to contextualize her agency in a wider context of common good and a value basis providing the justification for needs and desires. The "why" and "how" of business are then equally as important as the "what." Christian ethics would press for a commitment to ultimate values. In

68. See Harry G. Frankfurt, "Freedom of the Will and the Concept of a Person," in *The Importance of What We Care About: Philosophical Essays* (New York: Cambridge University Press, 1998), 11–25.

69. See Arbinger Institute, *Leadership and Self Deception: Getting Out of the Box* (San Francisco: Berrett-Koehler, 2010); Robert Trivers, *Deceit and Self Deception: Fooling Yourself the Better to Fool Others* (London: Allen Lane, 2011), esp. chapter 8.

70. Georges Enderle, "The Option for the Poor and Business Ethics," in *The Preferential Option for the Poor beyond Theology*, ed. Daniel G. Groody and Gustavo Gutiérrez (Notre Dame, Ind.: University of Notre Dame Press, 2014), 28–46.

this sense, Christian ethics calls for the primacy of the intangible over the tangible. Christian ethics works through an *understanding of ultimate questions* about the "why" and the "where to" by accepting the gravity of those questions as well as the mystery surrounding them. A prudent person according to Aquinas's understanding of the concept will have an idea of the *summum bonum* and will make decisions in light of this value commitment.[71] Dynamics such as these can be and should be reflected in business activities and decisions.

2. Love as a second pillar of Christian ethics will express itself in the quality of caring relationships within a business context, but also as the common good orientation of a business. This approach can heal the damages wrought by a spirit of toxic competitiveness. Business is carried out by groups of persons for a community of other persons. This constitutes a state of being between individuals and collectives; this state has been described by Jacques Maritain as the "third way" between individualism and collectivism.[72] Aquinas's understanding of a social order of love is based on the idea of a common-good orientation: "But many people cannot live a social life together unless someone is in charge to look after the common good."[73] This orientation gives profile and depth to a social entity: "If society is not a mere aggregate of subjects, it must have an end—its common good—which cannot be reduced to the particular good of its members."[74] The same can be said about a particular business. From a Christian perspective, love (as concern for the also spiritual well-being of the person) structures relationships *ad intra* and *ad extra*. This order also expresses itself by a business being committed to the common good, to being part of a communal, social, and political context that transcends the particular business context.

71. Thomas Aquinas, *Summa theologiae* (Cambridge: Cambridge University Press, 2006), II-II, qq. 47–55; hereafter *ST*.

72. Jacques Maritain, *The Person and the Common Good* (New York: Charles Scribner's Sons, 1947).

73. *ST* I, q. 96, a. 4.

74. Antonio Argandoña, "The Common Good," Working Paper 937, IESE Business School (2011), 3, http://dx.doi.org/10.2139/ssrn.1947309, accessed May 8, 2017.

The central role of love is located not only on a personal micro-level but on the macro-level of structures, too. We could call this the dynamics of "permeability"—the idea that the same moral grammar (values, virtues) permeates the different spheres of society. In other words, the rules we apply to ordering our private and personal relationships are not significantly different from the rules we use to co-ordinate our own conduct when confronted by that of strangers in the public sphere. Even more, the rules that we are called upon to use in ordering structures and institutions are based on this "personalist" account. The businessperson and the consumer are citizens residing in the same (civil) world, but maybe in different spheres.[75]

This translation of love as an ordering principle of micro-relationships into an ordering principle of macro-relationships can be based on the Catholic understanding of the permeability between the various spheres of human existence. These ideas are most notably expressed with a view to economics in chapter 3 of *Caritas in veritate*. Economics and civil virtues are presented as a unity, making use of some ideas developed in the civil economy approach.[76]

> The Church has always held that economic action is not to be regarded as something opposed to society.... The Church's social doctrine holds that authentically human social relationships of friendship, solidarity and reciprocity can also be conducted within economic activity, and not only outside it or "after" it. The economic sphere is neither ethically neutral, nor inherently inhuman and opposed to society. It is part and parcel of human activity.[77]

That is why economic activities need to be governed by overriding principles and must not be separated from ethical imperatives.[78]

75. See Jekaterina Kuzmina, "Usage of Christian Social Ethics in Business," *Journal of Economics, Business and Management* 1, no. 1 (2013): 6–10. Kuzmina works with Peter Ulrich's model of business as part of civil society.

76. Luigino Bruni and Stefano Zamagni, *Civil Economy: Efficiency, Equity and Public Happiness* (2004; Frankfurt: Peter Lang, 2007).

77. Benedict XVI, *Caritas in veritate*, no. 36.

78. See Pius XI, *Quadragesimo anno*, no. 133ff; John XXIII, Encyclical Letter *Mater et magistra* (May 15, 1961), no. 38.

Economic progress is to be linked to social progress,[79] and, we could even say, moral progress. *Caritas in veritate* invites us to think about the relevance of the category of "fraternity" and the category of "gift" for human coexistence and cooperation. Pope Benedict XVI suggests communion as a lens through which we can look at transactions and interactions, as a third—a "civil"—way between market and state:

> When both the logic of the market and the logic of the State come to an agreement that each will continue to exercise a monopoly over its respective area of influence, in the long term much is lost: solidarity in relations between citizens, participation and adherence, actions of gratuitousness, all of which stand in contrast with *giving in order to acquire* (the logic of exchange) and *giving through duty* (the logic of public obligation, imposed by State law). In order to defeat underdevelopment, action is required not only on improving exchange-based transactions and implanting public welfare structures, but above all on gradually *increasing openness, in a world context, to forms of economic activity marked by quotas of gratuitousness and communion.* The exclusively binary model of market-plus-State is corrosive of society, while economic forms based on solidarity, which find their natural home in civil society without being restricted to it, build up society. The market of gratuitousness does not exist, and attitudes of gratuitousness cannot be established by law. Yet both the market and politics need individuals who are open to reciprocal gift.[80]

The concept of "gift," an important dimension of our personal lives, is introduced as a pillar of social life. This is done on a theological basis reflecting upon the gift of grace.[81] It is an important element of "friendship citizenship" that prevents the complete contractualization of relationships.[82] This kind of "friendship citizenship" is the basis of civil society. Society is described as a society of persons.[83] The categories described to understand the human person are relevant on the level of institutional structures and economic activities as well.

79. John XXIII, *Mater et magistra*, no. 73.
80. Benedict XVI, *Caritas in veritate*, no. 39.
81. See Pontifical Council for Justice and Peace, *Compendium*, no. 26.
82. See John Paul II, *Centesimus annus*, no. 10.
83. Ibid., no. 43.

A business is a community of persons working for an economics of persons. This will nurture a desire to provide quality (a commitment that can be enhanced through proper competition) without creating a sense of toxic competitiveness that is primarily based on comparison and not the will to provide proper quality.

3. The third moral challenge in business named earlier was "ruthlessness," a one-dimensional business mind, a one-track mindset.[84] Christian ethics offers a perspective reflecting on ultimate values and "the point of business." Alisdair MacIntyre's well-known definition of practice ("any coherent and complex form of socially established co-operative human activity through which goods internal to that form of activity are realised in the course of trying to achieve those standards of excellence which are appropriate to, and partially definitive of that form of activity")[85] invites us to ask the question: just what goods should business practice produce? This is obviously a value question, a question concerning "conceptions of the desirable" (yet again pointing us toward interiority and a structure of desires); Christian ethics calls for a proper consideration of values in the light of ultimate values, in the light of "last things" and the search for meaning and the final answers to the question of point and telos of life.

A possible understanding of economy as "planned human activities in order to fulfill human needs by a scarcity of goods" makes us think about the concepts of needs and goods. Which products are really "goods" in an ethically acceptable sense? From a Christian perspective, goods are to be seen in the light of personhood. In other words, goods build the person, contribute to and express a person's identity. A helpful approach in this context is the understanding of identity economics: identity economics considers economic decisions

84. Herbert Marcuse's well-known consideration of the one-dimensional person can be applied not only to consumers, but also to business people; see Marcuse, *One-Dimensional Man* (Boston, Mass.: Beacon, 1991).

85. Alasdair MacIntyre, *After Virtue: A Study in Moral Theory*, 2nd ed. (Notre Dame, Ind.: Notre Dame University Press, 1997), 187.

as expressions of identity statements. It promotes the notion that decisions, significantly economic decisions, have to do with assumptions about self. As far back as 1987 the Hungarian economist László Garai had already given a great deal of thought to links between social identity and economies.[86] Manufacturers utilize their selling clout to codetermine individual identity via the products they sell. In 2000 George Akerlof and Rachel Kranton published their groundbreaking findings on identity economics;[87] identity is "a person's sense of self" and encompasses basic economic decisions he or she will make. Identity is a structure based on social categories, and each category creates particular social expectations which individuals try to fulfill. Our identity is the way we communicate and express ourselves in the outside world. Akerlof and Kranton construe a person's identity on the basis of a defining social category "C" that implies role expectations or prescriptions "P." We try to do justice to the social category we accept as identity-defining by following the respective prescriptions in our economic decisions. A person buying a tie will do so in order to fulfill expectations of the social category this person belongs to or desires to belong to. In a sense, we could say, whenever we buy something we buy "ourselves" ("our Selves"). Pierre Bourdieu has described the dynamics of changing "tastes" with changing social attachments in his important book *Distinction*.[88] Hence, business life can be reconstructed as identity work, and identity work can be understood as "living values."

Christian ethics lends itself to an understanding of economic goods as value-based because of its understanding of the sacramental structure of the world. Objects point to something invisible: economic products have a meaning, a deeper dimension; they respond to needs

86. László Garai, "Determining Economic Activity in a Post-Capitalist System," *Journal of Economic Psychology* 8, no. 1 (1987): 77–90.

87. George A. Akerlof and Rachel E. Kranton, "Economics and Identity," *Quarterly Journal of Economics* 115, no. 3 (2000): 715–53; Akerlof and Kranton, *Identity Economics: How Our Identities Shape Our Work* (Princeton, N.J.: Princeton University Press, 2010).

88. Pierre Bourdieu, *Distinction: A Social Critique of the Judgment of Taste* (London: Routledge, 1984).

and desires. "Things" are not flat; things have an outside and an inside representing certain values; things say a lot about the people who own them. The watch I was given for my Confirmation cannot be valued in tangible cash terms: it is intangibly priceless and invaluable beyond its face value or significance as a timepiece. Things have something to say; they have both message and meaning beyond their tangible surface. This is something that the British anthropologist Daniel Miller has discovered and revealed.[89] Miller looked at the subjective value of household articles in homes on one street in East London. The things we have in our homes are not as inanimate as they might look; they are not merely items stockpiled, but impact the behavior and attitudes of the people around them (their owners): they provide and make profound the stories they are part of and give meaning—add soul—to the human lives they share.[90] Christian ethics would invite producers and consumers to not only recognize the inner dimension of products as "goods," but also to link the understanding of something as "good" to an ultimate value debate: what is at stake when we live our lives as human beings? What are the ultimate immaterial values behind our valuing material goods? These questions can help to see the bigger picture necessary to run a business as a community of persons serving the common good by responding to well-justified needs and desires.

A CHRISTIAN SPIRITUALITY OF BUSINESS

Can you be a Christian and a businessperson? The three moral challenges of greed, toxic competitiveness, and ruthlessness share one common moral concern: a lack of limits. The three remedies suggest-

89. Daniel Miller, *The Comfort of Things* (Cambridge: Polity, 2009). See also Miller, *Stuff* (Cambridge: Polity, 2010).

90. Things are part of the human identities they help create. As human beings we identify with the things around us, and as humans we often cling to those external tangible objects that provide the affirmation we often need for that identity; they help us express certain aspects of life that would not be possible without the "things" in the corners, on the shelves of homes. Russell W. Belk has similarly shown the way in which we have an extended identity of self in the things we surround ourselves with and express ourselves through; Belk, "Possessions and the Extended Self," *Journal of Consumer Research* 15, no. 2 (1988): 139–68.

ed—well-ordered interiority, love as a business category, a sacramental view of the world—share one message: a sense of depth. This sense of depth can be translated into a commitment to the priority of the intangible over the tangible and the immaterial over the material, into the virtues of prudence and temperance and into a key imperative: "Do not maximize." This is fundamentally a matter of "business spirituality." It will not provide a definite answer to ethical challenges, but a direction and points of orientation for the ongoing struggle.

Andrew Gustafson gives an example of doing business as a Christian:

> When I came to Omaha, I bought a house, then an apartment, then another, and now, with the help of others, I have 18 houses and apartments. Most of these are buildings I have redeemed and restored, and renovated for moderate priced housing. I often work with people who lose their job to help them stay in their house or apartment, and employ a number of alcoholics who live on the edge of society—one was living in his truck when we first met. I see my work on these buildings in my neighborhood and my relationship with my "guys" as a faith commitment to redeem and restore, and I have hope in people and buildings in which others have lost faith.[91]

In order to stay in business, there has to be profitability orientation, but this has to be clearly distinguished from profit maximization. "Do not maximize" is the name of the Christian business game. It expresses a common-good orientation of a business as a community of persons responding to well-justified needs and desires. There are good reasons—such as the price of inequality or the human and moral cost for negative (social and environmental) externalities—not to leave profit unrestrained,[92] a warning expressed throughout the encyclical *Laudato si'*.

An influential example of a business culture clearly dedicated to the idea that "the intangible takes priority over the tangible" is the

91. Andrew Gustafson, "Business in the Service of the Common Good: A Christian Perspective," *Journal of Religion and Society*, Supplement Series, Supplement 10 (2014): 244.

92. See Kenneth Arrow, "Social Responsibility and Economic Efficiency," *Public Policy* 21, no. 3 (1973): 303–18.

Benedictine tradition. Benedictine monasteries have proven to be remarkably successful in economic terms. Studies have shown that the factors of good governance and value basis have contributed to this success.[93] Benedictine monasteries follow the imperative "do not maximize." The Benedictine tradition provides a framework that puts the spiritual before and above material needs and demands. How does such an intangible economy work? By adopting and applying absolute trust in God—any action taken by the abbot should be born of absolute trust in God: "Do not worry about any lack of monetary profit."[94] A Benedictine monastery will have at its disposal business structures and infrastructures, which are not a means in themselves nor the means to monetary gain. In other words, a monastic business is unlike any other company in that first and foremost it is a "spiritual business" with intangible spirituality as its overriding principle and concern; additionally, it engages in tangible trade to supply the monks it has to feed with their daily bread, so to speak. Chapter 57 of the *Regula* provides guidance for "Artisans in the monastery"—that is, those men who have learned and practiced a trade before entering the monastery. They may be allowed to continue their trade, *but* "if any one of them becomes conceited over his skill in his craft, because he seems to be conferring a benefit on the monastery, let him be taken from his craft."[95] Business success, profit, and gain in cash terms are subordinate to the overall spiritual good of the community.

The abbot and the entire community are oriented toward a perspective of ultimate values: monastic rules emphasize the fact that the abbot too will have to face the Final Judgment. The inner intangible structure of spirituality defines, determines, and defends any external

93. Katja Rost et al., "The Corporate Governance of Benedictine Abbeys: What Can Stock Corporations Learn from Monasteries?," *Journal of Management History* 16, no. 1 (2010): 90–115; Emil Inauen and Bruno S. Frey, "Benediktinerabteien aus ökonomischer Sicht: Über die ausserordentliche Stabilität einer besonderen Institution" [Benedictine Abbeys from an Economic Perspective: On the Extraordinary Stability of a Special Institution], Working Paper 388, Institute for Empirical Research in Economics, University of Zurich (2008), http://www.zora.uzh.ch/52341/, accessed May 8, 2017.

94. Benedict, *The Rule of Saint Benedict*, trans. Leonard Coyle (Collegeville, Minn.: Liturgical Press, 2001), 35.

95. Ibid., 57:2.

tangible infrastructures, meaning that the maximization of profit and yield is incommensurate with spiritual values and traditions. Similarly, in the sale of crafted goods, craftsmen must be careful: "And in the prices let not the sin of avarice creep in, but let the goods always be sold a little cheaper than they can be sold by people in the world."[96] Why? "That in all things God may be glorified."[97] If we take an inside look at this reason, we should first remember that it is referring to a monastery that is able to make a profit from the manufacture and sale of its own goods. So far so good. Why should the products not be sold? They can, but the dangers inherent in such trade are made clear: greed and avarice that will rob the manufacturer and salesperson of his or her spiritual wealth, which is a greater loss than any economic loss in financial terms could ever be. So, in the exchange of goods there has to be a limit, a boundary as to how far one can and should go to avoid the temptation of maximizing profit at any cost. We find similar guidelines on recruiting potential "company employees"—entrants to the monastery: "If she has any property, let her either give it beforehand to the poor or by solemn donation bestow it on the monastery, reserving nothing at all for herself";[98] note that there is no obligation or desire to maximize profit. The Benedictine "business" is governed by a principle other than making a maximum financial profit: workers should lay aside their tools at regular intervals during the day for inner spiritual reflection: "Then let all labor at the work assigned them until None. At the first signal for the Hour of None let everyone break off from her work."[99] Work in itself is not the point or overall aim; it is intangible infrastructures that guide, lead, and govern any work carried out. This primacy of the intangible over the tangible, the primacy of the spiritual over the material, is the foundation for a proper sense of proportion and for a commitment to a spirituality of nonmaximization. Even though, I may add, a global corporate business is not quite

96. Ibid., 57:7–8.
97. Ibid.; see 1 Pt 4:11.
98. Benedict, *The Rule*, 58:24.
99. Ibid., 48:12.

the same as a monastery, the importance of the very idea of a value-basis cannot be denied, especially if one accepts that any business is a "community of persons."

CONCLUDING COMMENT

The most difficult thing, one could say, looking at the pulling forces of *avaritia*, is to take less if you could take more. This is why we need a framework to nurture a sense of proportions, the big picture, and a sense of the point of business life. You need to have a clear idea of the good life in order to limit your own desires.[100] Greed, toxic competitiveness, and ruthlessness can be curbed with a spirituality of nonmaximization. This spirituality can best be cultivated with a sense of the inner, a commitment to love, and a sacramental view of reality. Spirituality is a matter of being, rather than doing. Business, as we have seen, can be presented as "identity work." For a Christian, identity is a gift based on a relationship with Jesus Christ.

BIBLIOGRAPHY

Adorno, Theodor W. "Education after Auschwitz." In *Critical Models: Interventions and Catchwords*, 191–204. New York: Columbia University Press, 2005.

Akerlof, George A., and Rachel E. Kranton. "Economics and Identity." *Quarterly Journal of Economics* 115, no. 3 (2000): 715–53.

———. *Identity Economics: How Our Identities Shape Our Work, Wages, and Well-Being*. Princeton, N.J.: Princeton University Press, 2010.

Aquinas, Thomas. *Summa theologiae*. Cambridge: Cambridge University Press, 2006.

Arbinger Institute. *Leadership and Self Deception: Getting Out of the Box*. San Francisco: Berrett-Koehler, 2010.

Argandoña, Antonio. "The Common Good." Working Paper 937. IESE Business School. 2011. http://dx.doi.org/10.2139/ssrn.1947309. Accessed May 8, 2017.

100. See the thesis developed in Robert Skidelsky and Edward Skidelsky, *How Much Is Enough? Money and the Good Life* (New York: Other Press, 2012).

Arrow, Kenneth. "Social Responsibility and Economic Efficiency." *Public Policy* 21, no. 3 (1973): 303–18.

Badaracco, Joseph L., Jr. *Tom Monaghan: In Business for God; Teaching Note*. Harvard Business School Teaching Note 392-140. May 1992.

Beed, Clive. "Jesus and Competition." *Faith and Economics* 45 (2005): 41–57.

Belk, Russell W. "Possessions and the Extended Self." *Journal of Consumer Research* 15, no. 2 (1988): 139–68.

Benedict. *The Rule of Saint Benedict*. Translated by Leonard Doyle. Collegeville, Minn.: Liturgical Press, 2001.

Benedict XVI. Encyclical Letter *Deus caritas est*. December 25, 2005.

———. Encyclical Letter *Caritas in veritate*. June 29, 2009.

Bourdieu, Pierre. *Distinction: A Social Critique of the Judgment of Taste*. London: Routledge, 1984.

Bruni, Luigino, and Stefano Zamagni. *Civil Economy: Efficiency, Equity and Public Happiness*. Frankfurt: Peter Lang, 2007. Originally published in 2004.

Cassian, John. "Institutes." In *A Select Library of Nicene and Post-Nicene Fathers of the Christian Church*, vol. 11, edited by Philip Schaff. Buffalo, N.Y.: Christian Literature, 1894.

Darwall, Stephen. *The Second-Person Standpoint: Morality, Respect and Accountability*. Cambridge, Mass.: Harvard University Press, 2006.

Enderle, Georges. "The Option for the Poor and Business Ethics." In *The Preferential Option for the Poor Beyond Theology*, edited by Daniel G. Groody and Gustavo Gutiérrez, 28–46. Notre Dame, Ind.: University of Notre Dame Press, 2014.

Francis. Apostolic Exhortation *Evangelii gaudium*. November 24, 2013.

———. Encyclical Letter *Laudato si'*. May 24, 2015.

Frankfurt, Harry G. "Freedom of the Will and the Concept of a Person." In *The Importance of What We Care About: Philosophical Essays*. New York: Cambridge University Press 1998, 11–25.

Garai, László. "Determining Economic Activity in a Post-Capitalist System." *Journal of Economic Psychology* 8, no. 1 (1987): 77–90.

Gustafson, Andrew. "Business in the Service of the Common Good: A Christian Perspective." *Journal of Religion and Society*. Supplement Series. Supplement 10 (2014): 242–56.

Inauen, Emil, and Bruno S. Frey. "Benediktinerabteien aus ökonomischer Sicht: über die ausserordentliche Stabilität einer besonderen Institution" [Benedictine Abbeys from an Economic Perspective: On the Extraordinary Stability of a Special Institution]. Working paper 388. Institute for Empirical Research in Economics, University of Zurich. (2008). http://www.zora.uzh.ch/52341/. Accessed May 8, 2017.

John XXIII. Encyclical Letter *Mater et magistra*. May 15, 1961.

John Paul II. Encyclical Letter *Centesimus annus*. May 1, 1991.

Johnson, Roger D. "Economics of Good and Evil: The Quest for Economic Meaning from Gilgamesh to Wall Street." (Review) *Faith and Economics* 59 (2012): 86–90.

Keenan, James F. *The Works of Mercy: The Heart of Catholicism*. Lanham, Md.: Rowman and Littlefield, 2008.

Kuzmina, Jekaterina. "Usage of Christian Social Ethics in Business." *Journal of Economics, Business and Management* 1, no. 1 (2013): 6–10.

Leonard, James. *Living the Faith: A Life of Tom Monaghan*. Ann Arbor: University of Michigan Press, 2012.

Lewis, C. S. *Mere Christianity*. New York: HarperCollins, 1980.

MacIntyre, Alasdair. *After Virtue: A Study in Moral Theory*. 2nd ed. Notre Dame, Ind.: Notre Dame University Press, 1997.

Marcuse, Herbert. *One-Dimensional Man*. Boston, Mass.: Beacon, 1991.

Maritain, Jacques. *The Person and the Common Good*. New York: Charles Scribner's Sons, 1947.

Miller, Daniel. *The Comfort of Things*. Cambridge: Polity, 2009.

———. *Stuff*. Cambridge: Polity, 2010.

Monaghan, Tom, with Robert Anderson. *Pizza Tiger*. New York: Random House, 1986.

Pfeil, Margaret. "Oscar Romero's Theology of Transfiguration." *Theological Studies* 72, no. 1 (2011): 87–115.

Pius XI. Encyclical Letter *Quadragesimo anno*. May 15, 1931.

Pontifical Council for Justice and Peace. *Compendium of the Social Doctrine of the Church*. Vatican City: Libreria Editrice Vaticana, 2004.

Rhee, Helen. *Loving the Poor, Saving the Rich: Wealth, Poverty, and Early Christian Formation*. Grand Rapids, Mich.: Baker Academic, 2012.

Rost, Katja, Emil Inauen, Margit Osterloh, and Bruno S. Frey. "The Corporate Governance of Benedictine Abbeys: What Can Stock Corporations Learn from Monasteries?" *Journal of Management History* 16, no. 1 (2010): 90–115.

Sedláček, Tomas. *Economics of Good and Evil: The Quest for Economic Meaning from Gilgamesh to Wall Street*. Oxford: Oxford University Press, 2011.

Sedmak, Clemens. *Lokale Theologien und globale Kirche: Eine erkenntnistheoretische Grundlegung in praktischer Absicht* [Local Theologies and Global Church: An Epistemological Foundation with Practical Aims]. Freiburg im Breisgau: Herder, 2000.

———. "Utility and Identity: A Catholic Social Teaching Perspective on the *Economics of Good and Evil*." *Studies in Christian Ethics* 28, no. 4 (2015): 461–77.

Siker, Louke van Wensveen. "Christ and Business: A Typology for Christian Business Ethics." *Journal of Business Ethics* 8, no. 11 (1989): 883–88.

Singleton, John D. "'Money Is a Sterile Thing': Martin Luther on the Immorality of Usury Reconsidered." *History of Political Economy* 43, no. 4 (2011): 683–98.

Skidelsky, Robert, and Edward Skidelsky. *How Much Is Enough? Money and the Good Life*. New York: Other Press, 2012.

Sloane, Julie, and Tom Monaghan. "Tom Monaghan Domino's Pizza: The Pioneering Pizza-Delivery Chain I Started Almost Didn't Make It Out of the Oven." *Fortune Small Business*, September 1, 2003.

Stump, Eleonore. "Second-Person Accounts and the Problem of Evil." In *Faith and Narrative*, edited by Keith E. Yandell, 86–103. New York: Oxford University Press, 2001.

———. *Wandering in Darkness: Narrative and the Problem of Suffering*. Oxford: Oxford University Press, 2010.

Sugar, Alan. *What You See Is What You Get: My Autobiography*. London: Pan Macmillan, 2011.

Trivers, Robert. *Deceit and Self Deception: Fooling Yourself the Better to Fool Others.* London: Allen Lane, 2011.

Vatican Council II. Pastoral Constitution *Gaudium et spes*. December 7, 1965.

Wogaman, J. Philip. *A Christian Method of Moral Judgment*. London: SCM, 1976.

7

GIFT, ECONOMICS, AND SOCIETY

Elements for an Open Debate

GERMÁN SCALZO

> Economic, social and political development, if it is to be authentically human, needs to make room for the *principle of gratuitousness* as an expression of fraternity.
>
> —Benedict XVI, *Caritas in veritate*, no. 34

INTRODUCTION: REDISCOVERING THE IDEA OF GIFT

In his speech inaugurating the 2013–14 academic year at the University of Navarra, Ángel Luis González emphasized that:

> In recent years (the last 25–30 years), the question of gift has achieved enormous attention in the fields of sociology, philosophy, psychology, economics, theology, general ethics, ethics of responsibility, ethics of dialogic responsibility, the ethics of care and of course many other so-called applied ethics. "Become a donor!" is a constant invitation.[1]

1. Ángel Luis González, *Persona, libertad, don* [Person, Freedom, Gift], Inaugural lecture of the 2013–14 academic year, Universidad de Navarra, Pamplona (September 6, 2013), 6, my translation. In the same work, against the large variety of prevailing approaches, the philosopher explains: "My contribution to this jumbled matter is based on a metaphysical explanation of the person and freedom because the gift, strictly speaking, is interpersonal and its condition of possibility is freedom" (7). For a complementary vision, see Ignacio Falgueras, "El dar, actividad plena de la libertad transcendental" [Giving, Full Activity of Transcendental Freedom], *Studia Poliana* 15 (2013): 69–108, and Rafael Alvira, "Tener y existir, reflexión y donación" [Having and Existing, Reflection and Donation], *Anuario Filosófico* 36, no. 3 (2003): 575–85.

Benedict XVI himself placed the logic of gift in the center of his social encyclical *Caritas in veritate*, saying that "*charity in truth* places man before the astonishing experience of gift" and that "it is the primordial truth of God's love, grace bestowed upon us, that opens our lives to gift and makes it possible to hope for a 'development of the whole man and of all men.'"[2]

Indeed, the presence of gift is fundamental in moving beyond the crossroads to which modern thought has brought us. Although mainstream economic theory has followed a different course, there are some isolated efforts to include this reality, which, although it is inherent in economic rationality, has been regarded as "extra-economic" by those who have mapped out a positivist intellectual itinerary.[3]

In one form or another, the notion of gift has been present in all human communities, especially in ancient societies. The work of Marcel Mauss, Émile Durkheim's nephew, is found halfway between sociology and cultural anthropology and was fundamental in reviving the topic in the mid-twentieth century. In his seminal work, titled in English *The Gift: Forms and Functions in Archaic Societies*, Mauss claims that gift, freedom, liberality, and interest in giving have re-emerged as a seminal notion after being long forgotten.[4]

In *The Enigma of the Gift*, Maurice Godelier critically dialogues with Mauss to conclude that "the giving of gift has become above all a subjective, personal and individual matter. It is the expression and the

2. Benedict XVI, Encyclical Letter *Caritas in veritate* (June 29, 2009), nos. 34 and 8, quoting John XXIII, Encyclical Letter *Pacem in terris* (April 11, 1963), no. 42.

3. In this regard, the development of the so-called civil economy is noteworthy and has mainly been developed by Italian thinkers Stefano Zamagni and Luigino Bruni. See, for example, Zamagni and Bruni, *Handbook on the Economics of Reciprocity and Social Enterprise* (Cheltenham, UK: Edward Elgar, 2013); Bruni and Zamagni, *Civil Economy: Efficiency, Equity and Public Happiness* (Frankfurt: Peter Lang, 2007); Zamagni, "Reciprocity, Civil Economy, Common Good," in *Pursuing the Common Good*, ed. Margaret S. Archer and Pierpaolo Donati (Vatican City: Pontifical Academy of Social Sciences, 2008), 467–502; Bruni, *Il prezzo della gratuità* [The Price of Gratuitousness] (Rome: Città Nuova, 2006); Bruni, *Reciprocity, Altruism and Civil Society* (London: Routledge, 2008).

4. See Marcel Mauss, *The Gift: Forms and Functions of Exchange in Archaic Societies* (1925; repr. London: Cohen and West, 1966). Although the original version is from 1924, Lévi-Strauss was responsible for its dissemination, having popularized Mauss's work after his death in 1950. Currently, the *Revue du Mauss*, edited by the Mouvement anti-utilitariste dans les sciences sociales (M.A.U.S.S. http://www.revuedumauss.com), shows the evolution of leading intellectual works on this matter.

instrument of personal relationships located beyond the spheres of the market and the state,"[5] which eventually became known as the third paradigm: "Today, given the scale of social problems, and the apparent inability of the market and the State to solve them, gift is becoming again a socially necessary objective condition for the reproduction of society."[6]

With the initiative of Alain Caillé—one of the main authors in gift studies today—the group Mouvement anti-utilitariste dans les sciences sociales (MAUSS) was founded in Paris, and its acronym makes an honorific reference to Mauss. This group has contributed to the fact that the French have taken the lead on the interpretation of gift.

Caillé is a great admirer of Mauss, who "showed that ritually codified, generous reciprocity constituted the dominant fact in relationships between groups in traditional societies and formed the very cement of the social bond."[7] The highlights of Caillé's work include the *Anthropologie du don: Le tiers paradigm*[8] and his collaboration in Jacques Godbout's work *L'esprit du don*,[9] a book that has become necessary to understand this movement, in the French tradition and in general.[10] For them, gift is "any provision of goods and services without obligation, guarantee or certainty of return, undertaken with the intent to create, maintain or regenerate a social relationship."[11]

Caillé is especially responsible for the study of social relations from the viewpoint of the logic of the gift as a "third paradigm," a multidimensional theory of action beyond the individualism proper to the market and holism of the state.[12] "The paradigm of the gift makes

5. Maurice Godelier, *The Enigma of the Gift* (Chicago: University of Chicago Press, 1999), 207.

6. Ibid., 295.

7. Alain Caillé, *Anthropologie du don: Le tiers paradigme* [Anthropology of Gift: The Third Paradigm] (París: Desclée de Brouwer, 2000), 107.

8. Ibid.

9. Jacques Godbout and Alain Caillé, *L'esprit du don* [The Spirit of Gift] (París: La Dècouverte, 1992).

10. See also Godbout, *Le don, le dette, l 'identité: Homo donator versus homo economicus* [Gift, Debt, Identity: Homo donator versus homo economicus] (París: La Découverte, 2000).

11. Caillé, *Anthropologie du don*, 124.

12. Ibid., 14–21. Holism points to the fact that the totality of the social sphere, which preexists individuals and their actions, explains by default everything that makes up the individual parts of

donation the first constitutive moment of human reality, the moment at which personal identity and social bonds are founded because of that donation."[13] In short,

> with different perspectives and diverse methods, it can certainly be said that many current interests in the humanities and social sciences are showing that the concept of gift, an ancient notion, whether rehabilitated or proposed anew, is an especially privileged key to understanding the person and human nature, as well as contemporary social and economic problems.[14]

Before proceeding, it is worth pausing to further consider the anthropology of gift developed by these authors and their relation with the genesis of economic thought.

THE ANTHROPOLOGY OF THE GIFT

The Ceremonial Gift

In his lectures on the philosophy of economics, Martínez Echevarría emphasizes that to understand the meaning of the economy, it is best to start from the differences that can be observed between animal and human life.[15]

While all animal species conform to certain rules for breeding and feeding, leaving no room for reflection or knowledge, in the case of human beings, this process is not necessarily fixed, but rather depends on culture and history. Moreover, these rules are not intended for the mere survival of the species, but rather aim to achieve the best way of life.

Human beings, therefore, do not live in the wild in the same way

---

society. From the scientific point of view, it has taken the form of functionalism, culturalism, structuralism, etc.; see Ángel Luis González, "Thomistic Metaphysics: Contemporary Interpretations," *Anuario Filosófico* 39, no. 2 (2006): 16.

13. Antonio Moreno Almárcegui, "Ensayo sobre el don" [Essay on Gift], *Actas del Seminario del grupo de investigación en Economía Política y Filosofía* (Pamplona: Universidad de Navarra, 2010), 7, my translation.

14. González, *Persona, libertad, don*, 15, my translation.

15. For a more extended development of this section, see Germán Scalzo, "A Genealogy of the Gift," in *Ethical Economy*, ed. Alexander Brink and Jacob Dahl Rendtorff, vol. 51, *Perspectives on Philosophy of Management and Business Ethics*, ed. Jacob Dahl Rendtorff (Basel, Switzerland: Springer Nature, 2016), 31–45.

that other living beings do; rather, humans inhabit their own world, in which the symbolic dimension of speech and discourse prevails within a community. In fact, man can only live in community, the most basic of which is the family, which is where the idea of economics acquires its meaning (etymologically *oikos-nomos* means household management)[16] as the acquisition and administration of the means for a good life.[17] Ethnographic studies and cultural anthropology pioneered by Mauss at the beginning of the last century revealed the evolution of the human bond between families and the resulting social structure.[18]

In general terms, in the ancient world there are three big stages in human groups that express progressively greater ownership of the natural habitat: the first was dedicated to hunting and gathering, the next was structured by grazing or an incipient kind of agriculture, and finally came the emergence of crafts and trade. In the first two stages, human bonds were founded on the practice of the ceremonial gift, regulated by vindictive justice. In the third phase, in which cities were consolidated, human bonds were based on political authority, regulated by arbitrational justice.

In the practice of the ceremonial gift, the bond of blood and honor or status of each person within the clan or tribe prevailed. Exchanges were conducted in order to establish and maintain partnerships between parental groups through their representatives; the delivery and reception of the gift—whether things or people—expressed mutual recognition. The ultimate expression of an alliance between different groups was marriage—that is, the delivery and reception of wives, which shows that the gift did not correspond to the delivery and reception of something neutral, but rather was a "pledge," something

16. This point goes beyond the scope of this essay. For an idea of economics in the ancient world, see Scalzo, "Génesis del pensamiento económico: Dos visiones en pugna" [Genesis of Economic Thought: Two Conflicting Visions], *Cauriensia* 9 (2014): 341–74.

17. See Ricardo Crespo, "'The Economic' according to Aristotle: Ethical, Political and Epistemological Implications," *Foundations of Science* 13, no. 3 (2008): 281–94.

18. Gift appears as something universal; Mauss analyzed its presence in Northwest America, Melanesia, Polynesia, the Samoan Islands, Trobriand, etc., as well as in Scandinavian, Celtic, Roman, Germanic and Indian societies; see Mauss, *Gift*.

that was of upmost importance to the parties involved.[19] A pledge is an object that is delivered as sign of fulfillment of an obligation toward someone, while it expresses what is most valuable and intrinsic to the subject that gives; it is the gift of self in the one who gives. The goods exchanged according to this logic are priceless assets; they focus on the relationship and constitute "the development of a powerful network of interpersonal bonds."[20]

Hénaff studied the evolution of the gift in *The Price of Truth: Gift, Money and Philosophy*, based on Mauss's studies of ceremonial gift in ancient societies, and he showed how, over time, it acquired some verticality with the practice of offering to the gods, which he called *ritual gift*.[21] He first used the case of the Maori tribe to show that giving creates the obligation to respond: "After giving something of himself, he must receive something of the other,"[22] but especially, that one *gives oneself* in that which he or she gives: "The implication of the giver in the thing given is not a metaphor: it involves a transfer of soul and substantial presence."[23]

The practice of the ceremonial gift was a way of ensuring the recognition of stable and public alliances between groups of families, and its name derives from the fact that this gift was carried out according to very detailed ceremonial rules. It is "total social fact" because it "creates a bond that holds people together."[24] The justice that corresponds

19. The exchange of useful goods developed in parallel, but it was not of great importance, since these groups' subsistence economies were, in principle, self-sufficient.

20. Marcel Hénaff, *The Price of Truth: Gift, Money and Philosophy* (Stanford, Calif.: Stanford University Press, 2010), 107.

21. The idea of sacrifice, although it is important in the history of the gift, exceeds the scope of this essay. See, for example, Hénaff, ibid., 156–202, as well as Alejandro Llano, *Deseo, violencia, sacrificio: El secreto del mito según René Girard* [Desire, Violence, Sacrifice: The Secret of the Myth according to René Girard] (Pamplona: Eunsa, 2004), and René Girard, *Violence and the Sacred* (Baltimore: John Hopkins University Press, 1977).

22. Hénaff, *Price*, 125.

23. Ibid., 127.

24. Hénaff gives the example of a kind of exchange called *kula*, which involves a three-month journey by ship between islands where one tribe goes to visit another, resulting in a competitive exhibition, and then an exchange of precious goods called *waygu'a* takes place: precious necklaces (*soulava*) that are viewed as masculine, but worn by women, are traded for armshells (*mwali*) that are viewed as feminine, but worn by men. The necklaces move east to west between the different

to these societies is vindictive justice, intended to restore, in the case of an offense, the order established by the ceremonial practice of gift-exchange.

The Moral Gift

In his gift genealogy, Hénaff makes it clear that the ceremonial gift is social, not moral.[25] The emergence of cities represented an important step in the evolution of human relationships and the structure of social organization. A central authority's law replaced mutual recognition, which had previously been established horizontally through partnerships between families. This signified a shift from vindictive justice to arbitrational justice. As part of vindictive justice, the fundamental mode of justice was revenge: "eye for an eye, tooth for a tooth." In contrast, in an arbitrational system, authority acts as a mediator that "administers the debt" of the community, which it evaluates and sanctions. However, "the difference between vindictive justice and arbitrational justice is not reduced to an opposition between violence and lawlessness on one side and rule of law and reasonable mediation on the other."[26] The key is not the relationship to justice, but rather the relationship to debt: in the case of the gift, there is a debt to pay back; in the latter, an exchange price is determined, resulting in parity between symbolic and financial debt.[27]

Aristotle was the first to perceive the passage from personal reciprocity proper to vindictive justice to the proportional reciprocity of arbitrational or political justice. While for the ceremonial gift, the gift's

islands, whereas the armshells move west to east, so that there is not equilibrium in exchange but "continuous gift." According to the trobiandés myth, *mwali* and *soulava* tend toward each other, as man tends toward woman. Exchange is a festive ceremony in which the giver is not seen as losing, but rather gaining. Moreover, he who rejected the gift was tantamount to spurning an invitation to alliance, which was equivalent to declaring war. The other example he uses is *potlatch*, one chief's celebration to honor another that he considered a rival, which augmented the rivalry because the more ostentatious the celebration, the more ostentatious the reciprocal recognition had to be; see Hénaff, *Price*, 116–38. See also Lewis Hyde, *The Gift: Creativity and the Artist in the Modern World* (New York: Random House, 2007), 17.

25. Hénaff, *Price*, 109–25.

26. Ibid., 297.

27. Ibid., 283–98.

symbolic value or pledge received from a group matters more than its utility, the new configuration of gift focuses on utility, and as a consequence exchange moves to center stage.

Aristotle devoted book V of the *Nicomachean Ethics* to justice. He distinguished universal justice from particular justice, and within the latter he parsed the difference between distributive justice—equality according to a geometric proportion—and corrective justice—equality according to an arithmetic proportion.[28] Immediately afterward, in chapter 5, and in the context of corrective justice, he addressed the issue of justice in exchanges—voluntary transactions—as a form of reciprocity: "In associations for exchange this sort of justice does hold men together—reciprocity in accordance with a proportion and not on the basis of equality."[29] The aim of this kind of justice is to correct the gains and losses that occur in exchanges to maintain proportional reciprocity, which is proper to the city.

In *Politics* I, Aristotle discussed the genesis of exchange and distinguished different forms: bartering, or exchange without the intermediation of currency; the use of money as a means to acquire something that is needed; buying and selling to make money; and lending money at interest, which is known as usury.

Aristotle examined the evolution of relationships of exchange over time while exploring the nature of exchange value and its effects on human behavior. In relation to the respective ends (*telos*) of these forms of exchange, he concludes that there are two types: one that is natural to the good life in community and another that is contrary to it.[30] The key to understanding the difference is made clear in his *Ethics* and is related to currency and the distinction between the use of goods to satisfy a need and their use for exchange.[31]

28. "Distributive justice is based on man's 'natural' inequality, while corrective justice is concerned with the equality of man, which is instituted by 'convention'"; Josef Soudek, "Aristotle's Theory of Exchange: An Inquiry into the Origin of Economic Analysis," *Proceedings of the American Philosophical Society* 96, no. 1 (1952): 47.

29. Aristotle, *Nicomachean Ethics* V. 1132b.

30. Aristotle, *Politics* I.1257a.

31. Aristotle's sharp distinction between exchange value and use value may lead to a certain

Oikonomiké deals with the acquisition of property necessary for the good life—that is, its purpose is provision, pointing to consumption or use.[32] Indeed, from this Aristotle distinguished *chrematistic*, which is guided by exchange value—that is, by the desire for money.[33] Exchange value quantifies things, gives them a logical category that differs from their inherent nature—that is, their use value.

When use value takes precedence, accumulation of goods is limited because "the amount of property which is needed for a good life is not unlimited."[34] When exchange value takes precedence, the search for profit is endless, as is shown in the following maxim Aristotle took from Solon: "No bound to riches has been fixed for man."[35] As Meikle points out, "The underlying thought at this point is that, since it is a quantity, exchange value (and its bodily form of money) has no inherent limit."[36]

Exchange arose "at first from what is natural, from the circumstance that some have too little, others too much."[37] The exchange of goods without the intermediation of money—bartering—"is not part of the wealth-getting art and is not contrary to nature, but is needed for the satisfaction of men's natural wants, and it was natural to complete self-sufficiency."[38] However, the other form of exchange grew out of this one, "when the inhabitants of one country became more dependent on those of another, and they imported what they needed, and exported what they had too much of, money necessarily came into use."[39]

---

ambivalence on this point, since the exchange value of a good does not correspond to its proper and peculiar use. However, Aristotle fails to say that the use of an object in exchange is "unnatural" (*para phusin*), precisely because using an object in a way other than its proper and peculiar use does not mean that this use is bad. See Scott Meikle, "Aristotle and the Political Economy of the Polis," *Journal of Hellenic Studies* 99 (1979): 57–73.

32. See Crespo, "'Economic,'" 281–94.

33. Aristotle, *Politics* I.1258b.

34. Ibid., I.1256b.

35. Ibid.

36. Meikle, *Aristotle's Economic Thought* (Oxford: Oxford University Press, 1995), 50.

37. Aristotle, *Politics* I.1257b.

38. Ibid., I.1257a.

39. Ibid.

Aristotle is lenient with this form of exchange because its purpose is consumption; however, he disapproves of money being an end in itself because in that case, someone's profit means someone else's loss, which is an affront to justice. These forms are different, and "the source of the confusion is the near connection between the two kinds of wealth-getting; in both, the instrument is the same, although the use is different, and so they pass into one another; for each is a use of the same property, but with a difference: accumulation is the end in the one case, but there is a further end in the other . . . to increase their money without limit, or at any rate not to lose it."[40] It is of key importance to distinguish between the two ends, because, "though they appear to be different ways of doing the same thing, they are really similar ways of doing different things."[41]

The fourth form of exchange is between money without the mediation of any good, known as usury. "The most hated sort, and with the greatest reason, is usury, which makes a gain out of money itself, and not from the natural object of it. For money was intended to be used in exchange, but not to increase at interest . . . of all modes of getting wealth this is the most unnatural."[42] For Athenians, moneylending was a sign of friendship whose end was to help cement bonds of *philia* for the stability of the polis.[43]

Indeed, justice in exchange is fundamental in Aristotle's analysis because, as Ritchie points out, it provides a form of *philia* in an activity (commerce) that could threaten the unity of the polis.[44] Aristotle was aware of how important exchange is for the unity and development of a community. Therefore, before analyzing proportionality, he mentions the *spirit of gratitude* (*kharis*):

40. Ibid., I.1257a, 1257b.

41. Meikle, *Aristotle's Economic Thought*, 88.

42. Aristotle, *Politics* I.1258b.

43. Paul Millet, *Lending and Borrowing in Ancient Athens* (Cambridge: Cambridge University Press, 1991); Meikle, *Aristotle's Economic Thought*, 65. See also Odd Langholm, *Wealth and Money in the Aristotelian Tradition* (Bergen: Universitetsforlaget, 1983).

44. David Ritchie, "Aristotle's Subdivisions of Particular Justice," *Classical Review* 8, no. 5 (1984): 185.

This is why they give a prominent place to the *temple of Graces*—to promote the requital of services; for this is characteristic of grace—we should serve in return one who has shown grace to us, and should another time take the initiative in showing it.[45]

Aristotle insisted that politics was based on the realm of the gift, which is why the Temple of Graces acted as a reminder of the obligation to give and receive in terms of mutual service, without which the city would be inconceivable:

Several conditions are requisite if there is to be a genuine *koinonia*: (1) the members must be free men; (2) they must have a common purpose, major or minor, temporary or of long duration; (3) they must have something in common, share something, such as place, goods, cult, meals, desire for a good life, burdens, suffering; (4) there must be *philia* (conventionally but inadequately translated "friendship"), mutuality in other words, and to *dikaion*, which for simplicity we may reduce to "fairness" in their mutual relations.[46]

Gift thus takes on a new perspective: "It had become a virtue and it was no longer a gesture of reciprocal recognition but had become a gesture of mutual assistance."[47] In his genealogy of the gift, Hénaff equates the moral gift to the Greek idea of *kharis*—that is, "an entire model of gift-giving as favor developed around the Greek notion of *kharis*."[48] This is especially important because this paradigm contains the essence of subsequent economic thought.[49]

The Personal Gift

With the notion of person introduced by Christianity,[50] the idea of the gift takes on a different hue, which does not depart from earlier

45. Aristotle, *Nicomachean Ethics* 1133a.

46. Moses Finley, "Aristotle and Economic Analysis," *Past and Present* 47 (1970): 8.

47. Hénaff, *Price*, 251.

48. Ibid., 246.

49. See Hénaff, "Religious Ethics, Gift Exchange and Capitalism," *European Journal of Sociology* 44, no. 3 (2003): 293–324.

50. Étienne Gilson, *Christian Philosophy: An Introduction*, trans. Armand Augustine Maurer (1960; repr. Toronto: Pontifical Institute of Mediaeval Studies, 1993).

traditions, but renews them, giving them a more solid foundation.[51] The revelation of the mysteries of creation and the incarnation introduce radical innovations in the way of understanding the relationship not only between God and human beings, but among human beings themselves. St. Thomas and his teacher St. Albert the Great are the most recognized representatives of medieval thought, and they were the first to consider that the gift had ontological significance—that is, that gift meant ontological Being.[52]

In Aristotle's work, Aquinas found an excellent basis for better understanding the Christian message. In fact, his treatment of economics is merely a commentary on Aristotle's vision with an added supernatural perspective. Aquinas added to Aristotle's political scheme the call to human perfection that all men and women have through civic friendship, as well as the call to full perfection—holiness—with the help of grace.

The person is not fully realized with the actualization of a form proper to his own nature, but rather has a supernatural end that transcends his own nature.[53] Furthermore, self-determination toward that end is free—one can draw closer to or further away from it, or what is the same, dignify or degrade oneself. The person can freely destine herself to realize her unique way of being, which has been received as a gift, and which she will only come to know if she lives according to it. The person starts with a received life that grows into a realized life through personal acceptance of the gift and contribution to it.[54]

51. Without the notion of creation, the idea of the person is unattainable because radical contingency and the distinction between being and nothingness go along with it, and essence and existence therefore cannot be distinguished. For a metaphysics of the person, see Leonardo Polo, *Antropología Trascendental*, vol. 1, *La persona humana* [Transcendental Anthropology, vol. 1, The Human Person] (Pamplona: Eunsa, 1999), and Fernando Haya, *El ser personal: De Tomás de Aquino a la metafísica del don* (Pamplona: Eunsa, 1997). For its anthropological and ethical implications, see Polo, *Presente y futuro del hombre* [Present and Future of Man] (Madrid: Rialp, 1993), and Polo, *Ética: Hacia una versión moderna de los temas clásicos* [Ethics: A Modern Version of Its Classic Themes] (Madrid: Aedos, 1997).

52. See Miguel Alfonso Martínez Echevarría, *Evolución del Pensamiento Económico* [Evolution of Economic Thought] (Madrid: Espasa Calpe, 1983), 15–18.

53. For other created beings, fulfilling that which they tend toward is necessary and completely determined by their nature. Their end is, therefore, a finite external consummation from an instinctive and unthinking tendency.

54. Polo, "Tener y dar" [Having and Giving], in *Sobre la existencia Cristiana* (Pamplona: Eunsa, 1996), 103–36.

People are created unique and unrepeatable, analog participations in God's uncreated love, beings who can freely live in community with other persons. In his moral theology, Aquinas considers nature and grace in such a way that man can reach his ultimate end: perfect happiness in the beatific vision. With a free response to grace—a divine gift—man can turn his service to the city into love for God and men since, as St. Augustine had already shown, men belong to two cities, one earthly and the other divine, which do not oppose each other, but are present simultaneously. Here we can anticipate a conclusion: the radical novelty of Christianity with respect to gift is found in considering that man, created in the image and likeness of God, can only be deeply understood as a gift.[55]

Understanding man and woman as persons implies recognizing that each one is essentially *a someone* open to relationships. A human person can achieve his or her end only in communion with others, in all dimensions of life. Knowledge and human love should be shared, reciprocated, and objectified in their manifestations. Communication is intrinsic to the human person, who, through language and work, carries out an expansion of his or her corporeality, thus realizing him- or herself incrementally. There are natural relationships between people—kinship, fraternity, parentage—that are manifested in giving and receiving. This existential community of exchange expands into society, which arise naturally because, through mutual help, people achieve their own perfection; through the care of others, people find a remedy for mutual needs, compassion and sympathy, gifts and exchanges, and other manifestations of the human need to love and be loved.[56] The social end par excellence is the common good, defines the necessary conditions for individuals and families to reach their high-

55. Juan Fernando Sellés, *Antropología para inconformes: Una antropología abierta al futuro* [Anthropology for Nonconformists: An Anthropology Open to the Future] (Madrid: Rialp, 2007), 618; see also 95–105 and 596–97.

56. As we saw, for Mauss, the gift system is the fundamental form in which human groups express relationships. It does not deal with giving, but rather with giving of oneself in whatever is given, which is the manifestation of personal being.

est development, conditions that we can summarize into three areas: peace, material well-being, and values.

Following the classical tradition of viewing society as a natural unity of order, Aquinas does not exclude gift from the field of justice,[57] although he relates it to liberality (justice gives the other what is his, while the posture of the gift gives what is one's own) and integrates it, therefore, in a paradigm of love and gratitude: "The word 'gift' imports an aptitude for being given. And what is given has an aptitude or relation both to the giver and to that to which it is given. For it would not be given by anyone, unless it was his to give; and it is given to someone to be his."[58] Thus, besides commutative and distributive justice, a way toward *transcendental justice* is opened up. In establishing justice within the order God imposed on the world, gift acquires a transcendent and personal basis through eternal or *divine law*, in which rational creatures participate through reason. It is the knowledge of the truth that gives full meaning to our freedom and is written on our hearts.

Under the basic premise that "love is superior to the good,"[59] Aquinas highlights two points that were present in classical reflections on gift: gratuity and love. As Aquinas notes,

> In proof of this we must know that a gift is properly an unreturnable giving, as Aristotle says (Topic. iv, 4)—i.e. a thing which is not given with the intention of a return—and it thus contains the idea of a gratuitous donation. Now, the reason of donation being gratuitous is love; since therefore do we give something to anyone gratuitously forasmuch as we wish him well. So what we first give him is the love whereby we wish him well. Hence it is man-

57. "*Charity goes beyond justice*, because to love is to give, to offer what is 'mine' to the other; but it never lacks justice, which prompts us to give the other what is 'his,' what is due to him by reason of his being or his acting. I cannot 'give' what is mine to the other, without first giving him what pertains to him in justice. If we love others with charity, then first of all we are just towards them. Not only is justice not extraneous to charity, not only is it not an alternative or parallel path to charity: justice is inseparable from charity, and intrinsic to it"; Benedict XVI, Encyclical Letter *Caritas in veritate*, June 29, 2009, no. 6.

58. Thomas Aquinas, *Summa theologiae* (Cambridge: Cambridge University Press, 2006) I, q. 38, a. 1; hereafter *ST*.

59. Sellés, *Antropología*, 596.

ifest that love has the nature of a first gift, through which all free gifts are given.[60]

Leonardo Polo claims that the human person is not only defined as being able to have, but especially as a being capable of giving, and this giving comes from his or her intimacy, which characterizes what it means to be a person. That the gift is free means that it is not mechanically caused; rather, it is a novelty:

> The phenomenology of the gift describes the manifestation of a reality that is not contained in antecedent conditions. The gift is not a gift if the gift giver is just waiting for it to be deployed or made explicit. The gift in action is gratuity in the sense that the gift giver has no need beforehand and the gift giver is only called as such in the very act of giving.[61]

This is the radical difference between the human person and other living beings—namely, the person has intimacy, and it is not closed but open. In Polo's words, "Intimacy is not an enclosed area, but rather is inwardly open in as much as the person is a gift. On the other hand, both operational immanence and virtue can be called modes of having. Human having is affirmed in giving."[62]

FROM GIFT TO CONTRACT

The Genesis of the Contractual Society

Just as the idea of classical society—that which pertains to Aristotelian-Thomistic philosophy—is based on gift, modern society is based on the idea of the contract.[63] This is evident in the so-called contractualist political philosophers—especially Hobbes—but it was already nascent in a change of course that thirteenth-century philosophy introduced with the last great figure of medieval scholasticism, John Duns Sco-

60. Aquinas, *ST* I, q. 38, a. 2.

61. Haya, *El ser personal*, 324.

62. Polo, *Antropología trascendental*, 208–9.

63. See Arnaud Berthoud, *Essais de Philosophie Économique: Platon, Aristote, Hobbes, A. Smith, Marx* [Essays on Economic Philosophy: Plato, Aristotle, Hobbes, A. Smith, Marx] (Arras-Lille: Presses Universitaires du Septentrion, 2002).

tus.[64] His thesis, while remaining within orthodoxy, contains a critical spirit that serves as the basis for later, more significant deviations, especially in the case of William of Ockham's nominalism.[65]

Nominalism changed the scholastic conception of man as a person by radically separating philosophy and theology, with the many social implications derived therefrom. It initiated a new path based on the will, submission to faith, the acceptance of revealed truths irrespective of reason, and naturalist tendencies. The cosmos, formerly the natural way toward the discovery of the truth and the good, eventually became "nature that does not tend toward anything," something like a mechanism or a set of physical forces without an end. The person's ultimate end became dehumanized and no longer passed through tending forces and rational deliberations, but rather purely and solely through every person's individual will.

The entire created universe, including the moral law, became contingent not only in its existence, but also in its essence. Anti-metaphysical empiricism was joined by another ethical principle: divine omnipotence. In this view, faith reveals an omnipotent God, whose will is beyond order, truth, or the good. The moral law does not come from a divine wisdom that moves his creatures from within, but rather from a heteronomous law-giving God who moves them from the outside. Therefore, an intrinsic morality of human acts does not exist; rather, the criterion is extrinsic: the divine will, expressed in mandates and sanctioned by a system of punishments and rewards. It then falls into a moral conventionalism of a theological kind: the person must submit him- or herself to the will of God by faith alone, and conscience becomes the first moral

64. Gilson, *Juan Duns Escoto: Introducción a sus posiciones fundamentales* [John Duns Scotus: Introduction to His Fundamental Positions] (Pamplona: Eunsa, 2007); Polo, *Nominalismo, idealismo y realismo* [Nominalism, Idealism, and Realism] (Pamplona: Eunsa, 2001); André de Muralt, *La apuesta de la filosofía medieval: Estudios tomistas, escotistas, ockhamistas y gregorianos* [The Wager of Medieval Philosophy: Thomist, Scotist, Ockhamist, and Gregorian Studies] (Madrid: Marcial Pons, 2008); Michael Gillespie, *The Theological Origins of Modernity* (Chicago: University of Chicago Press, 2008).

65. Behind this posture there is a rejection of Aristotelian thought, which was condemned first in 1270 by the bishop of Paris, Étienne Tempier, and then later, in 1277, by the archbishop of Canterbury, Robert Kilwardby.

standard that should always be followed. Ockham's voluntarism is an expression of an impulsive ethics of love: doing the good is an act of pure love for God, a completely autonomous self-determination without tendencies or a desire for happiness.

If God is the great lawgiver, who arbitrarily and from the outside imposes a law that is unrelated to nature or reason and who discloses himself to the human race through revelation, then absolute power, rather than divine wisdom, governs human beings through their actions. The idea of divine filiation is therefore replaced by that of slavery; God gives orders, rather than advice. The way in which the lawgiver's will is made known and its enactment become an essential element of paramount importance for this kind of moral system.

For nominalism, the city, like everything universal, is notional and exists as a predicate; reality consists in the individual members that make up the city and in their conflicting wills.[66] Society is not a good toward which the person tends naturally, but rather an unavoidable evil imposed from above by a unique and incommunicable divine will that attempts to remedy nature corrupted by sin. In the state of nature, men were in a state of equality; sin introduced inequality or singularity. The idea of the common good was replaced by a new concept of general interest, which aimed to prevent the conflict of individual interests that are prior to the very constitution of the city. The law does not follow the common good, but rather imposes the general interest, a rational a priori design deduced from universal principles of theoretical reason.[67]

Exchange began to rely solely on the subjective will of the individuals involved, endowed with rights they possessed at their origin. Exchange was thus transformed into a kind of balance between wills

66. See André de Muralt, *La estructura de la filosofía política moderna* [The Structure of Modern Political Philosophy] (Madrid: Istmo, 2002).

67. Radical individualism necessarily leads to a natural state of war, which, according to Hobbes, must be corrected by an absolute sovereign that governs the agreements that men reach. Hobbes's *Leviathan* attempted to lay the foundations for a just and lasting political order in the framework of modern science. The Leviathan, a theoretical construct that acts as a representative of God in the world, is the guarantor of peace. We find here a precedent to the modern state.

that depended on nothing more than the wills involved and thus lost its reference to the common good. Justice in trade—in this view—depends solely on a contract that resulted from a voluntary agreement. Price thus emerged from a hypothetical agreement of wills, and the notion of a just price—so central to medieval thought—was lost.

The dominance of subjective will led to a perception of the market as a struggle of wills. In addition, the path was opened for late conceptions of the market as an aggregate of impersonal transactions, as a mechanism with a legality of its own that is designed to restore balance in the distribution of property. This same mechanism, as a result of opposing forces, determines the balance of prices, reducing an ethical problem to a logical problem and detaching man from any liability.

Contract as a Substitute for Gift

This paradigm shift in worldview resulted in modern political philosophy's conception of society not as an ordered natural reality, but as a mechanical construction. It gradually led to what Weber called a "disenchanted world." This disenchantment is the result of the modern project to build a horizontal and secular society that ignores gift.

> A first look at European society since the early modern period suggests an overwhelming dominance of contractual relationships, which are organized according to commutative justice and the logic of *do ut des*, both of which are hegemonic in market relations, as well as present in many of the relationships derived from the State. *It could be said that modernity is an attempt to build a society based on the contract.*[68]

What are the main differences between gift and contract in terms of exchange? The first difference is gratuity. While a gift is free and forms part of the things that the subject values, exchange goods have a price that respond to a kind of equilibrium-equality logic. The sec-

68. Antonio Moreno Almárcegui, "Consanguinidad y gracia: El culto a María y José en Occidente; Siglos I–XX: El caso de España" [Kinship and Grace: Devotion to Mary and Joseph in the West; 1st–20th Centuries: The Case of Spain], in *Actas del Seminario del grupo de investigación en Economía Política y Filosofía* (Pamplona: Universidad de Navarra, 2015), 6, my translation.

ond difference is that, by putting something of oneself into the gift, the giver offers him- or herself for the recognition of the other; in the case of exchange, the goods are evaluated regardless of who buys or sells them. Giving a gift is a challenge because accepting it (the object and therefore the person) requires reciprocation (just as refusing a gift implies denying the giver). Exchange, in contrast, is the result of a negotiation in which the parties consider their own interests. The aim of an exchange based on gift is to found and sustain a bond or relationship that creates a new identity for both givers. Contractual exchange, on the other hand, is impersonal, and the involved parties appear as subjects of law; they aim at a situation of equilibrium (zero-sum). Proportional reciprocity emphasizes that there is no equality. Finally, the gift can withstand insurmountable debt because its object is a personal relationship, while the logic of the contract demands all debt be repaid.

In *Charisma: The Gift of Grace and How It Has Been Taken Away from Us*,[69] a revealing work, Philip Rieff shows the effects of a world in which grace no longer acts. It goes beyond the scope of this essay, but it is worth mentioning that the notion of grace that is derived from the Protestant tradition, which has its origin in divine predestination, has been essential for the gift's exile from the public sphere with the social consequences therefrom derived. While Kant to an extent already recognized this situation in his work, it was Max Weber who best captured the tragic spirit of this radical split between the public and the private sphere at the beginning of the last century.

Weber, in his attempt to develop a comprehensive sociology, warns of a structural change in the understanding of the world that is closely related to modern man's "disenchantment." It corresponds to a historical-religious process that, after having been freed of the influence of "Christian pathos," culminated in forms of modern capitalism characterized by the rational organization of work. This process, which is proper to the West, was the topic of Weber's oeuvre *The Protestant*

69. Philip Rieff, *Charisma: The Gift of Grace and How It Has Been Taken Away from Us* (New York: Pantheon, 2007).

Ethic and the Spirit of Capitalism, probably one of the most controversial and discussed theses of the twentieth century.[70] I do not intend to enter into this controversy, but rather show how Ockham's initial problem, which Luther continued and Kant affirmed, is quite clearly found here.

Commenting on Weber, Hénaff emphasized that the social relationship itself was at stake in Protestant ethics:

> Luther wants to eliminate the practice of charity as "good deeds" guaranteeing salvation. It is easy to understand how challenging that practice would conform to a theological notion of faith as an act of unconditional trust in the divine word ... the break created by the Reformation ... concerns the devalorization of the generous act supposedly essential to salvation and finally its presentation as an economically irrational act. *What is involved here is the form of social relations itself.* If the latter are supposed to be generated by the complementarity of tasks instead of the reciprocity of gifts, then the transformation mentioned by Weber is even more radical.[71]

Weber notes that in the process of Western rationalization practical, theoretical, and formal rationality dominated substantive rationality, which generally meant replacing the broader sapiential Judeo-Christian worldview with a scientific one with its accompanying effort to reductively subject reality to empirical observation, mathematical measurement, and calculation.[72] The antagonism between formal and substantive rationality should be construed as a tension between conflicting values: between calculation, efficiency, and impersonality on one side and fraternity, equality, and *caritas* on the other.[73]

70. Weber is interested in the origin of the rationalization of practical behavior, which he characterized with the vague concept of the "spirit of capitalism." His main argument is that in certain manifestations of ascetic, puritanical Protestantism, methodical and disciplined work, along with accumulation and reinvestment of capital through the command of a substantive ethical rationality, generated a systematic component in economic activity that lasted even after its axiological-rational impulse ceased. This impulse corresponded to a certain substantive rationality and in particular to the doctrine of predestination, in which the accumulation of wealth was seen as a sign of divine election.

71. Hénaff, *Price*, 300.

72. Max Weber, *The Protestant Ethic and the Spirit of Capitalism* (1905; repr. London: Allen and Unwin, 1956).

73. Rogers Brubaker, *The Limits of Rationality: An Essay on the Social and Moral Thought of*

Indeed, by denying the possibility of a unifying metaphysical foundation of reality, modern rationalization has rejected the logic of gift. The capitalist economy and the state are fragmented into autonomous cultural spheres,[74] including political, legal, aesthetic, economic, cultural, and scientific spheres, all of which tend to claim universal validity.[75] Yet, they are incapable of giving a unifying theoretical and practical meaning to action and are continually in an irresolvable conflict with each other because of their individual claims to being a comprehensive interpretation of reality and criteria for action. Each sphere's awareness and assertion of its own rules and laws induces it to advance without much interaction with other spheres, producing a fragmented and sometimes antagonistic structure of the world, eventually giving rise to the temptation of one sector imposing its own logic on the others. In modern capitalism, we are witnessing such a process, in which the logic of economic efficiency gradually overrides and transforms all other subsystems of society.[76]

In the Weberian analysis values are subjective, plural, and equally valid, which keeps them in constant conflict. As a result of this struggle, a break between the public and the private occurs, leaving the substantive sphere of conviction of what constitutes a good life to individual conscience. In addition to its reductive character, modern rationality is thus characterized by a split between reason and conscience as a result of the failure to reach an agreement on issues related to substantive rationality dealing with normative, axiological, and evalu-

Max Weber (London: Routledge, 2006), 41. This tension between formal rationality—instrumental, elective—and material rationality—substantive and normative—is manifested in action as a double ethic: responsibility versus conviction, according to how the result or the action's intrinsic value is favored, resulting from the loss of overall meaning of reality and the ability to offer a unifying meaning to life and action.

74. Spheres of value, although they change with emerging new forms of social life, have an objective existence and are not metaphysical or empirical, but theoretical: they are ideal types of orders of potentially conflicting life. Each sphere of value has its own norms, and there is no sphere that can arbitrate conflicts between them; rather, the individual himself must choose.

75. Brubaker, *Limits*, 71–73, 82.

76. Weber, *Protestant Ethic*. See also Germán Scalzo, "La racionalidad en Max Weber," *Cuadernos Empresa y Humanismo* 118 (Pamplona: Servicio de Publicaciones UNAV, 2012).

ative aspects.[77] Therefore, aware of a profound polytheism of values, through choosing his postulates of value, man *chooses* the meaning of his action and being rather than receiving it as a gift. Human action is the expression of individuals' intentional subjectivity—that is, the meaning of action is subjective and is given by the ends chosen by each individual as means of self-expression and self-assertion according to postulated value (the gift is restricted to the field of private relationships).[78]

Ultimately, approaching human rationality from the solipsistic individual is a kind of reductionism that should be overcome because "man does not exist just like that, but rather he coexists with others and with nature and this coexistence is his very existence. To be a human being means to coexist."[79] Understanding the notion of person is to accept that the human person is equally individual and relationship. He is "essentially individual and essentially relationship. As an individual, man is an absolute, master of himself and therefore free; as a relationship, man is a social being and can only live in community with others and again only then is he free."[80]

77. Weber, *Economy and Society: An Outline of Interpretative Sociology* (1922; repr. Berkeley: University of California Press, 1978).

78. See André Orléan, "Pour une aproche girardienne de l'*homo oeconomicus*" [A Girardian Approach to *Homo Oeconomicus*], *Cahiers de L'Herne* 89 (2008): 261–65, and Llano, *Deseo, violencia, sacrificio*. Girard analyzes this dual structure present in romantic literature, whose individualism Orléan equates with the neoclassical economic model of society. Without mediators, the relationship appears to be profoundly unstable. Antonio Moreno helped me reach this conclusion.

79. Ricardo Yepes Stork, *Fundamentos de antropología: Un ideal de la excelencia humana* [Foundations of Anthropology: An Ideal of Human Excellence] (Pamplona: Eunsa, 1977), 241. For Polo, anthropology is not reduced to metaphysics. Transcendental anthropology is the doctrine of man's being as coexistence. Man is not limited to being (as metaphysics proposed), but rather he is coexistence (co-being or being-with). The Greeks did not see man in his strictest peculiarity. Christianity discovered the idea of the person: man is a personal being. While it is a theological issue, the human being as a person can be seen as a philosophical issue as well. See Polo, *Antropología Trascendental*, and Polo, *Quién es el hombre: Un espíritu en el tiempo* [Who Is Man: A Spirit in Time] (Madrid: Rialp, 2003).

80. Rafael Alvira, "Intento de clasificar la pluralidad de subsistemas sociales, con especial atención al Derecho" [Attempt to Classify the Plurality of Social Subsystems, with Special Attention to Law], *Persona y Derecho* 33 (1995): 41.

CONCLUDING REMARKS: RETURNING TO THE GIFT

Talking of a return to gift is a contradiction because, beyond the fact that modern science and philosophy have veered off course, gift has always been present in human life and society, and it cannot be otherwise.

The spirit of gift has been hidden, but by no means absent from the economy since, were that so, society would have collapsed by now. It is hidden within the law, in the way in which family and friends distribute goods, as well as in business and labor relations. It is logical that it is not directly visible in the market since, by its very nature, the market is more geared toward contract and exchange, which is based on equivalence. But we must not forget that the law itself is a mutual gift, which is why gratuity cannot arise from law and cannot be imposed through law. The gift, recognition, respect, and admiration for the other constitute the foundation that underpins contract and exchange.[81]

However, academic interest in the logic of gift markedly increased after the publication in 2009 of *Caritas in veritate*, an encyclical whose wealth overflows any attempt to summarize it and that is presented as a continuation of Paul VI's *Populorum progressio* and John Paul II's *Solicitudo rei socialis*.[82] Against the progressive reductionism that modern rationality has undergone, Benedict XVI argues that "the 'broadening [of] our concept of reason and its application' is indispensable if we are to succeed in adequately weighing all the elements involved in the question of development and in the solution of socio-economic problems."[83] While he certainly clarifies that he does not intend to provide clear technical solutions or to get tied up in politics, he offers

81. Miguel Alfonso Martínez Echevarría, "Don y Desarrollo: Bases de la economía" [Gift and Development: Foundations of the Economy], *Scripta Theologica* 42, no. 1 (2010): 135–36; my translation.

82. See Rafael Rubio de Urquía and Juan José Pérez-Soba, eds., *La doctrina social de la Iglesia: Estudios a la luz de la encíclica "Caritas in veritate"* [The Social Doctrine of the Church: Studies in Light of the Encyclical "*Caritas in veritate*"] (Madrid: AEDOS-BAC, 2014); Benedict XVI, *Caritas in veritate*, nos. 8, 10–20.

83. Benedict XVI, *Caritas in veritate*, no. 31, quoting Benedict XVI, *Address at the University of Regensburg*, September 12, 2006.

some guidelines for social life that come from "*fidelity to the truth*, which alone is the *guarantee of freedom* (see Jn 8:32) and of *the possibility of integral human development*" under the premise that "both the market and politics need individuals who are open to reciprocal gift."[84]

Indeed, gift is the encyclical's main theme:

> *Charity in truth* places man before the astonishing experience of gift. Gratuitousness is present in our lives in many different forms, which often go unrecognized because of a purely consumerist and utilitarian view of life. The human being is made for gift, which expresses and makes present his transcendent dimension.[85]

From this perspective, "man's essence is found in having been invited to participate in the fullness of charity in truth."[86]

As we see in Weber and in modern thought in general, while the logic of gift and the contract are presented as two opposing fields, in *Caritas in veritate* the logic of gift is pervasive. From there it follows that contract logic is subordinate to gift logic:

> Ultimately, the gift must be understood as the principal reality that encompasses all others, however relevant they might be. The best explanation of the relationship between the individual and society is the doctrine of gift because it encompasses all other elements in the relational system that are embedded in and are explained through the bundle of relationships that arise with gifts.[87]

Contrary to typically modern political thought, "the *earthly city* is promoted not merely by relationships of rights and duties, but to an even greater and more fundamental extent by relationships of gratuitousness, mercy and communion."[88]

84. Benedict XVI, *Caritas in veritate*, nos. 9, 39.

85. Ibid., 34. See Carlos Sánchez de la Cruz, *Don y gratuidad en el pensamiento de Joseph Ratzinger: Claves para la teología moral* [Gift and Gratuitousness in the Thought of Joseph Ratzinger: Keys for Moral Theology] (Madrid: Perpetuo socorro, 2012).

86. Martínez Echevarría, "Don y desarrollo," 128, my translation.

87. González, *Persona, libertad, don*, 16–17, my translation.

88. Benedict XVI, *Caritas in veritate*, no. 6.

The encyclical takes up a long tradition of philosophical and theological thought that reminds us of a truth that has been forgotten: "Because it is a gift received by everyone, charity in truth is a force that builds community, it brings all people together without imposing barriers or limits."[89] Far from being a definitive answer, this proposal is an invitation to rethink the profound meaning of human action and its impact on different social realities that demand an urgent renewal of science in charity and truth, taking into account that

> the economic sphere is neither ethically neutral, nor inherently inhuman and opposed to society. It is part and parcel of human activity and precisely because it is human, it must be structured and governed in an ethical manner.... In *commercial relationships* the *principle of gratuitousness* and the logic of gift as an expression of fraternity can and must *find their place within normal economic activity*. This is a human demand at the present time, but it is also demanded by economic logic. It is a demand both of charity and of truth.[90]

From these statements, two basic proposals can be derived: economics is an ethical discipline, and there is a need for an "expansion of rationality." It is time to assert without reservation that man cannot be explained by himself, but by love; that is to say, that true humanism can only be founded on Christ:

> Without God man neither knows which way to go, nor even understands who he is.... Paul VI recalled in *Populorum progressio* that man cannot bring about his own progress unaided, because by himself he cannot establish an authentic humanism. Only if we are aware of our calling, as individuals and as a community, to be part of God's family as his sons and daughters, will we be able to generate a new vision and muster new energy in the service of a truly integral humanism. The greatest service to development, then, is a Christian humanism that enkindles charity and takes its lead from truth, accepting both as a lasting gift from God.[91]

89. Ibid., no. 34.
90. Ibid., no. 36.
91. Ibid., no. 78, referencing Paul VI, Encyclical Letter *Populorum progressio* (March 26, 1967), no. 42.

BIBLIOGRAPHY

Aquinas, Thomas. *Summa theologiae*. Cambridge: Cambridge University Press, 2006.

Alvira, Rafael. "Intento de clasificar la pluralidad de subsistemas sociales, con especial atención al Derecho" [Attempt to Classify the Plurality of Social Subsystems, with Special Attention to Law]. *Persona y Derecho* 33 (1995): 41–51.

———. "Tener y existir, reflexión y donación" [Having and Existing, Reflection and Donation]. *Anuario Filosófico* 36, no. 3 (2003): 575–85.

Aristotle. *The Complete Works of Aristotle: The Revised Oxford Translation*. Edited by Jonathan Barnes. Princeton, N.J.: Princeton University Press, 1984.

Benedict XVI. Encyclical Letter *Caritas in veritate*. June 29, 2009.

Berthoud, Arnaud. *Essais de Philosophie Économique: Platon, Aristote, Hobbes, A. Smith, Marx* [Essays on Economic Philosophy: Plato, Aristotle, Hobbes, A. Smith, Marx]. Arras-Lille: Presses Universitaires du Septentrion, 2002.

Brubaker, Rogers. *The Limits of Rationality: An Essay on the Social and Moral Thought of Max Weber*. London: Routledge, 2006.

Bruni, Luigino. *Il prezzo della gratuità* [The Price of Gratuitousness]. Rome: Città Nuova, 2006.

———. *Reciprocity, Altruism and Civil Society*. London: Routledge, 2008.

Bruni, Luigino, and Robert Sudgen. "Fraternity: Why the Market Need Not Be a Morality Free Zone." *Economics and Philosophy* 24, no. 1 (2008): 36–64.

Bruni, Luigino, and Stefano Zamagni. *Civil Economy: Efficiency, Equity and Public Happiness.* Frankfurt: Peter Lang, 2007. Originally published in 2004.

Caillé, Alain. *Anthropologie du don: Le tiers paradigme* [Anthropology of Gift: The Third Paradigm]. París: Desclée de Brouwer, 2000.

Crespo, Mariano. *El perdón: Una investigación filosófica* [Forgiveness: A Philosophical Investigation]. Madrid: Encuentro, 2004.

Crespo, Ricardo. "'The Economic' according to Aristotle: Ethical, Political and Epistemological Implications." *Foundations of Science* 13, no. 3 (2008): 281–94.

De Muralt, André. *La estructura de la filosofía política moderna* [The Structure of Modern Political Philosophy]. Madrid: Istmo, 2002.

———. *La apuesta de la filosofía medieval: Estudios tomistas, escotistas, ockhamistas y gregorianos* [The Wager of Medieval Philosophy: Thomist, Scotist, Ockhamist, and Gregorian Studies]. Madrid: Marcial Pons, 2008.

Falgueras, Ignacio. "El dar, actividad plena de la libertad transcendental" [Giving, Full Activity of Transcendental Freedom]. *Studia Poliana* 15 (2013): 69–108.

Finley, Moses. "Aristotle and Economic Analysis." *Past and Present* 47 (1970): 3–25.

Gillespie, Michael. *The Theological Origins of Modernity*. Chicago: University of Chicago Press, 2008.

Gilson, Étienne. *Juan Duns Escoto: Introducción a sus posiciones fundamentales* [John Duns Scotus: Introduction to His Fundamental Positions]. Pamplona: Eunsa, 2007. Originally published in 1952.

———. *Christian Philosophy: An Introduction*. Translated by Armand Augustine Maurer. Toronto: Pontifical Institute of Mediaeval Studies, 1993. Originally published in 1960.

Girard, René. *Violence and the Sacred*. Baltimore: John Hopkins University Press, 1977.

Godbout, Jacques. *Le don, le dette, l 'identité: Homo donator versus homo economicus* [Gift, Debt, Identity: Homo donator versus homo economicus]. París: La Découverte, 2000.

Godbout, Jacques, and Alain Caillé. *L'esprit du don* [The Spirit of Gift]. París: La Dècouverte, 1992.

Godelier, Maurice. *The Enigma of the Gift*. Chicago: University of Chicago Press, 1999.

González, Ángel Luis. "Thomistic Metaphysics: Contemporary Interpretations." *Anuario Filosófico* 39, no. 2 (2006): 401–37.

———. *Persona, libertad, don* [Person, Freedom, Gift]. Inaugural lecture of the 2013–14 academic year. Universidad de Navarra, Pamplona. September 6, 2013.

Haya, Fernando. *El ser personal: De Tomás de Aquino a la metafísica del don* [The Personal Being: From Thomas Aquinas to the Metaphysics of Gift]. Pamplona: Eunsa, 1997.

Hénaff, Marcel. "Religious Ethics, Gift Exchange and Capitalism." *European Journal of Sociology* 44, no. 3 (2003): 293–324.

———. *The Price of Truth: Gift, Money and Philosophy*. Stanford, Calif.: Stanford University Press, 2010.

Hyde, Lewis. *The Gift: Creativity and the Artist in the Modern World*. New York: Random House, 2007.

John XXIII. Encyclical Letter *Pacem in terris*. April 11, 1963.

Langholm, Odd. *Wealth and Money in the Aristotelian Tradition*. Bergen: Universitetsforlaget, 1983.

Llano, Alejandro. *Deseo, violencia, sacrificio: El secreto del mito según René Girard* [Desire, Violence, Sacrifice: The Secret of the Myth according to René Girard]. Pamplona: Eunsa, 2004.

Martínez Echevarría, Miguel Alfonso. *Evolución del Pensamiento Económico* [Evolution of Economic Thought]. Madrid: Espasa Calpe, 1983.

———. "Don y desarrollo, bases de la economía" [Gift and Development, Foundations of the Economy]. *Scripta Theologica* 42, no. 1 (2010): 121–38.

Mauss, Marcel. *The Gift: Forms and Functions of Exchange in Archaic Societies*. London: Cohen and West, 1966. Originally published in 1925.

Meikle, Scott. "Aristotle and the Political Economy of the Polis." *Journal of Hellenic Studies* 99 (1979): 57–73.

———. *Aristotle's Economic Thought*. Oxford: Oxford University Press, 1995.

Millet, Paul. *Lending and Borrowing in Ancient Athens*. Cambridge: Cambridge University Press, 1991.

Moreno Almárcegui, Antonio. "Ensayo sobre el don." [Essay on Gift]. *Actas del Seminario del grupo de investigación en Economía Política y Filosofía*. Pamplona: Universidad de Navarra, 2010.

———. "Consanguinidad y gracia: El culto a María y José en Occidente; Siglos I–XX. El caso de España" [Kinship and Grace: Devotion to Mary and Joseph in the West; 1st–20th centuries: The Case of Spain]. In *Actas del Seminario del grupo de investigación en Economía Política y Filosofía*. Pamplona: Universidad de Navarra, 2015.

Orléan, André. "Pour une aproche girardienne de l'*homo oeconomicus*" [A Girardian Approach to the *Homo Oeconomicus*]. *Cahiers de L'Herne* 89 (2008): 261–65.

Paul VI. Encyclical Letter *Populorum progressio*. March 26, 1967.

Polo, Leonardo. *Presente y futuro del hombre* [Present and Future of Man]. Madrid: Rialp, 1993.

———. "Tener y dar" [Having and Giving]. In *Sobre la existencia Cristiana*, 103–36. Pamplona: Eunsa, 1996.

———. *Ética: Hacia una versión moderna de los temas clásicos* [Ethics: A Modern Version of Its Classic Themes]. Madrid: Aedos, 1997.

———. *Antropología Trascendental*. Vol. 1, *La persona humana* [Transcendental Anthropology. Vol. 1, The Human Person]. Pamplona: Eunsa, 1999.

———. *Nominalismo, idealismo y realismo* [Nominalism, Idealism, and Realism]. Pamplona: Eunsa, 2001.

———. *Quién es el hombre: Un espíritu en el tiempo* [Who Is Man: A Spirit in Time]. Madrid: Rialp, 2003.

———. "Lo radical y la libertad" [The Radical and Freedom]. *Cuadernos de Anuario Filosófico*, no. 179. Pamplona, 2005.

Rieff, Philip. *Charisma: The Gift of Grace and How It Has Been Taken Away from Us*. New York: Pantheon, 2007.

Ritchie, David. "Aristotle's Subdivisions of Particular Justice." *Classical Review* 8, no. 5 (1984): 185–92.

Rubio de Urquía, Rafael, and Juan José Pérez-Soba, eds. *La doctrina social de la Iglesia: Estudios a la luz de la encíclica "Caritas in veritate"* [The Social Doctrine of the Church: Studies in Light of the Encyclical "*Caritas in veritate*"]. Madrid: AEDOS-BAC, 2014.

Sánchez de la Cruz, Carlos. *Don y gratuidad en el pensamiento de Joseph Ratzinger:*

Claves para la teología moral [Gift and Gratuitousness in the Thought of Joseph Ratzinger: Keys for Moral Theology]. Madrid: Perpetuo socorro, 2012.

Scalzo, Germán. "Génesis del concepto de interés propio" [Genesis of the Concept of Self-Interest]. *Cuadernos Empresa y Humanismo* 108. Pamplona: Servicio de Publicaciones UNAV, 2008.

———. "La racionalidad en Max Weber." [Max Weber on Rationality] *Cuadernos Empresa y Humanismo* 118. Pamplona: Servicio de Publicaciones UNAV, 2012.

———. "Génesis del pensamiento económico: Dos visiones en pugna" [Genesis of Economic Thought: Two Conflicting Visions]. *Cauriensia* 9 (2014): 341–74.

———. "A Genealogy of the Gift." In *Ethical Economy*, edited by Alexander Brink and Jacob Dahl Rendtorff, vol. 51, *Perspectives on Philosophy of Management and Business Ethics*, edited by Jacob Dahl Rendtorff, 31–45. Basel, Switzerland: Springer Nature, 2016.

Sellés, Juan Fernando. *Antropología para inconformes: Una antropología abierta al futuro* [Anthropology for Nonconformists: An Anthropology Open to the Future]. Madrid: Rialp, 2007.

Soudek, Josef. "Aristotle's Theory of Exchange: An Inquiry into the Origin of Economic Analysis." *Proceedings of the American Philosophical Society* 96, no. 1 (1952): 45–75.

Weber, Max. *The Protestant Ethic and the Spirit of Capitalism*. London: Allen and Unwin, 1956. Originally published in 1905.

———. *Economy and Society: An Outline of Interpretative Sociology*. Berkeley: University of California Press, 1978. Originally published in 1922.

Yepes Stork, Ricardo. *Fundamentos de antropología: Un ideal de la excelencia humana* [Foundations of Anthropology: An Ideal of Human Excellence]. Pamplona: Eunsa, 1977.

Zamagni, Stefano. "Reciprocity, Civil Economy, Common Good." In *Pursuing the Common Good*, edited by Margaret S. Archer and Pierpaolo Donati, 467–502. Vatican City: Pontifical Academy of Social Sciences, 2008.

Zamagni, Stefano, and Luigino Bruni. *Handbook on the Economics of Reciprocity and Social Enterprise*. Cheltenham, UK: Edward Elgar, 2013.

8

HOW TO IMPLEMENT THE LOGIC OF GIFT IN THE MANAGERIAL DECISION-MAKING PROCESS

JUAN LUIS MARTÍNEZ, JOSÉ MARÍA ORTIZ, AND MARTIN SCHLAG

Before becoming Pope Benedict XVI, Joseph Ratzinger said that the human person is a being for whom only excess is enough: when a man or woman gives him- or herself sincerely, he or she does so in excess and, thus, all types of giving imply an excess.[1] This argument should not be merely applied to social relations that do not serve economic purposes (friendships, familiar bonds), but also to those relationships that seek to achieve an objective that can be measured in economic terms. This is not an added feature, but an intrinsic attribute of every action. Knowing how to discover the implicit human character in any relationship between people is part of the secret that needs to be disclosed in order to overcome the fragmented access to reality that some forms of contemporary management impose on practitioners.

In his encyclical *Caritas in veritate*, Benedict XVI analyzed the "new economy" and established the bases to understand its challenges. This economy, says the pope emeritus, should integrate the exchange of value, wealth distribution, and reciprocity in order to avoid the mistakes of the past.

In this chapter we build on the work of other authors and specify that law, contract, and gift are the essential elements—taken individ-

1. Joseph Ratzinger, *Introduction to Christianity* (San Francisco: Ignatius Press, 2004), 257–62.

ually as well as in combination—that allow us to review the current economic model.[2] *Caritas in veritate*, nos. 36–38, brings the central aspect of this diagnosis to our attention:

> The great challenge before us, accentuated by the problems of development in this global era and made even more urgent by the economic and financial crisis, is to demonstrate, in thinking and behavior, not only that traditional principles of social ethics like transparency, honesty and responsibility cannot be ignored or attenuated, but also that in *commercial relationships* the *principle of gratuitousness* and the logic of gift as an expression of fraternity can and must *find their place within normal economic activity*.... *Economic life* undoubtedly requires *contracts*, in order to regulate relations of exchange between goods of equivalent value. But it also needs *just laws* and *forms of redistribution* governed by politics, and what is more, it needs works redolent of the *spirit of gift*.... Charity in truth, in this case, requires that shape and structure be given to those types of economic initiative which, without rejecting profit, aim at a higher goal than the mere logic of the exchange of equivalents, of profit as an end in itself.[3]

Here we find the key notions of what the pope emeritus has called a *civilization of the economy*,[4] which in its turn requires a civilization that integrates the whole range of noble human motivations in an economy influenced by the gift from within, without ignoring the advantages of maintaining a constant, open dialogue with the external dimensions that have helped explain its development. This kind of economy calls for a new, more inclusive, and humane management.

Management decisions are made by people and affect people, both directly and indirectly, whether as employees, shareholders, customers, suppliers, or mere passive citizens. These effects on others take place independently of the fact that the manager is fully aware of them or understands them. It is worth recalling that management decisions,

2. Antonio Argandoña, "The 'Logic of Gift' in the Business Entreprise," in *Human Development in Business: Values and Humanistic Management in the Encyclical "Caritas in Veritate,"* ed. Domènec Melé and Claus Dierksmeier (New York: Palgrave-Macmillan, 2012), 198–216.

3. Benedict XVI, Encyclical Letter *Caritas in veritate* (June 29, 2009), nos. 36–38.

4. See ibid., no. 38.

even though they refer to objects, also always have a nontransitory effect on the acting subject. We transform ourselves through our actions. Zagmani has put it in these words: "The object of the transaction cannot be separated from those who carry it out."[5] Their effect on our being is more or less deep, smaller or larger, depending on the intensity and depth of the action taken or being suffered. In our decisions, our being appears in its fullness. When we act we do not do so partially, but fully; our whole being is mobilized: even though the reason behind an individual action might be determined by one dominant force—for example, earning money—there remain collateral motivations that are always effectively present, though in a subordinate way. Denying or ignoring them, silencing or relativizing them will not make them disappear. Being aware of their existence and presence in their own right allows us to make better decisions. Understanding the complexity of the person allows us to make decisions based on this complexity and thus to broaden and refine the decision by enlarging its scope of motivations. Therefore, in our view, management is not a matter of optimization, but of plenitude.

Our goal in this chapter is to justify the need to integrate the logic of gift into the decision-making process to make management decisions more complete. This approach will require us to address the differences between possession and hoarding as well as the need to elaborate on the role of trust as a key element in entrepreneurial management.

The encyclical *Caritas in veritate* has elicited a proliferation of essays on reciprocity and gift, among which we identify some as seminal for the development of the new management vision we wish to propose. Such is the case of the books edited by Adrian Pabst, Macieij Zieba, and Daniel Finn,[6] as well as the special issues in the *Journal*

5. Stefano Zamagni, *Por una economía del bien común* [The Economy of the Common Good] (Madrid: Ciudad Nueva, 2013), 17, our translation.

6. Adrian Pabst, ed., *The Crisis of Global Capitalism: Pope Benedict XVI's Social Encyclical and the Future of Political Economy* (Eugene: Cascade, 2011); Maciej Zieba, *Papal Economics: The Catholic Church on Democratic Capitalism, from "Rerum Novarum" to "Caritas in Veritate"* (Wilmington: ISI,

of Business Ethics, *Communio*, and the various essays on *Caritas in veritate* published since 2010 in the *Journal of Markets and Morality*.[7]

As Chester Barnard stated in his book *The Functions of the Executive*,[8] management will not be conveniently run without a prior correct understanding of the human person. It is the only way to remain coherent, to avoid falling into a trap that breaks the link between what is thought and what is done. The need for an anthropological vision to rigorously and comprehensively study the gift approach calls for phenomenological personalism. Rationalist purism imposed by the prevailing positivist logic in academic journals regarding management has produced subjective and prudential contributions, which are relevant and valid only due to the fact that—and insofar as—they share a sound anthropological conception, which is not made explicit or acknowledged. Sometimes the desire to discover new forms of good business leadership and to show how to improve corporate governance and its results has had to break free from the grip imposed by a rigid positivist approach in academia and has had to "think outside the box"—a phrase used to refer to the creative capacity that goes beyond the established limits, discovering a blue ocean, finding new ways of growth, and identifying new business or innovation opportunities. It has had to break out from the mainstream academic discourse with its monopoly of promoting ideas, raising them to the status of official doctrines. We hold that there are sound epistemological and methodological bases upon which voice and vote in academic fora can and should be granted to the phenomenology of personal decision-making in institutions.

In order to find a management model that supports our vision, it could be helpful to reread the anthropological model of business

2013); Daniel K. Finn, ed., *The Moral Dynamics of Economic Life: An Extension and Critique of "Caritas in Veritate"* (New York: Oxford University Press, 2012).

7. The *Journal of Business Ethics* published a special supplement issue entitled *The Encyclical-Letter 'Caritas in Veritate': Ethical Challenges for Business*, (100, no. 1 Supplement [March 2011]). *Communio: International Catholic Review* published an issue entitled, *A Symposium on Caritas in Veritate* (37, no. 4 [Winter 2010]).

8. Chester Barnard, *The Functions of the Executive* (Cambridge, Mass.: Harvard University Press, 1968).

management proposed by Juan Antonio Pérez López, particularly in his book *Teoría de la Acción Humana en las Organizaciones* [Theory on Human Actions in Organizations].[9] Unfortunately this book has not yet been translated into English—a worthwhile undertaking as it combines a body of teaching compatible with the proposals of *Caritas in veritate* with a proven and consistent vision of management.[10] This vision refers not only to the human person, but also to value, profit, and justice. These perceptions are rooted in the theories of the School of Salamanca of the sixteenth century. Its theories on the common good, the justification of profit, and its vision of the principles that should govern exchange relations are solid sources for reflection on the application of the logic of gift. In our view, the debate on the enlarged view of management could be rendered fruitful by rereading authors such as Tomás de Mercado, Martín de Azpilcueta, Francisco de Vitoria, Francisco Suárez, and Juan de Mariana.

Our purpose with this essay is to clearly show, figuratively speaking, the tree on which our ideas grow. Its trunk is the social teaching of the church; the roots are ethical personalism with a phenomenological basis, as well as the proposals and conclusions of the School of Salamanca; and the branches are the management models based on the anthropology of entrepreneurial action. More than offering a comprehensive summary of the references behind our work, we wish to help the reader identify our sources of inspiration.

GIFT AND ITS ROLE IN THE DECISION-MAKING PROCESS

We begin our reflection on the logic of gift within the business decision-making process with a case. Juan González was a Honduran micro-entrepreneur and part of the Lenca community, which borders El Sal-

9. Juan Antonio Pérez López, *Teoría de la Acción Humana en las Organizaciones: La acción personal* [Theory of Human Action in Organizations: Personal Action] (Madrid: Rialp, 1991).

10. See ibid., 6–8.

vador, and produced pineapple wine, something more similar to vinegar than wine itself, a result of the fermentation of pineapples. This natural product can be perfectly used as a dressing and is rarely found in Western gourmet shops. He thought that it could be a fine product for more sophisticated markets and started packaging it and carrying out marketing efforts, initially through a series of informal networks and now also through the formal system.

Almost by chance, we had the opportunity to meet him at the early stage of his ambitious activity. He had countless questions, ranging from packaging to labeling issues, but it was when the conversation shifted to prices that we were left dumbstruck. We realized that those in highly institutionalized—and thus impersonalized—markets have a numb ability to perceive the value behind the assets in question. We gave him some advice regarding the generation of potential revenue. We saw his eyes filling up and thought he was moved by the joy of being able to increase his profits beyond what he had expected, applying in a rather disrespectful way the self-interest logic that completely prevails in our decision-making models. But to our surprise, spontaneously, without asking for an explanation, he told us, “I know what it takes to earn a dollar, the effort needed to bring some money home, and knowing that someone may be willing to spend that money you are talking about to purchase the product that I have made with my own hands and my work, well, it honors me.... I would never have thought that someone I don’t know and who I will never meet could value my activity so much, could value me so much.” With no time to formulate a politically correct answer, what Juan valued from the market was its inherent capacity to recognize the human value behind every transaction.

That story made us think that perhaps when we talk about applying the logic of gift, it is not a matter of doing different things, nor even more things, but doing them from a new perspective, an expanded approach: one that involves giving and giving ourselves, providing opportunities to others to go beyond the borders of the mere exchange of goods, beyond symbolism and reaching the true sources of reciprocity.

All types of giving are an excess. If we give what is fair, in positive-normative terms, what we do is an exchange. But when we give ourselves, we deliver more than what the other expects, more than what the other part strictly deserves in justice. It is not a commutative relation between equals, but a donation. This is what our micro-entrepreneur grasped, moving beyond the face-value perception.

Attention should be paid to the "surface phenomena," to use an expression from physics, to what simultaneously unites and separates the different features of knowledge. Otherwise, the panoramic view that allows us to detect totalities in a sound manner is lost. And this, applied to management, could pose a significant problem. The integration of perspectives and knowledge, linking them to the storyline of the individual, is mandatory in order to have increased possibilities of identifying opportunities for value creation. These cannot be detected within the complexity of a kaleidoscope; instead, they should be analyzed through synthesis, only achievable through people thanks to their particular way of being and being part of the world.

Optimization implies the maximization of a good that is standardizable and valid for a great number of people because, on average, it benefits everybody. Although there are statistical deviations due to individual preferences, a good that shares the same nature and is expressible in a quantitative manner could qualify as a measure. Profit maximization could be such a good, as it is the economic objective everyone seeks. We strive for it by reducing costs and increasing income. We can define aggregate functions of supply and demand that, because they are aggregates, cannot distinguish among individuals, even though they seek to meet the same objectives. Such a formal system establishes the differences regarding the preferences between individuals according to their various capacities, measured in terms of resources or means of production or consumption, but always has an inertia of its own that it must obey: maximization. There seems to be an inner constraint that cannot be overcome, which always prevails, which inexorably forces us to pursue the maximization of profit. This model makes us talk about the logic of interest, the need to be efficient and effective, the need to optimize. In this perspective, profit maximization appears as the only rational thing; it is what can be empirically and mathematically measured in an objective manner: everything beyond those borders is considered subjective—it is not part of positivist logic—or belongs to the realm of romantic emotionalism. Scientific objectivism is overpowering; it discards any other approach and constantly smothers other sources of rationality.

Human persons, however, seek the plenitude of organic and harmonious growth in all its dimensions. Men and women are beings that exist here and now and have a history and a project toward their aims. They are neither an artifact nor an event. They are not a what, but a who. To the extent that the "I" is not an essence, it cannot be defined but narrated, and narrating is giving sense to what is heterogeneous, conferring unity to what, otherwise, would be dispersed. Human acts cannot be judged or their motivations analyzed from the aseptic approach of what is valid only for the species. They need to be considered also in their specificity, which allows persons to see themselves and become unique. The optimal is "for everyone"; plenitude is "for me." Thus, there is an essential and intrinsic connection between the apparent dichotomies of gift and interest, optimization and plenitude, hoarding and possession, exchange and reciprocity. The link that connects all these notions is the way the human person—in our case, the manager—makes decisions.

Juan's reaction manifests a fact: there is something beyond the capacity of the models of aggregate analysis, and it is this something that really moves him in his business, not only in purely emotional terms but also in rational terms. This something is the feature he identifies as a characteristic of the other party (the recognition of his work), which in turn helps Juan to give himself—to dignify himself—with solidarity through the sale of pineapple vinegar at an accessible price. He does not deny his interest in doing business, but that interest is seen in an expanded, nonfragmented way. No extrinsic reasons are added to his business decision, nor is it subordinated to variables of a noneconomic nature that would complicate his decisions by combining incompatible realities. He merely breaks all the elements of his value system down into one reasonable act. The obsession for optimization obstructs the humanity of business people; it reduces them to a single dimension. It is not as if profit were not a legitimate objective; business motivation simply needs to be enlarged. And this enlargement can only be achieved in a qualitative and not a quantitative way. This enlargement is what we call "plenitude": humanized optimization, maximization from the perspective of practical wisdom.

Contractual relationships require the application of the virtue of justice in its commutative dimension, political relations must be governed by legal and distributive justice, and relationships based on gift require the implementation of *equitas*, the reasonable and humane application of justice. Humane application of justice goes beyond the normative-positive dimension and thus, without denying justice, fulfills it. Equity does not question regulations, it does not add anything to the virtue of justice, but simply takes it to plenitude. The logic of justice is equivalence, that of equity is overabundance; the former is ethical, the latter is supra-ethical.[11] It operates from within, providing texture, volume, and, thus, weight. It is tempered justice. It takes the person into account as a specific person. To understand what a gift is, we must understand reciprocity, and this we can do only through equity, because gift is not a matter of giving what is fair, of receiving what one strictly deserves, but to exceed it, to give more, not in quantity, but in being.

HOARDING VS. POSSESSING

In recent literature on the phenomenon, gift is commonly identified with gratitude. This is the case of James Franklin, Dennis McCann,

11. See Zamagni, *Por una economía*, 13–14.

and Faldetta.[12] However, we consider that gratitude is just one of the ways to materialize the logic of gift, and perhaps the best approach is not to question economic interest, but to broaden it and to give it its true human nature. In this sense, we consider the trail blazed by authors such as Flavio Felice to be more adequate.[13] Even though he does not address the notion of gift directly, Felice establishes a sound conceptual framework to harmonize (not coordinate) both gift and self-interest. Also Wolfgang Grassl and Gene R. Laczniak, Thomas A. Klein, and Patrick E. Murphy, from a more practical approach, recognize the importance of corporate interest and its satisfaction for management, without questioning or refuting the requirements of gift and reciprocity.[14] To explain our approach further we must distinguish between several types of goods within a company and how these can be effectively created. This distinction requires us to address the differences between possessing and hoarding.

There are three types of goods according to their form of possession.[15] In the first place, there are goods that, in order for me to enjoy them, need to be in my immediate power and possession. If I give them away, I lose them. This characteristic is inherent to all material goods.

12. James Franklin, "Caritas in Veritate: Economic Activity as Personal Encounter and the Economy of Gratuitousness," *Solidarity: The Journal of Catholic Social Thought and Secular Ethics* 1, no. 1 (2011): 1–9; Dennis McCann, "The Principle of Gratuitousness: Opportunities and Challenges for Business in 'Caritas in Veritate,'" *Journal of Business Ethics* 100, supplement 1 (2011): 55–66; Guglielmo Faldetta, "The Logic of Gift and Gratuitousness in Business Relationships," *Journal of Business Ethics* 100, supplement 1 (2011): 67–77.

13. See Flavio Felice, "The Ethical Foundation of the Market Economy: A Reflection on the Economic Personalism in the Thought of Luigi Sturzo," *Journal of Markets and Morality* 4, no. 2 (2001): 217–39; and Felice, *Persona, impresa e mercato: L'economia sociale di mercato nella prospettiva teorica del pensiero sociale cattolico* [Person, Business, and Market: The Social Market Economy in the Theoretical Perspective of Catholic Social Thought] (Rome: Lateran University Press, 2010), esp. chapter 2.

14. Wolfgang Grassl, "Hybrid Forms of Business: The Logic of Gift in the Commercial World," *Journal of Business Ethics* 100, supplement 1 (2011): 109–23; Grassl and André Habisch, "Ethics and Economics: Towards a New Humanistic Synthesis for Business," *Journal of Business Ethics* 99, no. 1 (2011): 37–49; Gene R. Laczniak, Thomas A. Klein, and Patrick E. Murphy, "*Caritas in Veritate*: Updating Catholic Social Teaching for Responsible Marketing Strategy," in *Marketing and the Common Good: Essays from Notre Dame on Social Impact,* ed. Patrick E. Murphy and John F. Sherry Jr. (New York: Routledge, 2014), 105–18; Thomas A. Klein and Gene R. Laczniak, "Implications of 'Caritas in Veritate' for Marketing and Business Ethics," *Journal of Business Ethics* 112, no. 4 (2013): 641–51.

15. Higinio Marín identifies these three goods throughout his book *Teoría de la cordura y de los hábitos del corazón* [Theory of Sanity and the Habits of the Heart] (Valencia: Pre-textos, 2010).

Second, there are goods that, in order to possess them, need to be given; it is not necessary for someone else to possess them, but if I want them, I need to give them. In fact, the more I give, the more I obtain. These types of goods are fundamentally of intellectual scope. For example, the acquisition of knowledge: the more we express it exteriorly, for example in written form, the more we receive. Knowledge is not only the result of the clarity of an idea, but emerges in our awareness when we express it in words. It should be noted that it is not necessary for anyone else to receive it; we merely need to express it, although normally knowledge will be acquired in communicative and therefore shared contexts of life. This brings us to the third group of goods: those that we possess in the degree in which we share them. Far from losing possession over them by the fact that others receive them, our share is enhanced. Our own possession of these relational goods is conditioned by their effective possession by others. The more I give, the more I receive. Examples of such spiritual and relational goods are friendship and trust. Friendship is by definition mutual, and trust either is reciprocated or does not last long.

These three types of goods are present in businesses and form important assets. Businesses need to own the means of production in order to decide on their use without undue strain or limitations; they must control their assets in order to organize and combine them with appropriate know-how, but they must also own spiritual goods that align and guide them in their decisions. It is the pursuit of an end that gives meaning to corporate action; it is the aim that mobilizes and brings the assets and capabilities into play—it is what ultimately justifies their possession. To the extent that the corporate aim of business integrates all the dimensions of human action, it is more complete, solid, and coherent. As such it combines will and motivations, fosters commitments, and grants sustained success. The logic of gift within the company does not necessarily mean gratuitousness in the general understanding of the concept as giving away things for free, but benefits that go beyond short-term profit.

None of the three required types of goods for enterprises can be achieved in an exclusive, isolating, and atomizing approach, as they are always means used to achieve a greater human end. The company is always a finalized institution; it is its mission, perspective, and objectives, which give it its own character and justify its implementation and development. A company is not a mere mechanism that coordinates production factors, a tool to create or manufacture products or services, a system to generate profits: it is all that and more. Everything is done for a larger purpose that fits into a social whole, which gives it meaning and governs the decision-making process.

The assets that the company must own in order to be able to work independently and freely, with the ability to justify its operations and in a spirit of responsibility, cannot merely be acquired and retained, but must be open for constant use and service in order to satisfy the purpose for which the company was established. There is a whole process or internal value chain: material goods are made available to the business through investment; intellectual goods consist in management criteria and skills that put the material assets to the service of those values that form the sense and the right direction for the company. The logic of gift in this process is intrinsically linked to the way in which decisions are made, not only because all material goods have to receive external influence in order to be processed (raw material is transformed by human labor that adds value), but also because of what was said earlier about relational goods: the integration of all elements into a single whole that gives it a meaning requires the insertion of a business's activities in the shared existence of society, defined by a common good. The goods of the company are not just *goods-of*, but also *goods-for*, and these two dimensions cannot be torn asunder.

Planning, organizing, leading, and controlling are the four basic tasks of management and thus of managerial decision-making. They call for the combination of science, technology, practical wisdom, and values. Indeed, it takes technical knowledge to know what must be done or what the problem is that needs to be solved. This dimension of knowledge is essential to face nonstructured challenges, where diagnosis is the most important element. Scientific know-how is required to find the technical solution. However, particularly when facing complex multifaceted problems, the therapy becomes more complex, and humanistic knowledge is necessary to discover the deeper human causes of the problems. Very often the problems and tensions in organizations are not of a technical but of a human kind. They can be tackled only on solid anthropological foundations, taking into account human nature, the values that motivate, and the virtues that give joy. This is where values and practical wisdom come in. Without the harmonization of these three points—technical skills, practical wisdom, and values—management will be neither effective nor efficient and will face a severe informational and cultural deficit.

Along this line of reasoning, it is essential to distinguish between possessing and hoarding. This will also help to understand what the logic of gift implies. We identify five points of distinction:

1. Possession, in our use of the word, ascribes goods exclusively to the owner, at the same time tying social responsibility to ownership; hoarding implies an individualistic and exclusionary sense of ownership.

2. Possession is in the *interest of all, and thus for the common good*; hoarding is selfish, it merely strives for *personal interest.*

3. Possession introduces goods into the public sphere; hoarding withdraws assets from circulation and locks them into the private domain.

4. Possession creates wealth for all; hoarding ends up being destructive.

5. Possession opens up new realities and possibilities; hoarding closes them.

Gift has to do with the distinction between exclusivity (possession) and exclusionary practices (hoarding). Exclusivity defines me in my difference; an exclusionary attitude isolates me from others. Each of us possesses exclusive features that all together and in a specific way make up who each of us is. In a certain sense, we do not "share" these qualities with anyone else. Indeed, there are things that make each one of us unique. This fact does not isolate us; it simply defines us. However, the lack of willingness to make our qualities and strengths available to others isolates and impoverishes me as a person. I cannot express my exclusive uniqueness without relational goods (for instance, a common language shared with others) and without communality (in which my uniqueness is recognized as such). We relate to other persons only on the basis of a common nature and culture. Whether it is from an alter-ego point of view (someone like me) or the Orteguian alter-you approach (I am similar to someone else), there is a disposition to remain open to receiving from other people the characteristics that make me exclusive. I am endowed with features that make me recognizable to others, and only through the recognition of others can I recognize myself. Only when I give myself can I understand what makes me unique. Only when I see the qualities and characteristics I have and others do not can I understand what makes me different. The same occurs when I discover things in others that I do not have. A mirror merely shows our reflection, yet from this reflection alone we would not be able to grasp how much of that is singular and what is shared by everyone (and vice versa). The more I share what is common, the better I can express what is unique. For example, the better I master the common language, the more exactly will I be able to voice my individuality. This reflects the open character of possession in contrast to hoarding. In an analogous way, business assets have to be exclusive, but not exclusionary. The owner should be able to use them freely, but in order to make his ownership meaningful and fulfilling they must be possessed, not hoarded in an exclusionary way.

The legitimate desire to possess is subject to strong competitive and egocentric temptations excluding others from benefits, thus degenerating into what we call "hoarding." In contrast, the antagonistic desire to communicate, include, and share with others makes more human sense but exercises a weaker attraction on our senses.

Gifts are given out of free will. A forced donation, imposed by obligation or duty, is not a gift. Force does not help me answer for my actions, and I cannot possess it or its consequences. I am not responsible for it. Thus we also renounce hoarding and exclusion out of free will. Inclusion through the free gift of openness to just relations is the virtuous dynamic behind the logic of gift.

Problems arise when, intentionally or unintentionally, hoarding is confused with possession in the business sphere. This is typically the case of the neoclassical *homo oeconomicus*: he hoards but does not possess. Many problems that make modern businesses suffer, both among their managers and in the relationships the business establishes with other people and institutions, have their origin in this confusion. Authors such as Grassl and Faldetta have pointed out that definitions of business that marginalize or ignore the logic of gift end up excluding the consideration for others and the openness toward the decision-making process.[16] The cliché that a "gift" is a mere lack of self-interest and thus cannot be part of business activity, belonging exclusively to one's private life, needs to be overcome: the logic of gift does not contradict business interest, but appropriately broadens it so as to make right decisions. Let us see how this is applied in a particular case of gift: trust.

TRUST AS A POSSESSION, RECIPROCITY, AND GIFT

Trust is an almost instinctive perception of the fact that the reality we are in is positive for us; a positive evaluation of the situation, an overall assessment that confirms that things are going smoothly. We call it "assessment," since the power we use to study it is merely "estimative," a cognitive-affective sphere in which we carry out an *urgency summary* of the reality around us.[17] We could say that it is the feeling

16. Grassl, "Hybrid Forms of Business," 113–14; Faldetta, "Logic of Gift," 73.

17. José Antonio Marina, *El laberinto sentimental* (Barcelona: Anagrama, 1996), 33, defines this

of security that a good transmits. Its opposite is fear, which alerts us of something harmful.

Mistrust and the fears it entails appear when our view of true goods has been fragmented. If we only hold a part of what our life means in relation to others, of goodness, of truth, if we hold onto that difficult-to-share part, trust gives in to fear. And this is precisely what the current socioeconomic paradigm has led to. If the relations we have with others are focused on what makes us different instead of what unites us, then the fear of others appears; we see them as enemies, which leads to conflicts or voluntary isolation. If having is more important than being, and if we focus on the desire of goods that are hard to share, love is reduced to desire. The fear of losing what we have or jealousy of those who have more are consequences of the cult of money, common in the logic of interest, when this is not influenced by the logic of gift. In the same way the fear of being dominated is consequence of the cult of power. Last, when our opinions, our ideas, and the desire to pretend take precedence over the love for truth, then the desire of pretending is more important than being. Fear, mistrust, suspicions that we could be used, manipulated or deceived, the fear of the truth of being exposed are all outgrowths the cult of image.

Trust is the result of fully possessing goods; *fully*, not a mere fragment that is difficult to share. One of the keys to understanding the socioeconomic paradigm that has marked recent years is to consider how it reduces the main goods to a nonshareable aspect; it simplifies and reduces relations, love, and truth to a dimension of utility, leaving aside what these things represent and focusing on the mere use they have. Trusting, however, implies the ability of sharing goods based on what makes them valuable in themselves (its basis is *honest* goods, rather than *useful* goods).

Being an important quality in all aspects of life, trust is particu-

urgency summary as "a conscious experience that synthesizes the data we have concerning the transactions between my desires, expectations or beliefs, and reality"; our translation.

larly crucial in the decision-making process. Fear paralyzes and leads to errors. In this sense, emphasis should be put on the statement by Domènec Melé in what he defines as the *Level 5 Development: favoring people's human flourishing, mutual esteem, and friendship-based reciprocity*, the top level of quality in his hierarchical pyramid of the "notion of human quality treatment."[18] From this enlarged perspective and enhancement in the treatment of others, the perspective where trust acquires organizational relevance is established. When we trust, the best of the other party is opened up to us as soon as it identifies an enhancement of the treatment within this relation and thus is more predisposed to strengthen the relation, putting an end to the "anthropological halt" that the fear of the unknown generates. When I trust, I do not doubt.

Undoubtedly, there are many occasions when fear is positive, as it puts us on alert to detect unsafe situations or helps us avoid dangers; but its apparition always indicates the presence of a flaw or limitation. We could also ask ourselves whether fear is a "tool" that can help us obtain specific results from third parties on specific occasions. And the answer is yes. As pointed out by Goleman, to instill fear or use a rather coercive management style may result in increased efforts and intensity in the short term.[19] But it has also been shown that trust entails better and more sustainable results. If we take a look at one of the most important sectors of our economic activity, the financial sector, we can see that trust is the key for its proper functioning. It brings savers and borrowers closer together, as they both trust the institution to which they lend money or from which they borrow. Most of our economy has become somewhat financial; since money is mainly information, it is one of the easiest goods to exchange anywhere around the world.[20] However, as highlighted by the study conducted by Hay-

18. Domenec Melé, "'Human Quality Treatment': Five Organizational Levels," *Journal of Business Ethics* 120, no. 4 (2014): 465–66.

19. Daniel Goleman, "Leadership That Gets Results," *Harvard Business Review*, March–April 2000, 78–93.

20. Vittorio Mathieu, *Filosofia del dinero* [Philosophy of Money] (Madrid: Rialp, 1990), 51–74.

Group on the types of leadership exerted by financial institutions, the efficiency ratio is positively correlated to a management style able to propose medium-term objectives, where members feel as if they can contribute—that is, two factors closely related to trust.[21]

WHAT RESULTS DOES TRUST ENTAIL?

Trust is the engine for everything and the key to sustaining the cycle of results that entails innovation, growth, and differentiation. In recent years, we have witnessed an important "rethinking" of what leadership means and the ideal managerial profiles: recommendations increasingly propose general profiles over technical ones; comprehensive leaders rather than analysts; more strategy-related directors instead of tactical ones; managers that act as "architects" and not "construction workers"; diplomats rather than warriors; and people able to set an agenda over troubleshooters. This is the approach explicitly expressed by Watkins, but also close to the work of Zenger and Folkman as regards the inspiring leader.[22] This expression—inspiring—could certainly be seen as a vague and unrealistic proposal, when in fact it mainly promotes the importance of transmitting a compelling future vision, which, according to these authors, is based on organization and planning, honesty and integrity, anticipating problems, seeing desired results clearly, providing effective feedback and development, establishing stretch goals and personal accountability, being quick to act, providing rewards and recognition, creating high-performance teams, marshaling adequate resources, and initiating innovation. The truth is that the global market calls for differentiation, and thus growth and innovation become two main pillars for achieving results (and, simi-

21. HayGroup, "Estilos de Liderazgo y Clima en el Equipo: Perfile de éxito de los directivos in España" [Leadership Styles and the Climate in Europe: Profile of the Success of the Directives in Spain], HayGroup, 2010, http://www.haygroup.com/downloads/es/Estilos_de_Liderazgo_y_Clima_en_el_Equipo.pdf. The reference appears on page 13 of the report.

22. Michael D. Watkins, "How Managers Become Leaders," *Harvard Business Review*, June 2012, 65–72; John H. Zenger, Joseph R. Folkman, and Scott K. Edinger, *The Inspiring Leader: Unlocking the Secrets of How Extraordinary Leaders Motivate* (New York: McGraw-Hill, 2009).

larly, the skills of leaders should include the capability to promote the two aforementioned features). But innovation and growth can only be obtained if they are based on trust.

In order to obtain different results we need to develop different behaviors, but behaviors only change when we look at our circumstances in a different manner. Positive intelligence implies seeing reality in a different way, to perceive what others have not yet realized. That is the most innovative talent. Without it, results might entail incremental improvements—"more of the same but better"—but they are still ultimately "more of the same." Innovation and results are the elements that enable growth. And a globalized world cannot accept behaviors that lack integrity. Without trust, an open, global society will not be possible. Trust is the cornerstone of this cycle formed by results, innovation, and growth. We need it to make the right decisions, since its opposite (mistrust) distorts reality. When Warren Buffet decided to purchase Walmart, McLane Distribution came up with a way to speed up the due diligence to save several months of time (and several million dollars). Instead of hiring an army of lawyers and auditors, both parts stated the following: "We trade in public markets, and therefore are subject to regulatory controls; hence, we have no reason to distrust what the other is saying." After a two-hour meeting and a handshake the operation was completed, and in less than a month the merger had already taken place. As we have previously seen in the field of the psychology of fear, the one that fears is more likely to be wrong.

We trust when we deal with someone reliable, predictable, who keeps his word. We trust because we want to produce and take part in the final result. The favorable or unfavorable nature of the reality is an almost instinctive consequence of how we feel. We know perfectly well whether the context is beneficial or harmful for our interest, and thus trust is an essential element in an increasingly diversified context. In short, without trust innovation cannot be achieved, since no one would propose innovative ideas or would invest in innovation. Without trust, results would never be different, because without trust not all skills are used, and with fear wrong decisions are made. Mistrust greatly hinders growth.

HOW CAN TRUST BE ACHIEVED?

Researchers David Schoorman (Purdue University), Roger Mayer, and James Davis (both from the University of Notre Dame), in a work that still remains the main reference on the subject, proposed that three conditions need to be met in order to achieve trust:[23] first, we trust someone when that person shows that he has the specific skills required for the role (we usually call them "emotional skills"). That is what defines professionalism: we trust people with the required skills, as it makes them predictable. Second, we trust someone when our relationship with that person is governed by integrity: we both have appropriate principles and are willing to preserve the stability of the conditions. We trust people that do what they say and say what they do without changing the rules of the game. Third, we trust people who act in a kind manner (promoting solidarity or generosity)—that is, when they do not merely or exclusively seek personal gain. This attitude leads to the perception that the situation is favorable: I know that I will gain something, I am sure that I will be fine. Therefore, ethics and professionalism are not enough. A trust crisis cannot be avoided with more ethics classes. In order to achieve trust, that third element is required, which we can characterize with notions like benevolence, generosity, solidarity, and other manifestations of human empathy that promote a different logic in and between markets and society.

In order to trust, there is a first situational factor (capabilities). We cannot trust someone merely because he is an honest person or

23. Roger C. Mayer, James H. Davis, and F. David Schoorman, "An Integrative Model of Organizational Trust," *Academy of Management Review* 20, no. 3 (1995): 709–34. As Francis Fukuyama highlights, in addition to the entrepreneurial virtues that apply to individuals (like capacity for hard work, frugality, rationality, innovativeness, and openness to risk), "there is as well a series of social virtues, like honesty, reliability, cooperativeness, and a sense of duty to others, that are essentially social in nature"; see Fukuyama, *Trust: The Social Virtues and the Creation of Prosperity* (New York: Free Press Paperbacks, 1966), 46).

because he wants to help us. If he lacks the required knowledge, skills, or capabilities, if his performance or the results are not satisfactory, he will not achieve our trust. The truth is that skills are not the only factor that generates trust, but neither is integrity sufficient by itself. It is true that a profound crisis is a crisis of values and that an ethical regeneration is required in order to overcome it; however, skills and ethics alone are not enough to recover trust.

The third required element is a perception only achievable when we no longer try to control and calculate everything; the field of what is strictly calculable is insufferable. In addition to professionalism and integrity, trust needs a third element: a minimum level of benevolence, gratitude, a predisposition to favor something or someone without it being strictly due or calculated (according to Stephen Long's comment on Milbank's theory, the economy of exchange is associated with contract and the logic of gift with trust).[24] Trust is the perception we have to find an asset, and thus it is logical for it to be present in all types of goods in which, the more we give, the more we get (for instance, life, not biological life, but life in relation to others, and love and wisdom). Trust consequently leads to giving, considering, and relating better.

As time passes we have an increasing amount of empirical evidence in relation to the need for generosity in economic relations. The study "Top Teams: Why Some Work and Some Do Not," carried out by Hay Group in 2005, showed that in all high-performance teams there is always someone willing to yield (not necessarily the leader of the team), a person who is willing to put the collective interest before his personal interest.[25] More recently, the works by Adam Grant, com-

24. "Christianity opposes capitalism because the gift can never be reduced to a contract with nicely calculated profit/loss ratios where individuals enter into exchanges without being fundamentally changed by those exchanges. The Christian life requires a gift economy in which a return is always expected—as it should be when one gives gifts— but never one that can be calculated such that the contract terminates and the relationship dissolves"; Stephen D. Long and Nancy R. Fox, *Calculated Futures: Theology, Ethics, and Economics* (Waco, Tex.: Baylor University Press, 2007), 177.

25. Hay Group, "Top Teams: Why Some Work and Some Do Not: Five Things the Best CEOs Do to Create Outstanding Executive Teams," Working Paper, Hay Group, 2005, http://www.haygroup.com/Downloads/uk/misc/Top_Teams_Working_Paper_UK.pdf. The reference appears on page 16 of the report.

pleted by Frank Flynn and Robert Cialdini, allow us to see how the productivity of an organization increases when its members engage in exchange and help each other.[26]

An extensive study based on the analysis of over two hundred works, carried out by Sonja Lyubomirsky, Laura King, and Ed Diener, shows how happy employees, on average, have 31 percent higher productivity, their sales are higher (37 percent), and their creativity is three times better.[27] What are the underlying behaviors of "happy" people? It is precisely trust and optimism, features that allow them to face the challenges with originality and flexibility. Also—and this is one of the most striking aspects of the study—happy people have a "pro-social" behavior based primarily on the positive perception they have regarding other people. When we have a positive perception of the people around us, our productivity improves. Trust is the best attribute an organization can have, and in order to preserve it, companies need to always picture the best possible outcome, think highly of others, and always expect everything based on the best-case scenario. Therefore, trust provides teams with a voluntary coordination well above any control mechanism. Personal affinity or sharing the same values allows people within an organization to know that what they expect of others will certainly come true.

The best version of ourselves is possible thanks to the conjunction of capacities and inclinations, challenges and trust, reaching an intrinsic motivation that does not call for external influence. When we discover the gift itself, when we discover the most important part of what we have (which has been given to us), our perspective of others changes, since they are no longer a mere useful good, but are also a good by themselves. All things considered, we all have something

26. Adam Grant, "In the Company of Givers and Takers," *Harvard Business Review*, April 2013, 90–97; Francis J. Flynn, "Francis Flynn: What Makes People Want to Help Others?," *Insights by Stanford Graduate School of Business,* November 21, 2013, https://www.gsb.stanford.edu/insights/francis-flynn-what-makes-people-want-help-others; Robert Cialdini, "The Uses (and Abuses) of Influence," *Harvard Business Review*, July–August 2013, 76–81.

27. Sonja Lyubomirsky, Laura King, and Ed Diener, "The Benefits of Frequent Positive Affect: Does Happiness Lead to Success?" *Psychological Bulletin* 131, no. 6 (2005): 803–55.

unique and unrepeatable, a gift. And it is always better to lay foundations based on strengths rather than weaknesses. Thus, it does not make much sense to anticipate potential problems, since they are just that—potentialities. When the likelihood of a situation being positive or harmful is similar, by picturing the worst-case scenario, not only do we go through a hard time, but also probably distort reality. The right view is the positive view. Being suspicious of people who are generous with their resources or time implies narrow-mindedness. Most of the exchanged goods have a particular nature; in general, the more we give, the less we have. As a relational good, trust does not work this way: the more we give, the more we receive. Trust promotes prosocial behavior; it makes us give the best of ourselves and fosters positive intelligence. The first step to trust is free, and that is the reason it is so important to build trust from the earliest stages of education. The logic of gift requires the dynamic of gift, and this is particularly true for trust.

In this chapter we have reflected on how possession, reciprocity, gift, and trust are essential to the managerial decision-making process. They are all relational goods where the more you give, the more you receive, as long as someone receives that gift. Relation requires reciprocity. And it is a good example of the meaning of building a new culture. If the cycle comprised of diversity, innovation, and results lays its foundations on the trusting relations that compel us give the best of ourselves, it is because we are aware of the need to change what Tocqueville defined as "the habits of the heart," the prevailing paradigms of our culture. If our time of change is leading to a change of time it is because we need to replace distance with closeness, neutrality with commitment, speed with patience, dominance with service, image with coherence, indifference with interest, and utilities with values. The culture created by people who discover and live according to the logic of gift could be called a "culture of encounter," as it is a true encounter when the gifts are exchanged.

BIBLIOGRAPHY

Argandoña, Antonio. "The 'Logic of Gift' in the Business Enterprise." In *Human Development in Business: Values and Humanistic Management in the Encyclical "Caritas in Veritate,"* ed. Domènec Melé and Claus Dierksmeier, 198–216. New York: Palgrave-Macmillan, 2012.

Barnard, Chester. *The Functions of the Executive*. Cambridge, Mass.: Harvard University Press, 1968.

Benedict XVI. Encyclical Letter *Caritas in veritate*. June 29, 2009.

Cialdini, Robert. "The Uses (and Abuses) of Influence," *Harvard Business Review*, July–August 2013, 76–81.

Faldetta, Guglielmo. "The Logic of Gift and Gratuitousness in Business Relationships." *Journal of Business Ethics* 100, supplement 1 (2011): 67–77.

Felice, Flavio. "The Ethical Foundation of the Market Economy: A Reflection on the Economic Personalism in the Thought of Luigi Sturzo." *Journal of Markets and Morality* 4, no. 2 (2001): 217–39.

———. *Persona, impresa e mercato: L'economia sociale di mercato nella prospettiva teorica del pensiero sociale cattolico* [Person, Business, and Market: The Social Market Economy in the Theoretical Perspective of Catholic Social Thought]. Rome: Lateran University Press, 2010.

Finn, Daniel K., ed. *The Moral Dynamics of Economic Life: An Extension and Critique of "Caritas in Veritate."* New York: Oxford University Press, 2012.

Flynn, Francis J. "Francis Flynn: What Makes People Want to Help Others?" *Insights by Stanford Graduate School of Business*. November 21, 2013. https://www.gsb.stanford.edu/insights/francis-flynn-what-makes-people-want-help-others.

Franklin, James. "Caritas in Veritate: Economic Activity as Personal Encounter and the Economy of Gratuitousness." *Solidarity: The Journal of Catholic Social Thought and Secular Ethics* 1, no. 1 (2011): 1–9.

Fukuyama, Francis. *Trust: The Social Virtues and the Creation of Prosperity*. New York: Free Press Paperbacks, 1966.

Goleman, Daniel. "Leadership That Gets Results." *Harvard Business Review*, March–April 2000, 78–93.

Grant, Adam. "In the Company of Givers and Takers." *Harvard Business Review*, April 2013, 90–97.

Grassl, Wolfgang. "Hybrid Forms of Business: The Logic of Gift in the Commercial World." *Journal of Business Ethics* 100, supplement 1 (2011): 109–23.

Grassl, Wolfgang, and André Habisch. "Ethics and Economics: Towards a New Humanistic Synthesis for Business." *Journal of Business Ethics* 99, no. 1 (2011): 37–49.

Hay Group. "Top Teams: Why Some Work and Some Do Not: Five Things the Best CEOs Do to Create Outstanding Executive Teams." Working Paper. Hay Group. 2005. http://www.haygroup.com/Downloads/uk/misc/Top_Teams_Working_Paper_UK.pdf.

———. "Estilos de Liderazgo y Clima en el Equipo: Perfile de éxito de los directivos in España" [Leadership Styles and the Climate in Europe: Profile of the Success of the Directives in Spain]. Hay Group, 2010. http://www.haygroup.com/downloads/es/Estilos_de_Liderazgo_y_Clima_en_el_Equipo.pdf.

Klein, Thomas A., and Gene R. Laczniak. "Implications of 'Caritas in Veritate' for Marketing and Business Ethics." *Journal of Business Ethics* 112, no. 4 (2013): 641–51.

Laczniak, Gene R., Thomas A. Klein, and Patrick E Murphy. "*Caritas in Veritate*: Updating Catholic Social Teaching for Responsible Marketing Strategy." In *Marketing and the Common Good: Essays from Notre Dame on Social Impact*, edited by Patrick E. Murphy and John F. Sherry Jr., 105–18. New York: Routledge, 2014.

Long, D. Stephen, and Nancy Ruth Fox. *Calculated Futures: Theology, Ethics, and Economics*. Waco, Tex.: Baylor University Press, 2007.

Lyubomirsky, Sonja, Laura King, and Ed Diener. "The Benefits of Frequent Positive Affect: Does Happiness Lead to Success?" *Psychological Bulletin* 131, no. 6 (2005): 803–55.

Marín, Higinio. *Teoría de la cordura y de los hábitos del corazón* [Theory of Sanity and the Habits of the Heart]. Valencia: Pre-textos, 2010.

Marina, José Antonio. *El laberinto sentimental* [The Emotional Labyrinth]. Barcelona: Anagrama, 1996.

Mathieu, Vittorio. *Filosofía del dinero* [Philosophy of Money]. Madrid: Rialp, 1990.

Mayer, Royer C., James H. Davis, and F. David Schoorman. "An Integrative Model of Organizational Trust." *Academy of Management Review* 20, no. 3 (1995): 709–34.

McCann, Dennis. "The Principle of Gratuitousness: Opportunities and Challenges for Business in 'Caritas in Veritate.'" *Journal of Business Ethics* 100, supplement (2011): 55–66.

Melé, Domenec. "'Human Quality Treatment': Five Organizational Levels." *Journal of Business Ethics* 120, no. 4 (2014): 457–71.

Pabst, Adrian, ed. *The Crisis of Global Capitalism: Pope Benedict XVI's Social Encyclical and the Future of Political Economy*. Eugene: Cascade, 2011.

Pérez López, Juan Antonio. *Teoría de la acción humana en las organizaciones: La acción personal* [Theory of Human Action in Organizations: Personal Action]. Madrid: Rialp, 1991.

Ratzinger, Joseph. *Introduction to Christianity*. San Francisco: Ignatius Press, 2004.

Watkins, Michael D. "How Managers Become Leaders." *Harvard Business Review*, June 2012, 65–72.

Zamagni, Stefano. *Por una economía del bien común* [The Economy of the Common Good]. Madrid: Ciudad Nueva, 2013.

Zenger, John H., Joseph R. Folkman, and Scott K. Edinger. *The Inspiring Leader: Unlocking the Secrets of How Extraordinary Leaders Motivate*. New York: McGraw-Hill, 2009.

Zieba, Maciej, ed. *Papal Economics: The Catholic Church on Democratic Capitalism, from "Rerum Novarum" to "Caritas in Veritate."* Wilmington: ISI, 2013.

BIBLIOGRAPHY

Abela, Andrew V. "Profit and More: Catholic Social Teaching and the Purpose of the Firm." *Journal of Business Ethics* 31, no. 2 (2001): 107–16.

Adorno, Theodor W. "Education after Auschwitz." In *Critical Models: Interventions and Catchwords*, 191–204. New York: Columbia University Press, 2005.

Agamben, Giorgio. *The Time That Remains: A Commentary on the Letter to the Romans*. Edited by Patricia Dailey. Stanford, Calif.: Stanford University Press, 2005.

———. *Opus Dei: An Archaeology of Duty*. Stanford, Calif.: Stanford University Press, 2013.

Akerlof, George A., and Rachel E. Kranton. "Economics and Identity." *Quarterly Journal of Economics* 115, no. 3 (2000): 715–53.

———. *Identity Economics: How Our Identities Shape Our Work, Wages, and Well-Being*. Princeton, N.J.: Princeton University Press, 2010.

Alford, Helen. "The Influence of Thomistic Thought in Contemporary Business Ethics." In *Handbook of the Philosophical Foundations of Business Ethics*, edited by Christoph Luetge, 227–50. Dordrecht: Springer, 2013.

Allison, Dale C. *The Sermon on the Mount: Inspiring the Moral Imagination*. New York: Crossroad, 1999.

Alvira, Rafael. "Intento de clasificar la pluralidad de subsistemas sociales, con especial atención al Derecho" [Attempt to Classify the Plurality of Social Subsystems, with Special Attention to Law]. *Persona y Derecho* 33 (1995): 41–51.

———. "Work, Social Structure and Leadership: Spirituality and the Problem of Employment." Paper presented at the Third International Symposium on Catholic Social Thought and Management Education: Rethinking the Spiritual and Social Life within Business. Goa, India. January 10–12, 1999.

———. "Tener y existir, reflexión y donación" [Having and Existing, Reflection and Donation]. *Anuario Filosófico* 36, no. 3 (2003): 575–85.

———. "Social Justice and the Common Good Within and Between Different Spheres of Society." In *Pursuing the Common Good: How Solidarity and Subsidiarity Can Work Together*, edited by Margaret S. Archer and Pierpaolo Donati, 605–17. Vatican City: Pontifical Academy of Social Sciences, 2008.

Andrews, Charles F. *Mahatma Gandhi: His Life and Ideas*. Woodstock, Vt.: Skylight Paths, 2003. Originally published in 1930.

Aquinas, Thomas. "Collationes de decem praeceptis." In *The Catechetical Instruc-*

tions of St. Thomas, translated by Joseph B. Collins, 69–116. New York: Wagner, 1939. Available online at http://dhspriory.org/thomas/TenCommandments.htm#5. Accessed June 21, 2017.

———. *Summa theologiae*. Cambridge: Cambridge University Press, 2006.

Arbinger Institute. *Leadership and Self Deception: Getting Out of the Box*. San Francisco: Berrett-Koehler, 2010.

Argandoña, Antonio. "Beyond Contracts: Love in Firms." *Journal of Business Ethics* 99, no. 1 (2011): 77–85.

———. "The Common Good." Working Paper 937. IESE Business School. 2011. http://dx.doi.org/10.2139/ssrn.1947309. Accessed May 8, 2017.

———. "The 'Logic of Gift' in the Business Enterprise." In *Human Development in Business: Values and Humanistic Management in the Encyclical "Caritas in Veritate,"* ed. Domènec Melé and Claus Dierksmeier, 198–216. New York: Palgrave–Macmillan, 2012.

Argyris, Chris. *Understanding Organizational Behavior*. Homewood, Ill.: Dorsey, 1960.

Aristotle. *The Complete Works of Aristotle: The Revised Oxford Translation*. Edited by Jonathan Barnes. Princeton, N.J.: Princeton University Press, Princeton, 1984.

Arrow, Kenneth. "Social Responsibility and Economic Efficiency." *Public Policy* 21, no. 3 (1973): 303–18.

Augustine. *Commentary on the Lord's Sermon on the Mount with Seventeen Related Sermons*. Translated by Denis J. Kavanagh, OSA. Washington, D.C.: The Catholic University of America Press, 1951.

Aumann, Jordan. *Christian Spirituality in the Catholic Tradition*. London: Bloomsbury, 1985.

———. *Spiritual Theology*. London: Bloomsbury, 1991.

Azcuy, Virginia R. "La espiritualidad como disciplina teológica: Panorama histórico, consensos y perspectivas actuales" [Spirituality as a Theological Discipline: Historical Panoramic, Consensus and Current Perspectives]. *Revista Teología* 47 (2011): 251–80.

Badaracco, Joseph L., Jr. *Tom Monaghan: In Business for God; Teaching Note*. Harvard Business School Teaching Note 392-140, May 1992.

Barnard, Chester. *The Functions of the Executive*. Cambridge, Mass.: Harvard University Press, 1968.

Baviera, Tomás, William English, and Manuel Guillén. "The 'Logic of Gift': Inspiring Behavior in Organizations beyond the Limits of Duty and Exchange." *Business Ethics Quarterly* 26, no. 2 (2016): 159–80.

Bay, Darlene, Kim McKeage, and Jeffrey McKeage. "An Historical Perspective on the Interplay of Christian Thought and Business Ethics." *Business and Society* 49, no. 4 (2010): 652–76.

Beed, Clive. "Jesus and Competition." *Faith and Economics* 45 (2005): 41–57.

Belk, Russell W. "Possessions and the Extended Self." *Journal of Consumer Research* 15, no. 2 (1988): 139–68.

Bell, Michael. "Teaching of the Elders." In *The Palgrave Handbook of Spirituality and Business*, edited by Luk Bouckaert and László Zsolnai, 187–96. Houndmills: Palgrave Macmillan, 2011.

Benedict. *The Rule of Saint Benedict*. Translated by Leonard Doyle. Collegeville, Minn.: Liturgical Press, 2001.

Benedict XVI. Encyclical Letter *Deus caritas est*. December 25, 2005.

———. Encyclical Letter *Caritas in veritate*. June 29, 2009.

Berthoud, Arnaud. *Essais de Philosophie Économique. Platon, Aristote, Hobbes, A. Smith, Marx* [Essays on Economic Philosophy: Plato, Aristotle, Hobbes, A. Smith, Marx]. Arras-Lille: Presses Universitaires du Septentrion, 2002.

Beschorner, Thomas. "Unternehmensethiken: Eine theoretische Einführung" [Business Ethics: A Theoretical Introduction]. In *Integritäts- und Umweltmanagement in der Beratungspraxis*, edited by Thomas Beschorner and Matthias Schmidt, 151–78. Munich: Mering, 2004.

Bonhoeffer, Dietrich. *The Cost of Discipleship*. New York: Macmillan, 1979.

Bornkamm, Günther. "Der Aufbau der Bergpredigt." *New Testament Studies* 24, no. 4 (1978): 419–32.

Bouckaert, Luk, and László Zsolnai, eds. *The Palgrave Handbook of Spirituality and Business*. Houndmills, UK: Palgrave-Macmillan, 2011.

Bourdieu, Pierre. *Distinction: A Social Critique of the Judgment of Taste*. London: Routledge, 1984.

Brubaker, Rogers. *The Limits of Rationality: An Essay on the Social and Moral Thought of Max Weber*. London: Routledge, 2006.

Brueggemann, Walter. *The Prophetic Imagination*. Philadelphia: Fortress, 1985. Originally published in 1978.

Bruni, Luigino. *Il prezzo della gratuità* [The Price of Gratuitousness]. Rome: Città Nuova, 2006.

———. *Reciprocity, Altruism and Civil Society*. London: Routledge, 2008.

Bruni, Luigino, and Robert Sudgen. "Fraternity: Why the Market Need Not Be a Morality Free Zone." *Economics and Philosophy* 24, no. 1 (2008): 36–64.

Bruni, Luigino, and Stefano Zamagni. *Civil Economy: Efficiency, Equity and Public Happiness*. Frankfurt: Peter Lang, 2007. Originally published in 2004.

———, eds. *Dizionario di economia civile* [Dictionary of Civil Economy]. Rome: Città Nuova, 2009.

———. *Civil Economy: Another Idea of the Market*. Newcastle upon Tyne: Agenda, 2016.

Büscher, Martin. "Economic Systems and Normative Fundaments: A Social Market

Economy in the Light of Economic Ethics." *Journal of Socio-Economics* 22, no. 4 (1993): 311–22.

Caillé, Alain. *Critica della ragione utilitaria: Manifesto del Movimento antiutilitarista nelle scienze sociali* [Critique of Utilitarian Reason: Manifesto of the Anti-Utilitarian Movement in the Social Sciences]. Turin: Bollati Boringhieri, 1991.

———. *Anthropologie du don: Le tiers paradigme* [Anthropology of Gift: The Third Paradigm]. París: Desclée de Brouwer, 2000.

Capps, Donald. "The Beatitudes and Erikson's Life Cycle Theory." *Pastoral Psychology* 33, no. 4 (1985): 226–44.

Case, Peter, Robert French, and Peter Simpson. "From T*heoria* to Theory: Leadership without Contemplation." *Organization* 19, no. 3 (2012): 345–61.

Case, Peter, and Jonathan Gosling. "The Spiritual Organization: Critical Reflections on the Instrumentality of Workplace Spirituality." *Journal of Management, Spirituality and Religion* 7, no. 4 (2010): 257–82.

Cassian, John. "Institutes." In *A Select Library of Nicene and Post-Nicene Fathers of the Christian Church*, vol. 11, edited by Philip Schaff. Buffalo, N.Y.: Christian Literature Company, 1894.

Catechism of the Catholic Church. Vatican City: Libreria Editrice Vaticana, 1993.

Cavanagh, Gerald F., and Mark R. Bandsuch. "Virtue as a Benchmark for Spirituality in Business." *Journal of Business Ethics* 38, no. 1 (2002): 109–17.

Chapman, Alan. "The Psychological Contract." *Businessballs.com*. http://www.businessballs.com/psychological-contracts-theory.htm. Accessed April 12, 2017.

Chesterton, G. K. *What's Wrong with the World*. Leipzig: Tauchnitz, 1910.

Cialdini, Robert. "The Uses (and Abuses) of Influence." *Harvard Business Review*, July–August 2013, 76–81.

Costa, Ericka, and Tommaso Ramus. "Italian Economia Aziendale as a Model Inspired by Catholic Humanism." In *Humanism in Economics and Business: Perspectives of the Catholic Social Tradition*, edited by Domènec Melé and Martin Schlag, 147–62. Dordrecht: Springer, 2015.

Crawford, Alleah, Susan S. Hubbard, Steven R. Lonis-Shumate, and Martin O'Neill. "Workplace Spirituality and Employee Attitudes within the Lodging Environment." *Journal of Human Resources in Hospitality and Tourism* 8, no. 1 (2009): 64–81.

Crespo, Mariano. *El perdón: Una investigación filosófica* [Forgiveness: A Philosophical Investigation]. Madrid: Encuentro, 2004.

Crespo, Ricardo. "'The Economic' according to Aristotle: Ethical, Political and Epistemological Implications." *Foundations of Science* 13, no. 3 (2008): 281–94.

Darwall, Stephen. *The Second-Person Standpoint: Morality, Respect and Accountability*. Cambridge, Mass.: Harvard University Press, 2006.

Davenport, Gene L. *Into the Darkness: Discipleship in the Sermon on the Mount*. Nashville: Abingdon, 1988.

De Bonald, Louis. *Théorie du pouvoir politique et réligeux* [Theory of Political and Religious Power]. Paris: Libraire D'Adrien Le Clere, 1854. Originally published in 1796.

De George, Richard T. "Theological Ethics and Business Ethics." *Journal of Business Ethics* 5, no. 6 (1986): 421–32.

Deci, Edward L., Richard Koestner, and Richard M. Ryan. "Meta-Analytical Review of Experiments Examining the Effects of Extrinsic Rewards on Intrinsic Motivation." *Psychological Bulletin* 125, no. 6 (1999): 627–68.

Delbecq, André L. "Christian Spirituality and Contemporary Business Leadership." *Journal of Organizational Change Management* 12, no. 4 (1999): 345–54.

Deleuze, Gilles. *Nietzsche and Philosophy*. New York: Columbia University Press, 1983. Originally published in 1962.

De Muralt, André. *La estructura de la filosofía política moderna* [The Structure of Modern Political Philosophy]. Madrid: Istmo, 2002.

———. *La apuesta de la filosofía medieval: Estudios tomistas, escotistas, ockhamistas y gregorianos* [The Wager of Medieval Philosophy: Thomist, Scotist, Ockhamist, and Gregorian Studies]. Madrid: Marcial Pons, 2008.

Denton, Elizabeth A., and Ian I. Mitroff. *A Spiritual Audit of Corporate America: A Hard Look at Spirituality, Religion, and Values in the Workplace*. San Francisco: Jossey-Bass, 1999.

"Didache." In *The Apostolic Fathers*, translated by Francis X. Glimm, Joseph M.-F. Marique, SJ, and Gerald G. Walsh, SJ. Washington, D.C.: The Catholic University of America Press, 1947.

Dumais, Marcel. *Il Discorso della Montagna: Stato della ricerca, Interpretazione, Bibliografia.* [The Sermon on the Mount: The State of Research, Interpretation, Bibliography]. Turin: Elledici, 1999.

Dyck, Bruno. *Management and the Gospel: Luke's Radical Message for the First and Twenty-First Centuries*. New York: Palgrave-Macmillan, 2013.

———. "Spirituality, Virtue, and Management: Theory and Evidence." In *Handbook of Virtue Ethics in Business and Management*, edited by Alejo J. G. Sison, Gregory R. Beabout, and Ignacio Ferrero, 919–28. Dordrecht: Springer, 2017.

Dyson, Robert W. *The Pilgrim City: Social and Political Ideas in the Writings of St. Augustine of Hippo*. Woodbridge: Boydell, 2001.

Echevarría, Javier. *Vivir la Santa Misa* [Living the Holy Mass]. Madrid: Rialp, 2010.

Enderle, Georges. "The Option for the Poor and Business Ethics." In *The Preferential Option for the Poor beyond Theology*, edited by Daniel G. Groody and Gustavo Gutiérrez, 28–46. Notre Dame, Ind.: University of Notre Dame Press, 2014.

"The Epistle to Diognetus." In *Patres Apostolici*, vol. 1, edited by F. X. Funk. Tubingen: H. Laupp, 1901. http://www.vatican.va/spirit/documents/spirit_20010522_diogneto_en.html.

Escrivá, Josemaría. *Friends of God*. New York: Scepter, 2002. Originally published in 1977.

———. *The Forge*. New York: Scepter, 2011. Originally published in 1988.

———. *Furrow*. New York: Scepter, 2011. Originally published in 1986.

Eucken, Walter. *Grundsätze zur Wirtschaftspolitik* [Principles of Economic Policy]. Edited by Edith Eucken and K. Paul Hensel. Tübingen: Mohr Siebeck, 2004. Originally published in 1952.

Faldetta, Guglielmo. "The Logic of Gift and Gratuitousness in Business Relationships." *Journal of Business Ethics* 100, supplement 1 (2011): 67–77.

Falgueras, Ignacio. "El dar, actividad plena de la libertad transcendental" [Giving, Full Activity of Transcendental Freedom]. *Studia Poliana* 15 (2013): 69–108.

Felice, Flavio. "The Ethical Foundation of the Market Economy: A Reflection on the Economic Personalism in the Thought of Luigi Sturzo." *Journal of Markets and Morality* 4, no. 2 (2001): 217–39.

———. *Persona, impresa e mercato: L'economia sociale di mercato nella prospettiva teorica del pensiero sociale cattolico* [Person, Business, and Market: The Social Market Economy in the Theoretical Perspective of Catholic Social Thought]. Rome: Lateran University Press, 2010.

Ferreiro, Alberto. "Introduction to the Twelve Prophets." In *Ancient Christian Commentary on Scripture*, edited by Thomas C. Oden. Vol. 14, *The Twelve Prophets*, edited by Alberto Ferreiro, xvii–xxv. Downers Grove, Ill.: InterVarsity, 2003.

Finley, Moses. "Aristotle and Economic Analysis." *Past and Present* 47 (1970): 3–25.

Finn, Daniel K., ed. *The Moral Dynamics of Economic Life: An Extension and Critique of "Caritas in Veritate."* New York: Oxford University Press, 2012.

Flynn, Francis J. "Francis Flynn: What Makes People Want to Help Others?" *Insights by Stanford Graduate School of Business*. November 21, 2013. https://www.gsb.stanford.edu/insights/francis-flynn-what-makes-people-want-help-others.

Francis. *Letter to H. E. Mr. David Cameron, British Prime Minister on the Occasion of the G8 Meeting (17–18 June 2013)*. June 15, 2013.

———. *Meditation: Dirty Bread of Corruption*. November 8, 2013.

———. Apostolic Exhortation *Evangelii gaudium*. November 24, 2013.

———. *Address to the Participants in the World Meeting of Popular Movements*. October 28, 2014.

———. *Message to the Executive Chairman of the World Economic Forum on the Occasion of the Annual Meeting at Davos-Klosters (Switzerland)*. January 17, 2015.

———. *Address to Representatives of the Confederation of Italian Cooperatives*. February 28, 2015.

———. Encyclical Letter *Laudato si'*. May 24, 2015.
———. Francis, *Address at the Conferral of the Charlemagne Prize*. May 6, 2016.
———. *Address to the Christian Union of Business Executives (UCID)*. October 31, 2015.
———. *Peace Message*. January 1, 2017.
Frankfurt, Harry G. "Freedom of the Will and the Concept of a Person." In *The Importance of What We Care About: Philosophical Essays*. New York: Cambridge University Press 1998, 11–25.
Franklin, James. "Caritas in Veritate: Economic Activity as Personal Encounter and the Economy of Gratuitousness." *Solidarity: The Journal of Catholic Social Thought and Secular Ethics* 1, no. 1 (2011): 1–9.
Frémeaux, Sandrine, and Grant Michelson. "'No Strings Attached': Welcoming the Existential Gift in Business." *Journal of Business Ethics* 99, no. 1 (2011): 63–75.
Frey, Bruno S. *Not Just for the Money*. Cheltemham: E. Elgar, 1997.
Friedman, Milton. "The Social Responsibility of Business Is to Increase Its Profits" [1970]. In *An Introduction to Business Ethics*, edited by George D. Chryssides and John H. Kaler, 249–54. London: Thomson Learning, 2006.
Fukuyama, Francis. *Trust: The Social Virtues and the Creation of Prosperity*. New York: Free Press Paperbacks, 1966.
Garai, László. "Determining Economic Activity in a Post-Capitalist System." *Journal of Economic Psychology* 8, no. 1 (1987): 77–90.
Geigle, David. "Workplace Spirituality Empirical Research: A Literature Review." *Business Management Review* 2, no. 10 (2012): 14–27.
Ghoshal, Sumantra. "Bad Management Theories Are Destroying Good Management Practices." *Academy of Management Learning and Education* 4, no. 1 (2005): 75–91.
Giacalone, Robert A., and Carole L. Jurkiewicz, eds. *Handbook of Workplace Spirituality and Organizational Performance*. Armonk, N.Y.: M. E. Sharpe, 2010.
———. "The Science of Workplace Spirituality." In *Handbook of Workplace Spirituality*, edited by Robert A. Giacalone and Carole L. Jurkiewicz, 3–26. Armonk, N.Y.: M. E. Sharpe, 2010.
Gillespie, Michael. *The Theological Origins of Modernity*. Chicago: University of Chicago Press, 2008.
Gilson, Étienne. *Christian Philosophy: An Introduction*. Translated by Armand Augustine Maurer. Toronto: Pontifical Institute of Mediaeval Studies, 1993. Originally published in 1960.
———. *Juan Duns Escoto: Introducción a sus posiciones fundamentales* [John Duns Scotus: Introduction to his Fundamental Positions]. Pamplona: Eunsa, 2007. Originally published in 1952.

Girard, René. *Violence and the Sacred*. Baltimore: John Hopkins University Press, 1977.

Godbout, Jacques, and Alain Caillé. *L'esprit du don* [The Spirit of Gift]. París: La Dècouverte, 1992.

Godbout, Jacques T. *Le langage du don* [The Language of Gift]. Montreal: Fides, 1996.

———. *Le don, le dette, l 'identité: Homo donator versus homo economicus* [Gift, Debt, Identity: Homo donator versus homo economicus]. París: La Découverte, 2000.

Godelier, Maurice. *The Enigma of the Gift*. Chicago: University of Chicago Press, 1999.

Goleman, Daniel. "Leadership That Gets Results." *Harvard Business Review*, March–April 2000, 78–93.

González, Ángel Luis. "Thomistic Metaphysics: Contemporary Interpretations." *Anuario Filosófico* 39, no. 2 (2006): 401–37.

———. *Persona, libertad, don* [Person, Freedom, Gift]. Inaugural lecture of the 2013–14 academic year. Universidad de Navarra, Pamplona. September 6, 2013.

González-Ayesta, Cruz. "Work as 'a Mass': Reflections on the Laity's Participation in the *Munus Sacerdotale* in the Writings of the Founder of Opus Dei." *Romana* 50 (2010): 192–206.

Grant, Adam. "In the Company of Givers and Takers." *Harvard Business Review*, April 2013, 90–97.

Grassl, Wolfgang. "Hybrid Forms of Business: The Logic of Gift in the Commercial World." *Journal of Business Ethics* 100, supplement 1 (2011): 109–23.

Grassl, Wolfgang, and André Habisch. "Ethics and Economics: Towards a New Humanistic Synthesis for Business." *Journal of Business Ethics* 99, no. 1 (2011): 37–49.

Greenman, Jeffrey P., Timothy Larsen, and Stephen R. Spencer, eds. *The Sermon on the Mount through the Centuries: From the Early Church to John Paul II*. Grand Rapids, Mich.: Brazos, 2007.

Grimaldi, Nicolas. *Introducción a la filosofía de la historia de Carlos Marx* [Introduction to the Philosophy and History of Karl Marx]. Madrid: Dossat, 1986.

Guelich, Robert A. *The Sermon on the Mount: A Foundation for Understanding*. Waco: Word, 1982.

Gustafson, Andrew. "Business in the Service of the Common Good: A Christian Perspective." *Journal of Religion and Society*. Supplement Series. Supplement 10 (2014): 242–56.

Habermas, Jürgen. "Religion in the Public Sphere." *European Journal of Philsophy* 14, no. 1 (2006): 1–25.

Hahn, Scott. *Ordinary Work, Extraordinary Grace: My Spiritual Journey in Opus Dei*. New York: Doubleday, 2006.

Hay Group. "Top Teams: Why Some Work and Some Do Not; Five Things the Best CEOs Do to Create Outstanding Executive Teams." Working Paper. Hay Group. 2005. http://www.haygroup.com/Downloads/uk/misc/Top_Teams_Working_Paper_UK.pdf.

———. "Estilos de Liderazgo y Clima en el Equipo: Perfile de éxito de los directivos in España" [Leadership Styles and the Climate in Europe: Profile of the Success of the Directives in Spain]. Hay Group, 2010. http://www.haygroup.com/downloads/es/Estilos_de_Liderazgo_y_Clima_en_el_Equipo.pdf.

Haya, Fernando. *El ser personal: De Tomás de Aquino a la metafísica del don* [The Personal Being: From Thomas Aquinas to the Metaphysics of Gift]. Pamplona: Eunsa, 1997.

Heath, Anthony. *Rational Choice and Social Exchange: A Critique of Exchange Theory*. Cambridge: Cambridge University Press, 1976.

Hegel, Georg Wilhelm Friedrich. *Elements of the Philosophy of Right* [1820]. Edited by Allen W. Wood. Cambridge: Cambridge University Press, 1991.

Hénaff, Marcel. "Religious Ethics, Gift Exchange and Capitalism." *European Journal of Sociology* 44, no. 3 (2003): 293–324.

———. *The Price of Truth: Gift, Money and Philosophy*. Stanford, Calif.: Stanford University Press, 2010.

Hicks, Douglas A. *Religion and the Workplace: Pluralism, Spirituality, Leadership*. Cambridge: Cambridge University Press, 2003.

Hittinger, Russell. "Social Pluralism and Subsidiarity in Catholic Social Doctrine." *Annales Theologici* 16 (2002): 385–408.

Hoevel, Carlos. *The Economy of Recognition: Person, Market and Society in Antonio Rosmini*. Dordrecht: Springer, 2013.

Höhn, Hans-Joachim. *Zeit und Sinn: Religionsphilosophie postsäkular* [Time and Meaning: Post-Secular Philosophy of Religion]. Paderborn: Schöningh, 2010.

Holtom, Jeremy. "Gandhi's Interpretation of the Sermon on the Mount." In *The Oxford Handbook of the Reception History of the Bible*, edited by Michael Lieb, Emma Mason, and Jonathan Roberts, 542–56. Oxford: Oxford University Press, 2013.

Homann, Karl. *Vorteile und Anreize* [Advantages and Incentives]. 2nd ed. Tübingen: Mohr Siebeck, 2002.

———. *Ethik in der Marktwirtschaft: Position Nr. 3* [Ethics in the Market Economy: Position No. 3]. Munich: Deutscher Instituts Verlag, 2007.

Houghton, Jeffery D., Christopher P. Neck, and Sukumarakurup Krishnakumar. "The What, Why, and How of Spirituality in the Workplace Revisited: A 14-Year Update and Extension." *Journal of Management, Spirituality and Religion* 13 (2016): 177–205.

Hudson, Richard. "The Question of Theoretical Foundations for the Spirituality at

Work Movement." *Journal of Management, Spirituality and Religion* 11, no. 1 (2014): 27–44.

Hyde, Lewis. *The Gift: Imagination and the Erotic Life of Property*. New York: Vintage, 1981.

———. *The Gift: Creativity and the Artist in the Modern World*. New York: Random House, 2007.

Ichniowski, Casey, and Kathryn L. Shaw. "Connective Capital as Social Capital: The Value of Problem-Solving Networks for Team Players in Firms." Working Paper n. 15619. National Bureau of Economic Research. December 2009. http://www.nber.org/papers/w15619.

Inauen, Emil, and Bruno S. Frey. "Benediktinerabteien aus ökonomischer Sicht: Über die ausserordentliche Stabilität einer besonderen Institution" [Benedictine Abbeys from an Economic Perspective: On the Extraordinary Stability of a Special Institution]. Working Paper 388. Institute for Empirical Research in Economics, University of Zurich. 2008. http://www.zora.uzh.ch/52341/. Accessed May 8, 2017.

Janssen, Maarten C. W, and Ewa Mendys-Kamphorst. "The Price of a Price: On the Crowding Out and In of Social Norms." *Journal of Economic Behavior and Organization* 55, no. 3 (2004): 377–95.

Jensen, Michael C. "Value Maximization, Stakeholder Theory, and the Corporate Objective Function." *European Financial Management* 7, no. 2 (2001): 297–317.

Jeremias, Joachim. *Die Bergpredigt* [The Sermon on the Mount]. Stuttgart: Calwer, 1965.

Joas, Hans. *Die Entstehung der Werte* [The Genesis of Values]. 2nd ed. Frankfurt: Suhrkamp, 1999.

John XXIII. Encyclical Letter *Mater et magistra*. May 15, 1961.

———. Encyclical Letter *Pacem in terris*. April 11, 1963.

John Paul II. *Homily for the Inauguration of His Pontificate*. October 22, 1978.

———. Encyclical Letter *Redemptor hominis*. March 4, 1979.

———. Encyclical Letter *Laborem exercens*. September 14, 1981.

———. *Address to the Participants in the National Congress of the Ecclesial Movement for Cultural Commitment*. January 16, 1982.

———. *Foundation Letter of the Pontifical Council for Culture*. May 20, 1982.

———. Encyclical Letter *Mulieris dignitatem*. August 15, 1988.

———. Apostolic Exhortation *Christifideles laici*. December 30, 1988.

———. Encyclical Letter *Centesimus annus*. May 1, 1991.

———. *Homily for the Beatification of Father Adolph Kolping*. October 27, 1991

———. Encyclical Letter *Ecclesia de Eucharistia*. April 17, 2003.

Johnson, Roger D. "Economics of Good and Evil: The Quest for Economic Meaning from Gilgamesh to Wall Street." Review. *Faith and Economics* 59 (2012): 86–90.

Karakas, Fahri. "Spirituality and Performance in Organizations: A Literature Review." *Journal of Business Ethics* 94, no. 1 (2010): 89–106.

Keenan, James F. *The Works of Mercy: The Heart of Catholicism*. Lanham, Md.: Rowman and Littlefield, 2008.

Kelsen, Hans. *The Essence and Value of Democracy*. Lanham, Md.: Rowman and Littlefield, 2013. Originally published in 1920.

———. *Pure Theory of Law*. Clark, N.J.: Lawbook Exchange, 2005. Originally published in 1934.

Klein, Thomas A., and Gene R. Laczniak. "Implications of 'Caritas in Veritate' for Marketing and Business Ethics." *Journal of Business Ethics* 112, no. 4 (2013): 641–51.

Koehler, Ludwig, and Walter Baumgartner, eds. *The Hebrew and Aramaic Lexicon of the Old Testament*. 5 vols. Leiden: Brill, 1995–2000.

Konz, Gregory N. P., and Francis X. Ryan. "Maintaining an Organizational Spirituality: No Easy Task." *Journal of Organizational Change Management* 12, no. 3 (1999): 200–10.

Koslowski, Peter. "Ethical Economy as the Economy of Ethics and as the Ethics of the Market Economy." In *Corporate Citizenship, Contractarianism and Ethical Theory: On Philosophical Foundations of Business Ethics*, edited by Jesús Conill Sancho, Christoph Luetge, and Tatjana Schönwälder-Kuntze, 149–68. Farnham: Ashgate, 2008.

Kreuzhof, Rainer, and Wolfgang Ockenfels. "On the Proper Essence of Christian Economic Ethics." *Management Revue* 21, no. 1 (2010): 82–94.

Kuzmina, Jekaterina. "Usage of Christian Social Ethics in Business." *Journal of Economics, Business and Management* 1, no. 1 (2013): 6–10.

Laczniak, Gene R., Thomas A. Klein, and Patrick E Murphy. "*Caritas in Veritate*: Updating Catholic Social Teaching for Responsible Marketing Strategy." In *Marketing and the Common Good: Essays from Notre Dame on Social Impact*, edited by Patrick E. Murphy and John F. Sherry Jr., 105–18. New York: Routledge, 2014.

Lambrecht, Jan. *The Sermon on the Mount: Proclamation and Exhortation*. Wilmington, Del.: Michael Glazier, 1985.

Langholm, Odd. *Wealth and Money in the Aristotelian Tradition*. Bergen: Universitetsforlaget, 1983.

Lapide, Pinchas. *Il discorso della montagna: Utopia o programma?* [The Sermon on the Mount: Utopia or Program for Action?]. Brescia: Paideia, 2003. Originally published in 1992.

Lawler, Edward J., and Shane R. Thye. "Bringing Emotions into Social Exchange Theory." *Annual Review of Sociology* 25 (1999): 217–44.

Lázaro, Raquel. *La sociedad comercial en Adam Smith: Método, moral y religión*

[Commercial Society in Adam Smith: Method, Morality and Religion]. Pamplona: Eunsa, 2002.

———. "Adam Smith: Anthropology and Moral Philosophy." *Revista Empresa y Humanismo* 13, no. 1 (2010): 145–84.

Leo XIII. Encyclical Letter *Rerum novarum*. May 15, 1891.

Leonard, James. *Living the Faith: A Life of Tom Monaghan*. Ann Arbor: University of Michigan Press, 2012.

Lewis, C. S. *Mere Christianity*. Vol. 3, *The Great Sin*. New York: HarperCollins, 1980.

Liddell, Henry George, and Robert Scott, eds. *A Greek-English Lexicon*. Oxford: Oxford University Press, 1968.

Ligo, Vivian. "Configuring a Christian Spirituality of Work." *Theology Today* 67, no. 4 (2011): 441–66.

Lips-Wiesma, Marjolein, Kathy Lund Dean, and Charles J. Fornaciari. "Theorizing the Dark Side of the Workplace Spirituality Movement." *Journal of Management Inquiry* 18, no. 4 (2009): 288–300.

Llano, Alejandro. *Deseo, violencia, sacrificio: El secreto del mito según René Girard* [Desire, Violence, Sacrifice: The Secret of the Myth according to René Girard]. Pamplona: Eunsa, 2004.

Lohfink, Gerhard. *Wem gilt die Bergpredigt? Beiträge zu einer christlichen Ethik* [To Whom Does the Sermon on the Mount Apply? Contributions to Christian Ethics]. Freiburg: Herder, 1988.

Long, Stephen D., and Nancy Ruth Fox. *Calculated Futures: Theology, Ethics, and Economics*. Waco, Tex.: Baylor University Press, 2007.

Luther, Martin. *D. Martin Luthers Werke: Kritische Gesammtausgabe* [D. Martin Luther's Works: Complete Critical Edition]. 120 vols. Weimar: Hermann Böhlaus Nachfolger, 1883–1938.

Lyubomirsky, Sonja, Laura King, and Ed Diener. "The Benefits of Frequent Positive Affect: Does Happiness Lead to Success?" *Psychological Bulletin* 131, no. 6 (2005): 803–55.

Machiavelli, Niccolò. *The Prince: With Related Documents* [1513]. Boston: Bedford and St. Martin's, 2016.

MacIntyre, Alasdair. *After Virtue: A Study in Moral Theory*. 2nd ed. Notre Dame, Ind.: Notre Dame University Press, 1997.

Mahoney, John. "Christian Perspectives on Business Ethics." *Studies in Christian Ethics* 2, no. 1 (1989): 20–40.

Marcic, Dorothy. "God, Faith and Management Education." *Journal of Management Education* 24, no. 5 (2000): 628–49.

Marcuse, Herbert. *One-Dimensional Man*. Boston, Mass.: Beacon, 1991.

Marín, Higinio. *Teoría de la cordura y de los hábitos del corazón* [Theory of Sanity and the Habits of the Heart]. Valencia: Pre-textos, 2010.

Marina, José Antonio. *El laberinto sentimental* [The Emotional Labyrinth]. Barcelona: Anagrama, 1996.

Maritain, Jacques. *The Person and the Common Good.* New York: Charles Scribner's Sons, 1947.

Marques, Joan, Satinder Dhiman, and Richard King. *Spirituality in the Workplace: What It Is, Why It Matters, How to Make It Work for You.* Fawnskin, Calif.: Personhood, 2007.

Martí, Pablo. "La espiritualidad cristiana en el Concilio Vaticano II" [Christian Spirituality in Vatican Council II]. *Scripta Theologica* 45, no. 1 (2013): 153–84.

Martínez Echevarría, Miguel Alfonso. *Evolución del Pensamiento Económico* [Evolution of Economic Thought]. Madrid: Espasa Calpe, 1983.

———. "Don y desarrollo, bases de la economía" [Gift and Development, Foundations of the Economy]. *Scripta Theologica* 42, no. 1 (2010): 121–38.

Maslach, Christina, Wilmar B. Schaufeli, and Michael P. Leiter. "Job Burnout." *Annual Review of Psychology* 52, no. 1 (2001): 397–422.

Mathieu, Vittorio. *Filosofía del dinero* [Philosophy of Money]. Madrid: Rialp, 1990.

Mauss, Marcel. *The Gift: The Form and Reason for Exchange in Archaic Societies.* London: Routledge, 1990. Originally published in 1925 as *Essai sur le don.*

Mayer, Roger C., James H. Davis, and F. David Schoorman. "An Integrative Model of Organizational Trust." *Academy of Management Review* 20, no. 3 (1995): 709–34.

McCann, Dennis. "The Principle of Gratuitousness: Opportunities and Challenges for Business in *Caritas in Veritate.*" *Journal of Business Ethics* 100, supplement 1 (2011): 55–66.

Meikle, Scott. "Aristotle and the Political Economy of the Polis." *Journal of Hellenic Studies* 99 (1979): 57–73.

———. *Aristotle's Economic Thought.* Oxford: Oxford University Press, 1995.

Melé, Domènec. "Integrating Personalism into Virtue-Based Business Ethics: The Personalist and the Common Good Principles." *Journal of Business Ethics* 88, no. 1 (2009): 227–44.

———. "The Christian Notion of Αγάπη (Agápē): Towards a More Complete View of Business Ethics." In *Leadership through the Classics: Learning Management and Leadership from Ancient East and West Philosophy*, edited by Gregory P. Prastacos, Fuming Wang, and Klas Eric Soderquist, 79–91. Heidelberg: Springer, 2012.

———. "The Firm as a 'Community of Persons': A Pillar of Humanistic Business Ethos." *Journal of Business Ethics* 106, no. 1 (2012): 89–101.

———. "Scholastic Thought and Business Ethics: An Overview." In *Handbook of the Philosophical Foundations of Business Ethics*, edited by Christoph Luetge, 133–58. Dordrecht: Springer, 2013.

———. "'Human Quality Treatment': Five Organizational Levels." *Journal of Business Ethics* 120, no. 4 (2014): 457–71.

Melé, Domènec, and Claus Dierksmeier, eds. *Human Development in Business: Values and Humanistic Management in the Encyclical "Caritas in Veritate."* New York: Palgrave-MacMillan, 2012.

Melé, Domènec, and Martin Schlag, eds. *Humanism in Economics and Business: Perspectives of the Catholic Social Tradition*. Dordrecht: Springer, 2015.

Milbank, John, and Adrian Pabst. *The Politics of Virtue: Post-Liberalism and the Human Future*. London: Rowman and Littlefield, 2016.

Millán-Puelles, Antonio. *La libre afirmación de nuestro ser: Una fundamentación de la ética realista* [The Free Affirmation of Our Being: A Foundation of Realist Ethics]. Madrid: Rialp, 1994.

Miller, Daniel. *The Comfort of Things*. Cambridge: Polity, 2009.

———. *Stuff*. Cambridge: Polity, 2010.

Miller, John H. "The Nature and Definition of the Liturgy." *Theological Studies* 18, no. 3 (1957): 325–56.

Millet, Paul. *Lending and Borrowing in Ancient Athens*. Cambridge: Cambridge University Press, 1991.

Milliman, John, Andrew J. Czaplewski, and Jeffery Ferguson. "Workplace Spirituality and Employee Work Attitudes: An Exploratory Empirical Assessment." *Journal of Organizational Change Management* 16, no. 4 (2003): 426–47.

Molyneaux, David. "'Blessed Are the Meek, for They Shall Inherit the Earth'—An Aspiration Applicable to Business?" *Journal of Business Ethics* 48, no. 4 (2003): 347–63.

Monaghan, Tom, with Robert Anderson. *Pizza Tiger*. New York: Random House, 1986.

Moreno Almárcegui, Antonio. "Ensayo sobre el don" [Essay on Gift]. In *Actas del Seminario del grupo de investigación en Economía Política y Filosofía*. Pamplona: Universidad de Navarra, 2010.

———. "Consanguinidad y gracia: El culto a María y José en Occidente; Siglos I–XX. El caso de España" [Kinship and Grace: Devotion to Mary and Joseph in the West; 1st–20th centuries: The Case of Spain]. In *Actas del Seminario del grupo de investigación en Economía Política y Filosofía*. Pamplona: Universidad de Navarra, 2015.

Morrow, Jeffrey. "Work as Worship in the Garden and the Workshop: Genesis 1–3, the Feast of St. Joseph the Worker, and Liturgical Hermeneutics." *Logos* 15, no. 4 (2012): 159–78.

Moule, Charles F. D. *The Birth of the New Testament*. London: Adam and Charles Black, 1981. Originally published in 1962.

Múgica, Luis Fernando. *Tradición y Revolución: Filosofía y sociedad en el pensamien-*

to de Louis de Bonald [Tradition and Revolution: Philosophy and Society in the Thought of Louis de Bonald]. Pamplona: Eunsa,1988.

Naughton, Michael. "Thinking Institutionally about Business: Seeing Its Nature as a Community of Persons and Its Purpose as the Common Good." In *Humanism in Economics and Business: Perspectives of the Catholic Social Tradition*, edited by Domènec Melé and Martin Schlag, 179–99. Dordrecht: Springer, 2015.

Naughton, Michael J., Jeanne G. Buckeye, Kenneth E. Goodpaster, and T. Dean Maines. *Respect in Action: Applying Subsidiarity in Business*. St. Paul, Minn.: University of St. Thomas, 2015.

Neal, Judy. *Handbook of Faith and Spirituality in the Workplace: Emerging Research and Practice*. New York: Springer, 2013.

Neschen, Albena. "Hegel on Modern Economics and Business." In *Handbook of the Philosophical Foundations of Business Ethics*, edited by Christoph Luetge, 415–29. Dordrecht: Springer, 2013.

Novak, Michael. *Business as a Calling*. New York: Free Press, 1996.

Orléan, André. "Pour une aproche girardienne de l'*homo oeconomicus*" [A Girardian Approach to the *Homo Oeconomicus*]. *Cahiers de L'Herne* 89 (2008): 261–65.

Pabst, Adrian, ed. *The Crisis of Global Capitalism: Pope Benedict XVI´s Social Encyclical and the Future of Political Economy*. Eugene: Cascade, 2011.

Paul VI. Encyclical Letter *Populorum progressio*. March 26, 1967.

———. *Message for the World Day of Peace*. January 1, 1977.

Pérez López, Juan Antonio. *Teoría de la acción humana en las organizaciones: La acción personal* [Theory of Human Action in Organizations: Personal Action]. Madrid: Rialp,1991.

Pfeil, Margaret. "Oscar Romero's Theology of Transfiguration." *Theological Studies* 72, no. 1 (2011): 87–115.

Philippe, Jacques. *Time for God*. New York: Scepter, 2008. Originally published in 1992.

Pieper, Josef. *Leisure: The Basis of Culture*. Translated by Gerald Malsbary. South Bend, Ind.: St. Augustine's Press, 1998. Originally published in 1948.

Pinckaers, Servais. *The Sources of Christian Ethics*. Washington, D.C.: The Catholic University of America Press, 1995.

Pius XI. Encyclical Letter *Quadragesimo anno*. May 15, 1931.

Polo, Leonardo. *Presente y futuro del hombre* [Present and Future of Man]. Madrid: Rialp, 1993.

———. "Tener y dar" [Having and Giving]. In *Sobre la existencia Cristiana*, 103–36. Pamplona: Eunsa, 1996.

———. *Ética: Hacia una versión moderna de los temas clásicos* [Ethics: A Modern Version of Its Classic Themes]. Madrid: Aedos, 1997.

———. *Antropología Trascendental.* Vol. 1, *La persona humana* [Transcendental Anthropology. Vol. 1, The Human Person]. Pamplona: Eunsa, 1999.

———. *Nominalismo, idealismo y realismo* [Nominalism, Idealism, and Realism]. Pamplona: Eunsa, 2001.

———. *Quién es el hombre: Un espíritu en el tiempo* [Who Is Man: A Spirit in Time]. Madrid: Rialp, 2003.

———. "Lo radical y la libertad" [The Radical and Freedom]. *Cuadernos de Anuario Filosófico*, no. 179. Pamplona, 2005.

Pontifical Council for Justice and Peace. *Compendium of the Social Doctrine of the Church*. Vatican City: Libreria Editrice Vaticana, 2004.

———. *The Vocation of the Business Leader*. Vatican City: Pontifical Council for Justice and Peace, 2012.

Ratnakar, Rajesh, and Shreekumar Nair. "A Review of Scientific Research on Spirituality." *Business Perspectives and Research* 1, no. 1 (2012): 1–12.

Ratzinger, Joseph. *Introduction to Christianity*. San Francisco: Ignatius Press, 2004.

Rego, Arménio, and Miguel Pina E. Cunha. "Workplace Spirituality and Organizational Commitment: An Empirical Study." *Journal of Organizational Change Management* 21, no. 1 (2008): 53–75.

Rhee, Helen. *Loving the Poor, Saving the Rich: Wealth, Poverty, and Early Christian Formation*. Grand Rapids, Mich.: Baker Academic, 2012.

Rieff, Philip. *Charisma: The Gift of Grace and How It Has Been Taken Away from Us*. New York: Pantheon, 2007.

Ritchie, David. "Aristotle's Subdivisions of Particular Justice." *Classical Review* 8, no. 5 (1984): 185–92.

Rodríguez Lluesma, Carlos. *Los modales de la pasión: Adam Smith y la sociedad comercial* [Domesticated Passions: Adam Smith and the Commercial Society]. Pamplona: Eunsa, 1997.

Roof, Richard A. "The Association of Individual Spirituality on Employee Engagement: The Spirit at Work." *Journal of Business Ethics* 130, no. 3 (2015): 585–99.

Röpke, Wilhelm. "Ethik und Wirtschaftsleben" [Ethics and Economic Life] [1955]. In *Wilhelm Röpke: Marktwirtschaft ist nicht genug; Gesammelte Aufsätze*, edited by Hans-Jörg Hennecke, 270–88. Leipzig: Waltrop, 2009.

Rosmini, Antonio. *Opere inedite di politica* [Unpublished Works on Politics]. Edited by Giovanni Battista Nicola. Milan: Tenconi, 1923.

———. *Saggi di Scienza Politica: Scritti inediti* [Essays on Political Science: Unpublished Works]. Edited by Giovanni Battista Nicola. Turin: Paravia, 1933.

———. "Esame delle opinioni di Melchiorre Gioia in favor della moda" [Examination of the fashionable opinions of Melchiorre Gioia]. In *Opere edite e inedite di Antonio Rosmini*, vol. 49, *Frammenti di una Storia della empietà e scritti vari*, edited by Rinaldo Orecchia, 97–145. Padova: Cedam, 1977.

———. *The Philosophy of Right*. 6 vols. Edited by Denis Cleary and Terence Watson. Durham, N.C.: Rosmini House, 1993–96.

———. *The Philosophy of Politics*. 2 vols. Edited by Denis Cleary and Terence Watson. Durham, N.C.: Rosmini House, 1994.

Rost, Katja, Emil Inauen, Margit Osterloh, and Bruno S. Frey. "The Corporate Governance of Benedictine Abbeys: What Can Stock Corporations Learn from Monasteries?" *Journal of Management History* 16, no. 1 (2010): 90–115.

Rousseau, Denise M. "Psychological and Implied Contracts in Organizations." *Employee Responsibilities and Rights Journal* 2, no. 2 (1989): 121–39.

Rubio de Urquía, Rafael, and Juan José Pérez-Soba, eds. *La doctrina social de la Iglesia: Estudios a la luz de la encíclica "Caritas in veritate"* [The Social Doctrine of the Church: Studies in Light of the Encyclical "*Caritas in veritate*"]. Madrid: AEDOS-BAC, 2014.

Sánchez de la Cruz, Carlos. *Don y gratuidad en el pensamiento de Joseph Ratzinger: Claves para la teología moral* [Gift and Gratuitousness in the Thought of Joseph Ratzinger: Keys for Moral Theology]. Madrid: Perpetuo socorro, 2012.

Sánchez, Manuel Diego. *Historia de la espiritualidad patrística* [History of Patristic Spirituality]. Madrid: Editorial de espiritualidad, 1992.

Scalzo, Germán. "Génesis del concepto de interés propio" [Genesis of the Concept of Self-Interest]. *Cuadernos Empresa y Humanismo* 108. Pamplona: Servicio de Publicaciones UNAV, 2008.

———. "La racionalidad en Max Weber." [Max Weber on Rationality] *Cuadernos Empresa y Humanismo* 118. Pamplona: Servicio de Publicaciones UNAV, 2012.

———. "Génesis del pensamiento económico: Dos visiones en pugna" [Genesis of Economic Thought: Two Conflicting Visions]. *Cauriensia* 9 (2014): 341–74.

———. "A Genealogy of the Gift." In *Ethical Economy*, edited by Alexander Brink and Jacob Dahl Rendtorff. Vol. 51, *Perspectives on Philosophy of Management and Business Ethics*, edited by Jacob Dahl Rendtorff, 31–45. Springer Nature, 2016.

Schlag, Martin. *The Business Francis Means*. Washington, D.C.: The Catholic University of America Press, 2017.

Schnackenburg, Rudolf. *Von Jesus zur Urkirche* [From Jesus to the Early Church]. Vol. 1, *Die sittliche Botschaft des Neuen Testaments*. Freiburg: Herder, 1986.

Schneiders, Sandra. "Theology and Spirituality: Strangers, Rivals, or Partners?" *Horizons* 13, no. 2 (1986): 266–67.

Schockenhoff, Eberhard. *Die Bergpredigt: Aufruf zum Christsein* [The Sermon on the Mount: A Call to Being a Christian]. Freiburg: Herder, 2014.

Schoorman, F. David, Roger C. Mayer, and James H. Davis. "An Integrative Model of Organizational Trust: Past, Present, and Future." *Academy of Management Review* 32, no. 2 (2007): 344–54.

Sedláček, Tomas. *Economics of Good and Evil: The Quest for Economic Meaning from Gilgamesh to Wall Street*. Oxford: Oxford University Press, 2011.

Sedmak, Clemens. *Lokale Theologien und globale Kirche: Eine erkenntnistheoretische Grundlegung in praktischer Absicht* [Local Theologies and Global Church: An Epistemological Foundation with Practical Aims]. Freiburg im Breisgau: Herder, 2000.

———. "Utility and Identity: A Catholic Social Teaching Perspective on the *Economics of Good and Evil*." *Studies in Christian Ethics* 28, no. 4 (2015): 461–77.

Sellés, Juan Fernando. *Antropología para inconformes: Una antropología abierta al futuro* [Anthropology for Nonconformists: An Anthropology Open to the Future]. Madrid: Rialp, 2007.

Sen, Amartya. "Does Business Ethics Make Economic Sense?" *Business Ethics Quarterly* 3 (1993): 45–54.

Siker, Louke van Wensveen. "Christ and Business: A Typology for Christian Business Ethics." *Journal of Business Ethics* 8, no. 11 (1989): 883–88.

Singleton, John D. "'Money Is a Sterile Thing': Martin Luther on the Immorality of Usury Reconsidered." *History of Political Economy* 43, no. 4 (2011): 683–98.

Sison, Alejo José G. *Happiness and Virtue Ethics in Business*. Cambridge: Cambridge University Press, 2015.

Skidelsky, Robert, and Edward Skidelsky. *How Much Is Enough? Money and the Good Life*. New York: Other Press, 2012.

Sloane, Julie, and Tom Monaghan. "Tom Monaghan Domino's Pizza: The Pioneering Pizza-Delivery Chain I Started Almost Didn't Make It Out of the Oven." *Fortune Small Business*, September 1, 2003.

Smith, Adam. *An Inquiry into the Nature and Causes of the Wealth of Nations* [1776]. London: Dent, 1910.

Smith, Janet E. "The Importance of the Concept of 'Munus' to Understanding *Humane Vitae*." In *"Humanae Vitae": 20 Anni Dopo*, 677–90. Milan: Edizioni Ares, 1989.

Smith, Nancy R. *Workplace Spirituality: A Complete Guide for Business Leaders*. Lynn, Mass.: Axial Age, 2006.

Solomon, Robert C. *Ethics and Excellence: Cooperation and Integrity in Business*. New York: Oxford University Press, 1993.

Soudek, Josef. "Aristotle's Theory of Exchange: An Inquiry into the Origin of Economic Analysis." *Proceedings of the American Philosophical Society* 96, no. 1 (1952): 45–75.

Spohn, William C. "Spirituality and Ethics: Exploring the Connections." *Theological Studies* 58, no. 1 (1997): 109–23.

Stump, Eleonore. "Second-Person Accounts and the Problem of Evil." In *Faith and Narrative*, edited by Keith E. Yandell, 86–103. New York: Oxford University Press, 2001.

———. *Wandering in Darkness: Narrative and the Problem of Suffering*. Oxford: Oxford University Press, 2010.

Sugar, Alan. *What You See Is What You Get: My Autobiography*. London: Pan Macmillan, 2011.

Titmuss, Richard. *The Gift Relationship*. London: Allen and Unwin, 1970.

Tolstoy, Leo. *The Kingdom of God Is within You*. [1894]. Doylestown, Pa.: Wildside, 2005.

Tourish, Dennis. *The Dark Side of Transformational Leadership: A Critical Perspective*. London: Routledge, 2013.

Tourish, Dennis, and Naheed Tourish. "Spirituality at Work, and Its Implications for Leadership and Followership: A Post-Structuralist Perspective." *Leadership* 6, no. 2 (2010): 207–24.

Trivers, Robert. *Deceit and Self Deception: Fooling Yourself the Better to Fool Others*. London: Allen Lane, 2011.

Ulrich, Peter. "Integrative Wirtschaftsethik: Grundlagenreflexion der ökonomischen Vernunft" [Integrative Business Ethics: Foundational Reflections on Economic Rationality]. *Ethik und Sozialwissenschaft* 11, no. 4 (2000): 555–66.

———. "Auf der Suche nach der ganzen ökonomischen Vernunft: Der St. Galler Ansatz der integrativen Wirtschaftsethik" [In Search of the Whole of Economic Rationality: The St. Gallen Approach to Integrative Business Ethics]. In *Moral und Kapital: Grundfragen der Wirtschafts- und Unternehmensethik*, edited by Wolfgang Kersting, 61–75. Paderborn: Mentis, 2008.

———. "Zivilgesellschaft: Dritter Sektor oder Dritter Weg? Zur wirtschaftsethischen Bedeutung des Bürgerengagements" [Civil Society: Third Sector or Third Path? The Relevance of Civic Involvement for Business Ethics]. *Zeitschrift für Wirtschafts- und Unternehmensethik* 9, no. 3 (2008): 331–36.

Underhill, Kristen. "When Extrinsic Incentives Displace Intrinsic Motivation: Designing Legal Carrots and Sticks to Confront the Challenge of Motivational Crowding-Out." *Yale Journal on Regulation* 33, no. 1 (2016): 213–79.

Vatican Council II. Dogmatic Constitution *Lumen gentium*. November 21, 1964.

———. Decree *Apostolicam actuositatem*. November 18, 1965.

———. Pastoral Constitution *Gaudium et spes*. December 7, 1965.

———. Decree *Presbyterorum ordinis*. December 7, 1965.

Vaughan, Genevieve. *For-Giving: A Feminist Criticism of Exchange*. Austin, Tex.: Anomaly Press and Plain View Press, 2002. Originally published in 1997.

Vaughan, Genevieve, ed. *Women and the Gift Economy: A Radically Different Worldview Is Possible*. Toronto: Innana, 2007.

Von Rad, Gerhard. *The Message of the Prophets*. London: SCM, 1969. Originally published in 1967.

Wadell, Paul J. *Friendship and the Moral Life*. Notre Dame, Ind.: University of Notre Dame Press, 1989.

Watkins, Michael D. "How Managers Become Leaders." *Harvard Business Review*, June 2012, 65–72.

Weber, Max. *The Protestant Ethic and the Spirit of Capitalism*. London: Allen and Unwin, 1956. Originally published in 1905.

———. *Economy and Society: An Outline of Interpretative Sociology*. Berkeley: University of California Press, 1978. Originally published in 1922.

Weigel, George. *Witness to Hope: The Biography of Pope John Paul II*. New York: HarperCollins, 1999.

Whyte, William H. *The Organization Man*. Philadelphia: University of Pennsylvania Press, 2002. Originally published in 1956.

Wieland, Josef. *Die Ethik der Governance* [The Ethics of Governance]. Marburg: Metropolis, 1999.

Williams, Peter, and Stuart Allen. "Faculty Perspectives on the Inclusion of Spirituality Topics in Nonsectarian Leadership and Management Education Programs." *International Journal of Management Education* 12, no. 3 (2014): 293–303.

Wogaman, J. Philip. *A Christian Method of Moral Judgment*. London: SCM, 1976.

Wojtyla, Karol. *Consilium de Laicis, quid dicis de teipso?* December 3, 1968. http://www.laici.va/content/laici/en/media/notizie/doc_wojtyla.html. Accessed June 8, 2017.

———. *Sign of Contradiction*. New York: Seabury Press, 1979. Originally published in 1977.

———. *Sources of Renewal: The Implementation of Vatican II*. Translated by P. S. Falla. San Francisco: Harper and Row, 1980. Originally published in 1972.

Wood, Ralph C. *Flannery O'Connor and the Christ-Haunted South*. Grand Rapids, Mich.: William B. Eerdmans, 2004.

Yepes Stork, Ricardo. *Fundamentos de antropología: Un ideal de la excelencia humana* [Foundations of Anthropology: An Ideal of Human Excellence]. Pamplona: Eunsa, 1977.

Zamagni, Stefano. "Introduction." In *The Economics of Altruism*, edited by Stefano Zamagni, xv–xxii. Aldershot: Edward Elgar, 1995.

———. *Non profit come economia civile* [Non-Profit as Civil Economy]. Bologna: Il mulino, 1999.

———. "Reciprocity, Civil Economy, Common Good." In *Pursuing the Common Good*, edited by Margaret S. Archer and Pierpaolo Donati, 467–502. Vatican City: Pontifical Academy of Social Sciences, 2008.

———. "Caritas in Veritate." Observations presented at the conference "Civilizing the Economy: A New Way of Understanding Business Enterprise?" Faith and Work Initiative of Princeton University. Princeton, N.J., April 8–9, 2010.

———. *Impresa responsabile e mercato civile* [Responsible Business and Civil Market]. Bologna: Il mulino, 2013.

———. *Por una economía del bien común* [The Economy of the Common Good]. Madrid: Ciudad Nueva, 2013.

Zamagni, Stefano, and Luigino Bruni. *Handbook on the Economics of Reciprocity and Social Enterprise*. Cheltenham, UK: Edward Elgar, 2013.

Zenger, John H., Joseph R. Folkman, and Scott K. Edinger. *The Inspiring Leader: Unlocking the Secrets of How Extraordinary Leaders Motivate*. New York: McGraw-Hill, 2009.

Zieba, Maciej, ed. *Papal Economics: The Catholic Church on Democratic Capitalism, from Rerum Novarum to Caritas in Veritate*. Wilmington: ISI, 2013.

CONTRIBUTORS

RAFAEL ALVIRA is emeritus professor of philosophy at the University of Navarra, Spain.

MARKUS KRIENKE is professor of social doctrine of the church on the Theological Faculty of Lugano and professor of philosophical anthropology at the Pontifical Lateran University in Rome.

JUAN LUIS MARTÍNEZ is strategy and development director at the Pontifical University of Salamanca and professor of marketing at IE Business School.

DOMÈNEC MELÉ holds the Chair of Business Ethics, IESE Business School, University of Navarra, Spain.

JOSÉ MARÍA ORTIZ is dean of the School of Law and Business at Universidad Francisco de Vitoria, Madrid.

ELIZABETH REICHERT is a research assistant at the Markets, Culture and Ethics Research Centre at the Pontifical University of the Holy Cross, Rome.

GERMÁN SCALZO is research professor in the School of Economics and Business at Panamerican University, Mexico.

MARTIN SCHLAG is professor of Catholic social thought, holds the Alan W. Moss endowed Chair for Catholic Social Thought at the Center for Catholic Studies, University of St. Thomas (Minnesota), and is director of the John A. Ryan Institute for Catholic Social Thought.

CLEMENS SEDMAK is professor of social ethics at the University of Notre Dame.

CARDINAL PETER K. A. TURKSON is prefect of the Dicastery for Promoting Integral Human Development.

INDEX OF NAMES

GENERAL INDEX

A Catholic Spirituality for Business: The Logic of Gift was designed in Minion with Hypatia Sans display type and composed by Kachergis Book Design of Pittsboro, North Carolina. It was printed on 60-pound House Natural Smooth and bound by Sheridan Books of Chelsea, Michigan.